MODERN SOUTH AFRICA
IN WORLD HISTORY

MODERN SOUTH AFRICA IN WORLD HISTORY

BEYOND IMPERIALISM

Rob Skinner

Bloomsbury Academic
An imprint of Bloomsbury Publishing Plc

B L O O M S B U R Y
LONDON • OXFORD • NEW YORK • NEW DELHI • SYDNEY

Bloomsbury Academic
An imprint of Bloomsbury Publishing Plc

50 Bedford Square
London
WC1B 3DP
UK

1385 Broadway
New York
NY 10018
USA

www.bloomsbury.com

BLOOMSBURY and the Diana logo are trademarks of Bloomsbury Publishing Plc

First published 2017

British Library Cataloguing-in-Publication Data
A catalogue record for this book is available from the British Library.

ISBN: HB: 978-1-4411-2272-8
PB: 978-1-4411-0844-9
ePDF: 978-1-4411-5964-9
ePub: 978-1-4411-6476-6

Library of Congress Cataloging-in-Publication Data
Names: Skinner, Rob, 1966– author.
Title: Modern South Africa in world history: beyond imperialism / Rob Skinner.
Description: London; New York: Bloomsbury Academic,
an imprint of Bloomsbury Publishing, 2017. |
Includes bibliographical references and index.
Identifiers: LCCN 2016038798| ISBN 9781441122728 (hardback) |
ISBN 9781441108449 (paperback)
Subjects: LCSH: South Africa–History. | BISAC: HISTORY / Africa / South / General. |
HISTORY / Modern / General. | HISTORY / World.
Classification: LCC DT1787. S55 2017 | DDC 968–dc23
LC record available at https://lccn.loc.gov/2016038798

Cover design by Catherine Wood
Cover image © Africa Media Online / Alamy Stock Photo

Typeset by Newgen Knowledge Works (P) Ltd., Chennai, India
Printed and bound in India

CONTENTS

LIST OF MAPS

CHAPTER 1
INTRODUCTION

In August 2002, nearly two centuries after she had left South Africa, the remains of Sara Baartman were buried near the site of her birthplace in the Eastern Cape. Speaking at her funeral, the then president of South Africa, Thabo Mbeki, described her life as a symbol of the physical, cultural and moral dispossession of black South Africans by colonialism: 'as a people without a past, except a past of barbarism, who had no capacity to think, who had no culture, no value system to speak of and nothing to contribute to human civilisation'.[1] Born around 1789, little is known of Baartman's life prior to 1810, but much has been written of the final five years of her life, spent in Britain and France where she was exhibited as an exotic curiosity to a fascinated public and equally mesmerized scientific community.[2] Her body – and her sexual anatomy in particular – was the focus of attention, both in life and in death, when she became the subject of a post-mortem conducted by the naturalist and pioneer of palaeontology, Georges Cuvier. Her remains were added to the scientist's personal collection and subsequently placed on public display in the Musée de l'Homme in Paris until the 1970s. Although calls had been made for the repatriation of her remains prior to the 1990s, it was not until the ANC (African National Congress) came to power in 1994 that an official request was made to the French authorities for her return.

Since 1810, the image of Baartman's body has been deployed in various ways as a representation of Africa. For Cuvier, her anatomy confirmed the near-bestiality of Africans, his analysis an early illustration of the biological determinism that shaped the social assumptions of the architects of segregation and apartheid.[3] During the 1980s, she again became the focus of academic attention as contemporary images of her body were scrutinized as examples of nineteenth-century European constructions of racial and gender stereotypes.[4] Again, Baartman was presented not for what she was, but for what she embodied in the minds of European observers. And then, in 1994, the primary impetus behind calls for the return of her remains came from the Griqua National Conference, for whom Baartman was an icon of indigenous culture.[5] In their recent account of her life, Clifton Crais and Pamela Scully argue that, despite her return in 2002, Baartman was still 'ensnared by diverse people's expectations, by histories that remain traumatic'.[6]

For Mbeki, an account of Baartman's history needed to be rooted in South African experience, not framed with reference to Europe. Returning Baartman's remains to South Africa was part of a process of renewal: it was a reclamation of African dignity in the face of colonial humiliation, not a reconstitution of the South African past that sought to reconcile African and European elements, or indigenous and settler histories.

Another interpretation might suggest, however, that the story of Baartman's exile and return was inherently transnational, an individual's life and death that was shaped by – but also symbolically re-enacted – transnational connections.[7] The history of modern South Africa, likewise, might be regarded as a transnational history. That, at least, is the starting point from which the following narrative account departs; that South African history is in many significant ways a transnational experience, not isolated or exceptional but fundamentally inscribed by people, processes and projects that 'thrived in between, across and through polities and societies'.[8] South African history has been marked by global contacts, exchanges and interactions, and its national culture is in significant ways a composite of the complex interplays between the domestic and the foreign.

As Saul Dubow has recently argued, 'the struggle for South Africa has always been, and in many ways continues to be, a struggle to become South African'.[9] This, rightly, focuses attention on the claims to citizenship rights that have moulded the region since the nineteenth century. The predominant forces acting on South African history might be regarded as the struggle between competing nationalisms – Afrikaner and African – that sought in disparate ways to displace British imperial power. Read in this manner, the history of modern South Africa becomes an account of a struggle for ideological and moral hegemony within the political, social and economic structures of a modern nation state. But, as a struggle that had its genesis in a settler society within the British Empire, individual and collective identities were shaped by an Anglo-European agenda, and also by 'the reality of encountering indigenous peoples with highly differentiated political, cultural and social structures'.[10] Post-apartheid projects have nevertheless sought to overturn the effects of the 'persuasive attempt to colonize consciousness' that were enacted by missionaries, administrators and other colonial agents, but South Africa has, like the continent, more widely remained subject to forces of globalization and a 'paradigm of extraversion'.[11] The African Renaissance has thus appropriated and reinvented global influences as much as it has rejected them; the struggle to become South African has never taken place in a vacuum.

Alongside the ideological construction of modern South Africa, transnational forces have played a critical role in the development of the economic and social structures that have defined the modern South African state. Imperialism and capitalism prepared the ground for the Union of South Africa in 1910 and provided the framework within which the politics of segregation and apartheid emerged. But the dominance of these transnational influences was never complete. It was the case that South Africa remained an outpost of empire, of marginal importance in networks of imperial trade until the 1860s, its strategic significance determined by its position on the sea route to India. The dynamic shift of importance that came with the development of diamond and gold mining industries in the last three decades of the century should not imply, however, that South Africa was the construct of entrepreneurs and imperial agents alone. The Union of South Africa that emerged in 1910 was an 'imperial creation', and yet the limits of capitalist influence were also determined by 'pre-industrial societies, both black and white'.[12]

Similarly, imperial identities never entirely supplanted colonial identities, but often sat alongside each other. A shared concept of 'Britishness' has been placed at the centre of recent revisions of imperial history into accounts of a 'British world', but a concept of imperial belonging supplemented a sense of being – or desire to become – 'South African'. An imperial 'Britishness' was therefore a 'composite, rather than an exclusive, form of identity'.[13] Nineteenth-century Cape politicians could describe themselves as British even as they rejected plans for federation under the British Empire; African nationalists embraced the values of the British world in idealized terms that reflected affinities forged in the discourses of mission and school. To a significant extent, the influence worked the other way around too; the pre-eminent South African political figure of the mid-twentieth century Jan Smuts became a 'philosopher of race' for the metropolitan centre, helping to define 'whiteness' just as a post-war immigration began to forge a new, multicultural Britain.[14]

But it was not the British Empire that made southern Africa transnational. Recent attention has focused on the seventeenth-century interconnections and networks that established the Cape as part of a wider Indian Ocean world, and the ways in which the Dutch East India Company provided a form of 'imperial network' comparable with those that shaped the politics and culture of the nineteenth century.[15] The movements of sailors, convicts and officials through the networks established by the Dutch East India Company was supplanted in the nineteenth and twentieth centuries by Indian Ocean networks centred on 'British' India. This was a transnational world that connected South African cities such as Durban with key centres in India and East Africa, as well as important nodes of transoceanic sea routes such as Mauritius. South Africa, viewed in this context, becomes a point of intersection between imperial and Indian Ocean worlds and a focal point of frictions between white settler culture and identities and those of Greater India.[16] Africa became a point of reference for Indian nationalists, often subject to contradictory discourses of African 'otherness' and Afro-Asian solidarity. Thus, paternalist imperial visions of Africa continued to shape Indian perceptions even as Indians sought to disengage from the cultures of empire.[17]

The story of modern South Africa which follows provides a broad overview of key historical developments from the turn of the nineteenth century until the turn of the twenty-first century. This narrative of events is underpinned by a transnational perspective that seeks to highlight the cosmopolitan nature of modern South Africa and the global influences that have enabled and constrained social, political and economic experiences over the past two centuries. These influences fall broadly into three strands, the first of which is concerned with the ways in which modern South Africa has been shaped by – and has reshaped – ideologies that centred on a universal human subject, drawing the multifarious groups and actors into a singular 'South African' field of social and political interaction. These included the complex impact of Christian religion, forged out of the cultural exchange and resistance of the colonial mission encounter, as well as notions of humanitarianism that both served to legitimate colonial expansion and conquest and provided a point of reference for resistance against white domination both within South Africa and across the globe. Against these universalizing discourses,

South Africa was of course deeply marked by the impact of the divisive language and ideologies of race and colonialism.

The second strand encompasses the transnational influences discussed earlier, namely, the networks of exchange that have shaped South African politics, society and economy. Pre-eminent among these have been imperial networks and economies of empire, but a transnational history of South Africa must take account of forces beyond those rooted in imperialism. Finally, the history of modern South Africa should also reflect the position of the country within a regional and continental framework. South Africa has always been part of Africa, just as it has always been at the limits of the continent.

Further reading

Beinart, William. *Twentieth-Century South Africa*. Oxford: Oxford University Press, 1994.
Clark, Nancy L. and William H. Worger. *South Africa: The Rise and Fall of Apartheid*. Harlow: Longman, 2011.
Davenport, Rodney. *The Birth of the New South Africa*. London: University of Toronto Press, 1998.
Davenport, Rodney and Christopher C. Saunders. *South Africa: A Modern History*. New York: St. Martin's Press, 2000.
Feinstein, C. H. *An Economic History of South Africa: Conquest, Discrimination and Development*. Cambridge: Cambridge University Press, 2005.
Hamilton, Carolyn, Bernard K. Mbenga and Robert Ross, eds. *The Cambridge History of South Africa*. Vol. 1: *From Early Times to 1885*. New York: Cambridge University Press, 2010.
Ross, Robert. *A Concise History of South Africa*. Cambridge: Cambridge University Press, 2008.
Ross, Robert, Anne Kelk Mager and Bill Nasson, eds. *The Cambridge History of South Africa*. Vol. 2: *1885–1994*. Cambridge: Cambridge University Press, 2011.
Shepherd, Nick and Steven Robins, eds. *New South African Keywords*. Johannesburg: Jacana, 2008.
South African Democracy Education Trust, ed. *The Road to Democracy in South Africa*. Cape Town: Zebra Press, 2004.
Worden, Nigel. *The Making of Modern South Africa: Conquest, Segregation and Apartheid*. Oxford: Blackwell, 1994.

CHAPTER 2
SOUTH AFRICA IN THE COLONIAL WORLD

The development of southern African societies

For centuries, the outward connections of southern African societies had looked east, through networks of exchange that bound together an Indian Ocean 'world'.[1] The establishment of significant trading centres such as Mapungubwe and Great Zimbabwe speak of the twin processes of socio-political stratification and the intensification of trade contacts with East African coastal centres.[2] From the sixteenth century, transoceanic influences were deepened and sharpened following the establishment of contacts between African communities and Portuguese, Dutch and British traders further south around Delagoa Bay. In the seventeenth and eighteenth centuries, new transitional zones of interaction emerged as European colonialism established a foothold around Cape Town and its expanding hinterland. By 1800, southern Africa had been incorporated into global networks of economic and cultural exchange, that – despite the significant influences and new communities that had been fostered by trade links with and settlement from Europe – remained embedded in the Indian Ocean world. Colonial society at the Cape mixed European, South and Southeast Asian influences in a new context, but did so in the service of mercantile enterprises centred on trade with Asia.

The relationship between southern African societies and the wider world changed dramatically from the sixteenth century with the arrival of Portuguese ships at the Cape. It was in the following century, however, that contact with Europeans intensified, with the establishment of routes via the Cape to the Dutch mercantile outposts around the Indian Ocean, centred on Batavia (Indonesia). Cape Town was founded in the mid-seventeenth century as a supply station for the Dutch East India Company (VOC), but by the end of the century, the Cape had been identified as zone for potential expansion, in part to establish agricultural production. By 1700, Cape Town had become established as significant urban centre and, supplied from Madagascar and Indonesia, a slave-holding society, split between company- and privately-owned slaves, which numbered over 7,000 in the 1770s. By the mid-eighteenth century, Cape farms were producing a sufficient surplus of wheat for export, in the main to the VOC Indian Ocean outposts. Colonial society brought Christianity from Europe, although churches undertook little missionary activity; connections across the Indian Ocean did, however, result in the establishment of Sufi Islam through slaves as well as Indonesian leaders exiled to the Cape. It has been suggested that, rather than race, the major social distinctions during the Dutch colonial period were dichotomies defined by Christian versus heathen, between slave and free, or between various classes of status in colonial society.

Colonial expansion had a particularly negative impact on the Khoisan, whose social cohesion was founded on the basis of patronage connected to wealth in livestock, the loss of which to colonial trade resulted in declining power. The breakdown of indigenous political independence was compounded by increased competition over water sources that came with the expansion of colonial agriculture; when smallpox broke out in the colony in 1713, it sealed the fate of the Khoisan in the Western Cape. The Khoisan, along with outlying San hunter-gatherer communities gradually merged into a colonial lower order supplying labour to farms, as colonial expansion continued northwards towards the Gariep River and east as far as the Zuurveld, where Trekboer farmers came into contact – and conflict – with amaXhosa pastoralist lineage groups. By the final decade of the eighteenth century, colonial society in the Cape was well established. It was centred on the commercial economy of Cape Town and its immediate environs, characterized by an interdependent social order of colonial master and slaves and free labourers, with more scattered colonial farming communities and Khoisan in the interior.[3]

However, the history of southern Africa in the late eighteenth and early nineteenth centuries must be viewed from multiple perspectives – not simply from Cape Town. A historical account that centres on the expansion of the colonial frontier, while illuminating the terms by which colonialism in southern Africa was integrated into a wider global expansion of European political, economic and cultural power, cannot provide a complete picture of the interplay among the array of peoples that shaped the history of the subcontinent in the nineteenth century. The Cape and later Port Natal and Delagoa Bay were, of course, significant entry points for global influences in nineteenth-century southern Africa. Colonial travellers facilitated cultural change, such as the transmission of hybrid musical instruments like the *velvioool* (a form of violin) to Tswana peoples by the travelling party of naturalist William Burchell on his journeys into the Cape 'interior' during 1810–15.[4] But a narrative that sets transnational influences within the framework of the expansion, incursion or penetration of an African hinterland by western influences simply reproduces the ethnocentric assumptions of colonial society itself.[5]

Until the late twentieth century, histories of African societies in the late-eighteenth and early nineteenth centuries had centred on the emergence of the Zulu kingdom under Shaka and its supposedly exceptional expansion. A narrative of Zulu-led warfare, known as the *mfecane*, with its metaphorical allusions to 'chaos', 'strife' and dispossession, dominated histories until the late 1980s. This narrative, however, located the political and social transformations of the early nineteenth century in political and military developments, and defined the series of complex dramatic upheavals as purely a consequence of struggles *internal* to African polities, reinforcing a sense of separation between colonial and African historical trajectories. By the early twenty-first century, a new historical consensus had begun to emerge, which sought to present a broader analysis of continuity and change in African societies in the so-called interior. New interpretations of political and social transformations in the late-eighteenth and early-nineteenth centuries have placed emphasis on the changing nature of links with the Portuguese colonial world via Delagoa Bay, which extended and intensified trade links and the introduction of new crops such as maize.[6] Political changes were characterized by an apparent centralization of power under ruling lineages who claimed allegiance from subordinate client groups, although these alliances and networks of patronage were at the same time fluid and contingent.

The expansion of the Cape under Dutch rule led to the emergence of new groups that mingled Khoisan, San and Batswana with former slaves and others on the margins of colonial society. By the end of the eighteenth century, the Kora and Griqua, with access to guns and horses, developed a foothold in the region of the Orange River, and focused in part on cattle-raiding, but equally on livestock farming and trade with the Cape. In the region of Delagoa Bay, rising trade in the final decades of the century led to competition between chiefdoms, exacerbated, some have argued, by an increased focus on the trade in slaves, as West Africa became less viable as a source for transatlantic slavers following British abolition in 1807.[7] Similar fluctuations in power have been identified among various Batswana groups to the north of the Cape, and in the region around the Vaal River. African politics in the period centred on contest within structures of 'chiefly power', control over cattle and the ability to maintain patronage, all of which might be susceptible to the vagaries of the environment and the actions of rival leaders. Rather than seeing early-nineteenth-century power struggles as a singular catastrophic event, it has instead been suggested that we should think in terms of shifting patterns of allegiance associated with the movement of 'chiefly families and their followers'.[8]

During the 1820s, the politics of the eastern coastal region were shaped by three principal kingdoms of the abakwaNdwandwe, abakwaGaza and amaZulu. Recent accounts have questioned the mythology of Zulu power under Shaka, not least the extent to which Shaka's forces conquered vast swathes of territory. Zulu authority was a matter of cultural influence as much as regional conquest. But the 1820s did see the emergence of a dominant, highly militarized state under Shaka centred on the region around the Thukela River in present-day KwaZulu-Natal. Contacts between the amaZulu and European traders at Port Natal developed, with the latter providing military assistance in the Zulu defeat of Ndwandwe forces in the mid-1820s. The break-up of the Ndwandwe kingdom transformed the political landscape of the interior, most notably in creating space for the emergence of the amaNdebele – supporters of the Khumalo leader, Mzilikazi. Under Mzilikazi, the Ndebele established a power base in the region of present-day Pretoria, and by late 1830s, conflict with European Voortrekkers pushed Mzilikazi and his people north into what is now south-western Zimbabwe. A further consequence of the end of Nwandwe power, coupled with the assassination of Shaka in 1828, was the re-establishment of Pedi, Swazi and Gaza kingdoms to the east of the region. Elsewhere on the highveld, competition between African powers and Griqua raiders and the incipient influence of colonial forces led to the creation of yet further new leaders, in particular, the emergence of Moshoeshoe as the dominant force in the Caledon Valley.[9]

The consolidation of the Zulu kingdom under Shaka was, furthermore, narrated through interwoven accounts rooted in African oral traditions and the reports of European traders who began to establish a base at Port Natal (Durban) around 1824 (the same year that Moshoeshoe established his base at Thaba Bosiu). These accounts tended to serve particular political agendas, not least those associated with Shaka's half-brother Dingane, who came to control the Zulu kingdom after Shaka's assassination in 1828. The first colonial reports about a powerful Zulu kingdom began to filter back to the Cape in the early 1820s, and efforts to establish trade with Shaka began with the expeditions of Henry Francis Fynn and Francis Farewell in 1824. These individuals had close connections with the mercantile trade in Cape Town and the Eastern Cape, and pioneered transport routes between Graham's Town and Natal. Close connections with Shaka were required in order to facilitate trade, notably in ivory, and, as Carolyn Hamilton has noted, before his death in 1828, depictions of Shaka and the Zulu in colonial accounts tended to be positive and benign. Negative accounts of Zulu despotism and tyranny began to emerge in colonial accounts in the 1830s, following Shaka's death and the acceleration of campaigns to extend formal colonial control to Natal. The negative depiction of Shaka was not, Hamilton argues, simply an invention designed to serve the interests of colonial traders, but was equally rooted in African oral traditions, testimony to the struggles of power and resistance within African societies within the region.[10]

Over the course of the nineteenth century, the long-established African communities in the coastal regions of the southeast and in the interior faced increasing exposure to European colonialism, which was itself in the process of becoming the primary channel of political and economic interactions across the globe. Colonial administrative and trade networks formed the site of global interactions as much as they were channels of communication. Colonialism was thus both a means of establishing relations between peoples and the organizing principle upon which those relationships were based. Between 1800 and 1850, colonial South Africa became established as part of a vastly expanding web of connections dominated by, and in the service of, the expansion of European economic and political power.

Political and economic transitions at the Cape

The southern tip of Africa had never been isolated from the wider world, but from around 1800 the tempo and quality of global influences were transformed, largely as a consequence of the British occupations of the Cape. The British seizure of control in the Cape, and the subsequent establishment of imperial authority, took place in the context of the eastward shift of British global ambitions, as a 'second British empire' was forged in the context of revolutionary wars and emerging nationalism.[11] In South Asia, the extension of the power of the British East India Company in Mughal India and the invasion of the Indonesian territories of the Batavian republic (allied to Napoleonic France) gave the Cape a new significance in the minds of British officials. The imposition of British rule in southern Africa came, then, as a consequence of a 'global' conflict between nascent European empires.

As part of the Dutch mercantile empire, Cape Town and its environs had been shaped by both influences from Europe as well as those of the colonial system centred on Indonesia. As such, the Cape faced east as much as it faced north, despite the key demographic, political and economic connections with the Netherlands. And, despite the establishment of British hegemony, longer-term connections between the Cape and the Indian Ocean world continued to exert an economic and social influence. Nevertheless, British rule connected southern Africa to wider networks of empire, bringing the Cape more firmly within the world economy of empire and establishing a more formal and 'efficient' political administration. Although its influence was uneven, the singular strength of Britain, in terms of its economic reach and the power (both 'soft' and 'hard') that followed, was a defining factor in the reshaping of colonial south Africa in the half century after 1800.

While the Cape economy was a relatively minor part of the overall imperial trading and financial enterprise, the arrival of British merchant interests laid a platform for economic growth and the further extension of the influence of Cape Town in ways that paralleled the growth of colonial cities across the globe.[12] Newcomers such as John and Francis Collison, with close connections to London trading circles, could be seen as members of a 'cosmopolitan mercantile diaspora', advocates of free trade and linked to the wider imperial economy through personal and commercial networks.[13] Collison's 'respectable distillery' in Cape Town exploited preferential tariffs on wine trade introduced by British authorities in order to produce fine brandy for export to Europe.[14] The volume of trade declined rapidly when these preferences were abolished in 1825, however, and by the 1830s the focus of commercial ventures had shifted towards agricultural production in the east of the Cape. With demand driven by the expanding textile industry in Britain, the Cape interior provided an opportunity for new export-oriented commercial endeavours. Wool production in the Cape expanded significantly, with exports reaching beyond 3 million pounds in 1835 and increasing to 12 million in 1855. In the process, wool transformed the relationship between southern Africa and the British Empire.[15] It brought new animal inhabitants – in the form of merino sheep – into the region, making it part of an ovine colonialism that integrated the Cape into an imperial economy that traced a route from New Zealand, through the Cape to Britain. The networks of trade that supplied the raw resources of the woollen trade also brought the resulting products back to Africa, and blankets manufactured in northern England became a valued commodity among both colonial and African societies.[16]

The economic transformation of the Cape was built, however, upon the establishment of political authority that combined a process of military conquest with cultural transformations, mediated primarily through missionary activities, which facilitated the construction of a new political order. At the turn of the nineteenth century, nascent British authority had been threatened by a series of rebellions by frontier colonists, Khoisan and Xhosa. The revolts of 1799–1803 presaged intermittent conflict along the frontier throughout the first half of the nineteenth century, resulting in a colonial state with a decidedly military character.[17] In the first half of the nineteenth century then, the British administration was shaped by a 'war culture' rooted in a military-aristocratic elite.[18] By 1810, the British military force in the Cape numbered over 6,000, and in addition, a 'Hottentot corps' was created, deploying tactics developed during the Peninsular War in Europe as part of a strategy to integrate some indigenous groups into the system of colonial governance.[19] In 1811–12, Cradock used this force, alongside a settler militia and supported by British troops, to drive Xhosa communities across the Fish River, creating a frontier that was monitored by a series of forts.[20] Again, the transnational politics of empire had a role to play, as the establishment of British control under Cradock came at a moment of crisis in Britain itself, when wartime anxieties combined with fears of a rising radicalism to engender authoritarian and repressive style to government – both at the imperial 'centre' and its newest colonial margin.[21]

The war culture was a source of great profit for colonial merchants and traders, who provided transport, provisions and other material support for imperial forces despatched to the Eastern Cape in order to suppress Xhosa incursions or to engage in efforts to extend colonial territorial influence. The militarization of the eastern frontier was not simply a question of protection, it was also an economic boon – or to put in another way, a process that would 'facilitate primitive accumulation'.[22] Military interventions in the east of the colonial territory signalled the intentions of the administration to more assertively protect settler interests against the Xhosa. But, alongside militarism, the governing mentality of the British was shaped by a new conception of power that diminished the privileges of status that had marked Dutch colonial rule. The displacement of brutal authority by the 'rule of law', powerfully symbolized by the public destruction of slave torture instruments on the advent of British rule was, as Lester points out, a direct statement of British intent to bring 'civilization' to southern Africa.[23] Under the Earl of Caledon and John Cradock, the first two governors of the Cape after 1806, policies were introduced that espoused a benevolent and 'progressive' attitude towards indigenous populations, albeit one that was double-edged in practice. The 'Hottentot Proclamation' of 1809 insisted on formal contracts between masters and servants, simultaneously affording protection for indigenous workers and enforcing forms of regulation – such as documents to prove an individual's right of movement – that were a precursor of the 'pass systems' of the segregationist and apartheid systems of the twentieth century. Despite its tendency towards reform, the new colonial state was, for indigenous workers, 'more intrusive than Dutch East India Company rule had ever been'.[24]

The construction of a more efficient, ordered colonial regime was strongly influenced by humanitarian ideologies mediated through the efforts of missionaries whose world view was moulded by the Industrial Revolution in Britain. But, metropolitan visions of a civilizing mission also fostered alternative colonial ideologies that had a greater interest in commerce than in Christianity and civilization. Prompted by fears of growing radicalism within Britain, the British government initiated a settlement scheme in the vicinity of the Great Fish River, beginning with the arrival of some 4,000 settlers in 1820. With the hope of regulating the eastern border of the colony and creating a defensive bulwark against its Xhosa neighbours, the scheme envisaged the creation of an idealized rural society of gentleman farmers. Instead, the majority of the immigrants were artisans and traders, who established themselves as a nascent middle-class centred on Graham's Town, some 100 kilometre inland from the newly established town of Port Elizabeth. The new settlers created a commercial centre in the Eastern Cape that came to rival Cape Town, its culture shaped by Methodism and an 'ethic of individual redemption, discipline, self-improvement, austerity and frugality'.[25] Rather than 'stabilize' the frontier, the new zone of settlement would exacerbate conflict between the settler population and indigenous polities. By the end of the 1820s, the Eastern Cape was far from an idealized replica of the English countryside, but a site for a new form of colonial struggle between, on the one hand, humanitarian ideals of progress and 'civilization', and on the other, the desire for wealth, economic growth and a steady supply of labour.[26]

Missionaries, humanitarianism and settler colonialism

Mission Christianity at the Cape had its roots in the popular evangelicalism of late eighteenth-century Britain, a nonconformist 'revival' movement that caught the spiritual mood of a period of social and political transformation. Centred on the belief in the necessity of a personal relationship with God and the need to sanctify that relationship via a 'useful' life, Evangelical Christianity was both a progressive force – measuring the value of individuals by their talents and actions, rather than social station – but also aligned with the values and interests of industrial capitalism. During the first half of the nineteenth century, missionaries constituted the primary channels of colonial influence among indigenous Khoisan and Xhosa communities. Sharing ideological roots with the reformist ideas that informed the new colonial administration at the Cape, missionaries performed a function that was in the service of colonial conquest, but at the same time a source of new ideas that could be – and were – mobilized by Africans for their own ends.[27] Missionaries brought new religious values, frameworks of knowledge and models of social organization that had been shaped by industrialization in Britain, but were renegotiated in their encounters with African communities.[28]

The itinerant Protestant preachers of eighteenth century Britain became the architects of a rapid expansion of overseas missionary work, focused initially on the Khoisan communities that had been at the centre of resistance to colonial rule in the early years of British control. The Khoisan were nominally free, but had largely lost any semblance of independence and were subservient to Boers in conditions akin to slavery. Initial missionary activity provided centres of refuge for Khoisan, such as Bethelsdorp in the Eastern Cape, established by Johannes Van der Kemp of the London Missionary Society in 1802. Van der Kemp arrived in the Cape in 1799 and convinced British authorities to allow the construction of a mission station that might promote reconciliation between the Khoisan and colonial society. Van der Kemp, along with his London Missionary Society (LMS) colleague James Read elaborated what Elizabeth Elbourne has described as a 'compelling theology of evil that furnished an explanation for the apparently meaningless oppression of the Khoisan'.[29] The mutual hostility felt by colonial settlers

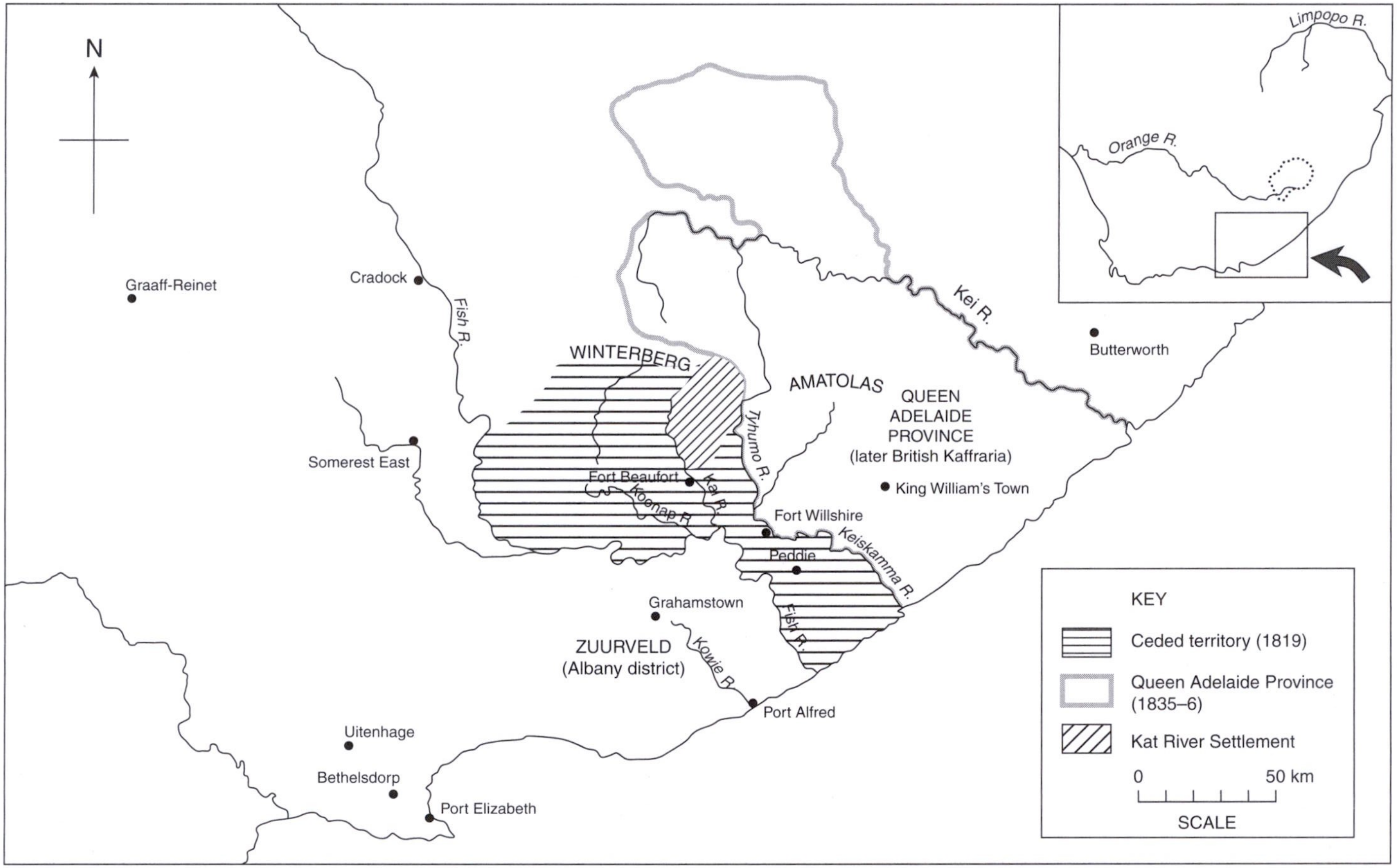

Map 1 The Eastern Cape in the 1820s and 1830s.

Source: 'The NE Cape frontier': Timothy J. Keegan, *Colonial South Africa and the Origins of the Racial Order*. Cape Town: David Philip Publishers, 1996, p. 130.

and radical missionaries such as Van der Kemp were thus rooted in contradictory world views. On the part of settlers this was founded upon fear of the indigenous population as the source of unremitting threat to life and livelihood, while missionaries at Bethelsdorp offered an inclusive vision of colonial society that provided an egalitarian counterpoint to the master–servant relations that underpinned the Boer social order.[30]

For Van der Kemp and Read, the desire to protect the Khoisan was not simply the product of an intellectual belief in equality and justice, but was imbued with a spiritual and personal *identification* with their Khoisan followers.[31] Both married Khoisan converts and lived culturally hybrid lifestyles that were viewed by contemporary critics as markers of their deviation from European norms of civility. Their model of syncretic Christianity had its detractors, not least Robert Moffat, head of the LMS mission to the Tswana-speaking Barolong peoples of the Northern Cape, who held a firm belief that the primary aim of the mission was to bring the undoubted benefits of European civilization.[32] With the extension of colonial control after the war of 1811–12, missionaries were drawn closer to the colonial government, as agents of 'respectable Christianity' that might serve the assimilation of the Xhosa on the eastern borders of the colony.[33]

In the 1820s, evangelical Christians therefore found themselves more closely aligned with reformers within the metropolitan political elite. This alliance was most firmly associated in the public mind, both at the Cape and in London, with Read's successor as head of the LMS, John Philip. The son of a Scottish weaver, he had become a Congregationalist minister at the turn of the nineteenth century and was appointed to the new post of resident director of the LMS in Cape Town in 1819. His intellectual influences were rooted in the Scottish Enlightenment and he brought to the role of director a firm belief in the essential connection between spiritual salvation and civilized behaviour. In contrast to Van der Kemp and Read, Philip thus set British norms and values at the heart of the missionary enterprise at the Cape – an agenda which went as far as to insist upon the reconstruction of Bethelsdorp on the lines of a decent and well-ordered Scottish village.[34] It was, however, as a conduit for metropolitan influence on the politics of the Cape – and on the rights of its indigenous population – for which Philip has been remembered.

The influence of Cape humanitarians can in part be attributed to Philip's connections with powerful networks in London who had shaped debates around slavery in the late 1820s and early 1830s. During extended visits to Britain in 1823 and 1826, and through the publication of his *Researches in South Africa* (1828), a polemical account of colonial depredations, he called on the British government to bring 'liberal institutions, and just and equal laws' to the indigenous peoples of the Cape.[35] On the one hand, his scathing criticism of the failure of the new British administration to improve the conditions of life for Khoisan and Xhosa was highly influential in metropolitan circles, but, on the other, the book was met with dismay from Cape settlers. As Lester has argued, the main problem for humanitarians – both in London and at the Cape – was that British authority appeared more concerned with the establishment of unity within the disparate sections of the settler community, rather than the development of a 'humane policy' towards the indigenous peoples in the new colony.[36]

During the 1820s, though, humanitarian and settler interests often seemed in alignment. Colonial administration was reshaped from the mid-1820s, under the metropolitan influence of a liberal Toryism concerned with the establishment of 'regulated, principled and consistent' government. Campaigns against restrictions on trade and a free press brought humanitarians and merchants together in a local reformist movement in the Cape with powerful connections with influential groups in London.[37] The leading abolitionist William Wilberforce had pressed for the establishment of the Commission of Eastern Inquiry by the British Colonial Office in 1822, which examined administration in the Cape alongside Indian Ocean bases in Sri Lanka and Mauritius. The Commission was one of a series of attempts to investigate and reformulate colonial rule following the Napoleonic Wars, and Wilberforce's sponsorship was indicative of the ways in which humanitarian networks sustained calls for colonial reform.[38] Ultimately, these reforms resulted in the 'inevitable dismantling of the old Dutch mercantilist system' and establishment of liberal orthodoxies at the Cape.[39] While principles of free trade and the liberties of the press found common cause with Cape humanitarians and merchants, reforms nonetheless revealed points of tension between metropolitan and settler interests.

A key example of missionary intervention was that of Philip's role in the passing of Ordinance 50 of 1828, a decree that sought to regulate the legal status and conditions of employment for Khoisan. Based on the reformist principle of free labour, the new regulations sought to construct a Khoisan labouring class in preference to the employment of Xhosa workers moving across the border into the eastern districts around Albany (Grahamstown).[40] The legislation, introduced by the Whig reformer Richard Bourke, and strongly supported by Philip and Read, came to be viewed as a cornerstone of colour-blind and exceptional 'Cape Liberalism', but the reforms of the 1820s might properly be regarded as part of a process of rationalization and regulation of labour and land across Britain's diverse colonial territories. Bourke's subsequent efforts to consolidate state control over land controlled by indigenous peoples in Australia reflected the similar concerns regarding the ambivalent legal status of indigenous groups and the dual-edged character of humanitarianism.[41] In the Cape, as elsewhere in the British Empire, the desire to 'protect' set limits on the legal rights and freedoms of indigenous groups. The culmination of early-nineteenth-century metropolitan humanitarianism came with the abolition of slavery in the British Empire in 1834, albeit moderated by a four-year period of 'apprenticeship' and compensation for slave-owners. In the Cape, emancipation provided the ultimate expression of the new form of colonial government that, for settlers, disrupted the established patterns of status and hierarchy and intensified discontent.[42]

By 1834, humanitarians such as Philip began to look beyond the northern and eastern boundaries of the Cape, and increasingly advocated a frontier policy based on the recognition of local chiefs, regulated through treaty. When Benjamin D'Urban arrived as the new governor in the Cape in 1834, he brought with him a plan for the establishment of a network of alliances with African chiefs in the Eastern Cape that had been forged in consultation with leading figures in the LMS.[43] His arrival coincided however with renewed hostilities in the Eastern Cape, as Xhosa forces launched a series of attacks on the colony in December 1834. Rather than simply expelling the Xhosa from the colony, the British commander, Colonel Harry Smith, launched a brutal retaliatory campaign, sending his forces across the Kei River into direct confrontation with the paramount Xhosa leader, Hintsa, who was taken prisoner, killed and mutilated by colonial forces.[44] In the aftermath of the war, D'Urban established colonial control over the territory between the Fish and Kei rivers, declaring a new 'Queen Adelaide Province' of the Cape. In the process, the colonial administration established a new colonial frontier zone, occupied by African intermediaries, who were cast as refugees from servitude among the Xhosa and increasingly defined as a homogenous group known collectively as 'Mfengu'.[45]

Smith, a veteran of the Napoleonic Wars and the War of 1812, represented another early-nineteenth-century imperial network whose efforts to elaborate methods of colonial administration paralleled (and cut across) that of the humanitarians. Focused on direct control and the dilution of the power of chiefs, Smith's programme for the administration of Queen Adelaide Province envisaged that missionaries would play a central role in the acculturation of those Xhosa who were given leave to remain. The establishment of Queen Adelaide Province was met with approval by Philip, who saw it as a step towards the transformation of African society. The 1834–35 war nevertheless prompted humanitarians in London, led by the veteran abolitionist Thomas Fowell Buxton, to establish an official Select Committee on Aborigines, which between 1836–37 undertook a broad-ranging investigation into the treatment of indigenous populations throughout the British Empire.[46] The Committee represented, perhaps, the height of the influence of the metropolitan humanitarian lobby on policies in South Africa. This was the moment at which the question of 'frontier' policy in the Cape became transnational politics, where relations between settler and Xhosa became a discussion of 'the processes of British colonialism *per se*'.[47] In addition to the Cape, the remit of the committee covered policies across North America and Australasia, while its discussions centred on two basic principles: the importance of 'legitimate economic practice', and the necessity of an interventionist colonialism. As such, it articulated the belief that humanitarian principles should be tied to profitable enterprise, but that a 'properly constituted governmental order' was necessary to protect indigenous populations from depredations at the hands of settlers.[48] Through the Select Committee, the colonial politics of the Cape in the early nineteenth century helped sketch the contours of the British 'civilizing mission'.

South Africans had a direct engagement with and impact on the workings of the Select Committee. Philip, of course, played a central role in communicating information about developments in the Cape. He travelled to London in 1835, together with Read and two African converts, Andries Stoeffels and Jan Tzatzoe (Dyani Tshatshu). Tzatzoe provided a living embodiment of the civilizing mission: a convert from a minor ruling lineage, he had studied under Read at Bethelsdorp before working with LMS missionary John Brownlee. Working in partnership with LMS missionaries to translate biblical texts into Xhosa, Tzatzoe's career encapsulated the twin processes of assimilation and reinterpretation of Western knowledge and intellectual tradition experienced by African intermediaries in the colonial encounter.[49] In London, Philip feted him as representative of the redemptive possibilities of humanitarianism and impressed audiences of supporters across the country; settlers in the Eastern Cape, in contrast, saw him merely as a tool of the humanitarian lobby. Tzatzoe's appearance before the committee certainly illustrated the ambiguities of his position, as he sought to articulate African frustrations and complaints.[50] Tzatzoe's efforts to present the agenda of the Xhosa notwithstanding, the Select Committee represented something of a highpoint for humanitarian interests. Before its hearings were complete, the evangelical Colonial Secretary, Lord Glenelg, had ordered the withdrawal from control of Queen Adelaide Province in December 1835. In the five years that followed the death of Hintsa, policies seeking to ensure the 'protection' of indigenous peoples were written into British colonial administrations throughout the Southern Hemisphere, while in 1837 the Aborigines' Protection Society was formed in London as a focus of metropolitan humanitarianism.[51]

While tensions between 'colonial' and 'humanitarian' opinion predated the issue of Queen Adelaide Province, Philip had already become established as an opponent within settler opinion, particularly in Grahamstown, which had become the centre of an emerging colonialist identity. The Eastern Cape settlers emerged as a community whose material interests saw them align themselves emphatically with the more established Dutch-Afrikaner settlers; although crude self-interest cannot fully explain the congruence between settler ideologies at the Cape in the 1820s and 1830s. The experience of the 1834–35 war was a particularly significant moment in the creation of settler identities on the Eastern Cape, whose contours were articulated by Godlonton's *Narrative of the Irruption of the Kafir Hordes* (1836). Godlonton, one of the 1820s settlers, embodied the general trajectory of the new colonists, in abandoning attempts at farming before establishing himself as a printer (his trade in London) in the early 1830s. The primary editorial voice of the *Graham's Town Journal*, Godlonton's writings, emphasized the role of the settler in the civilization of the 'wild' South African landscape and the establishment of a metropolitan form of social order. The construction of South African settler identities relied upon a simultaneous construction of Africans as the inverse of the European self-image – as uncivilized and indolent subjects who constituted a threat to colonial society without constant discipline and control.[52] Settler identities thus emerged around the construction of a negative stereotype of black 'barbarians', which revealed as much about white insecurities and their 'collective anxiety as colonists in an insecure frontier space'.[53]

Humanitarians played an equally important role in this process. The first three heads of the LMS at the Cape encapsulated the transnational qualities of mission humanitarianism. Van der Kemp the multilingual libertine, Read the charismatic egalitarian and Philip the political operator and agent of metropolitan humanitarianism, all sought to cross borders – both literally and figuratively – in their professional careers and personal lives. The network of social relationships that they created, and that sustained their work, were both imperial and transnational, in the sense that mission dissolved the boundaries between the colonial and the world beyond its self-determined boundaries. While the tensions between humanitarians and settlers such as Godlonton reveal something of the contradictions of colonialism in southern Africa, both colonists and their critics played a part in the laying the foundations for the struggle over land and labour that would become the dominant characteristic of colonial South Africa. Meanwhile, Jan Tzatzoe's frustrated efforts to present the full extent of Xhosa antipathy demonstrated the challenge that Africans would face in asserting agency, even among those who purportedly sought to protect their interests.

Trekkers, amaZulu and Natal

As in the east, the northern frontier of the Cape had never been fixed in reality – the boundaries of colonial control were always indistinct and permeable. By the turn of the nineteenth century, Boer farmers had already begun to extend colonial settlement northward into arid zone of the Karoo. Further north, across the Gariep River, groups of mixed settler and Khoisan ancestry had come to establish hegemony over Sotho-Tswana lineage groups and who might be considered as the vanguard of colonial expansion in the northern interior.[54] To a degree, the Griqua *were* the frontier between colonial and African society. In social and cultural terms, the Griqua were both geographically and symbolically marginal: 'they were blacks who appeared to possess some of the powers of whites'.[55] In the first decade of the nineteenth century, the Griqua became a particular focus of attention for LMS missionaries, who established a centre at Griquatown in 1801. During the 1820s, Griqua groups became engaged in struggles for control over trade and territory that overlapped to a degree with the contests over power between Sotho, Tswana and, latterly, Ndebele groups on the Highveld.[56] For the humanitarian lobby led by Philip, the Griqua represented a key to the establishment of British control over the interior, and he promoted the claims of the Griqua chief Andries Waterboer as the paramount ruler in the frontier region, a status that was bolstered by formal recognition by the Cape authorities and the appointment of a government representative in Griquatown in 1834.[57] Further north again, the LMS missionary Robert Moffat had established a mission station among the Tswana-speaking peoples at Kuruman in 1822. As political intermediaries, missionaries became a potent source of power for African chiefs, and requests for missionaries proliferated in the late 1820s and early 1830s, not because of any evangelical fervour, but because the examples of Moffat and others appeared to demonstrate the protective power of the missionary.[58] As brokers of cultural power, missionaries enabled chiefs to reinforce their standing and reputation – as such they became participants in the political struggles that were reshaping the relations of power in the South African heartland.

Alongside access to missionaries, the best way of ensuring control over the means of protection for African chiefs, was to secure a supply of arms, ammunition and horses. And one of the conduits for arms and ammunition from the Cape were the trekboers who, from the early 1830s, had begun to move their activities north of the Orange and Gariep rivers. By the mid-1830s, the practice of moving livestock into pastures beyond the colonial 'frontier' in the summer months had been superseded by a permanent exodus from the Cape. From 1834, increased numbers of trekboers began to cross the northern border of the Cape, aiming to place themselves beyond the reach of British imperial authority. By 1840, it is estimated that some 15,000 colonists had left the Cape, around 10 per cent of the white population.[59] Standard explanations for the 'Great Trek', as the exodus would later become known, focus on the abolition of slavery, while contemporary accounts cited the decision by Glenelg to withdraw from Queen Adelaide Province as the primary catalyst. Recent accounts have tended, however, to focus on the array of political and social transformations that British rule had fostered, which together undermined the networks of patronage that had regulated settler society at its eastern and northern margins. Anglicization of legal processes further entrenched perceptions of Boer disempowerment. Added to this were pressures on land, exacerbated by corrupt and inefficient establishment of tenure under British control, and the pre-eminence of British merchants and traders in the Eastern Cape economy after 1820.[60]

With the technological capacity to withstand attacks from African kingdoms, illustrated by successes against forces controlled by the Ndebele leader Mzilikazi at Vegkop in 1836 and the Mosega Valley early in 1837, the trekkers became established as a powerful new force in Highveld power struggles.[61] Moreover, despite their antipathy towards the colonial authorities, many of the leading trekkers saw their departure as an extension of colonial influence rather than a decisive break. Thus, while some groups of trekkers moved ever further northward into land beyond the Vaal River, many looked to the territory controlled by the Zulu king, Dingane, in what would become known as Natal. A trading post had been established on the coast at Port Natal (Durban) in 1824, opening a route to Grahamstown. By 1834, leading figures in the Cape were calling on the British government to establish formal control in Natal, while the arrival of American missionaries in the Zulu kingdom in 1835 brought an additional dimension to the burgeoning colonial society in Natal.[62] In 1837, a large party of trekkers associated with Piet Retief made contact with Dingane, hoping to secure the right to occupy lands within the control of the Zulu king. Diplomatic niceties deteriorated into disputes over the loss of cattle and Dingane launched a pre-emptive attack, killing Retief and his main supporters in early 1838. Trekker settlement in Natal was, however, secured under the leadership of Andries Pretorius later that year, with a decisive military victory against a Zulu army at the Ncome River. The battle was a significant defeat for Dingane, and a catalyst for the fracture of the Zulu kingdom when his brother, Mpande, withdrew his allegiance and entered a negotiated alliance with the Boers.[63]

The trekkers declared the formation of an independent Republic of Natalia, centred on Pietermaritzburg, some fifty miles inland from Port Natal, a move that provoked the British authorities under the new Governor at the Cape, Sir George Napier, to bring Natal under formal imperial control. The idea of British colonial expansion in the region began to arouse public enthusiasm in Britain, and a Natal Association was established in London in 1839, and in 1842 the British authorities despatched a military force to secure Port Natal. When the territory was formally annexed to Britain in the following year, most Boer land claims were confirmed, although a sizeable number of trekkers, including Andries Pretorius, retreated north across the Drakensberg mountains.[64] The annexation of Natal presaged a new phase of British imperial policy in South Africa. Thereafter, the interests of settlers would prevail over the waning influence of humanitarians, reinvigorating calls for further colonial expansion in the Eastern Cape.[65] Moreover, the newly established British authorities in Natal were obliged to regulate relations between settlers and an indigenous population living on the same land, foregrounding the 'importance of local impulses rather than grand imperial forces in extending the British empire'.[66]

Securing colonial hegemony

In the decade following Emancipation, the pendulum of ideological power had swung decisively towards the settler in the Cape. Connected with the rise of settler power, the 1840s saw the expansion of wool production in the Eastern Cape, increasingly concentrated in the hands of a land-holding elite. Over the course of the decade, wool exports, largely serving the demands of the British textile industry, had risen fivefold to 5.5 million pounds.[67] The burgeoning significance of large-scale agricultural production, entwining the colonial economy more firmly within imperial networks of trade, has been characterized by many as a decisive moment in South African history, when the colonial 'old regime' gave way to settler capitalism. Humanitarianism, which had done so much to foster the transformation of settler society, retreated in the face of settler visions of 'civilization' increasingly defined through a language of racial difference.[68] During the 1840s, new regulations to control labour were introduced, along with the reform of the colonial civil administration under John Montagu, who brought his experience as administrator of the colony of Tasmania to bear in the service of major improvements to the Cape's transport infrastructure with the use of convict labour.[69]

From the mid-1840s, a series of renewed conflicts with amaXhosa lineage groups resulted in the re-establishment of British control in the former Queen Adelaide Province. As in previous conflicts, settler agitation for the extension of colonial territory, together with amaXhosa raids – exacerbated by drought – raised tensions. In 1846, British military intervention was sparked by a dispute between the colonial authorities and the chief of the Rharhabe Xhosa, Sandile. Initially conceived as simply another 'punitive expedition', the war of 1846–47 differed in significant ways from earlier conflicts between the Xhosa and the Cape. The former opponents of the settlers, Andries Stockenstrom and John Philip both supported the military action in 1846, with Stockenstrom leading a commando of Khoisan, Boer and Mfengu. Jan Tzatzoe, former ally of Philip, aligned himself with Sandile, alongside the majority of African leaders in Xhosa territory. Furthermore, in contrast to earlier conflicts, the military response of the Xhosa was enhanced by significant numbers of fighters equipped with firearms, who were able to strike at the supply lines of the invading force, and engage in guerrilla-style actions from bases in the Amatola Mountains.[70] The British forces resorted to scorched-earth tactics, destroying villages and crops to ensure that Xhosa chiefs had been 'sufficiently humbled'.[71] As Etherington notes, it was British 'war culture' that ultimately subdued the amaXhosa – and even then, peace was finally secured only with the capture of Sandile in 1847.

The final humiliation of the Xhosa chiefs was enacted in January 1848, when the military commander of 1834–35, Harry Smith, returned as Governor of the Cape. In the intervening period, Smith had earned plaudits as a highly effective military commander in India, and returned to the Cape determined to use his enhanced reputation to set right what he clearly perceived as the wrongs of Glenelg's policies of the 1830s. He began by publically humiliating principal Xhosa leaders, a 'boorish act of self-assertion' intended to crush the resistance of the amaXhosa.[72] After tearing up the former treaties, Smith announced the reoccupation of the former Queen Adelaide Province, now rechristened British Kaffraria, and introduced a series of prescriptive regulations designed to 'reform' Xhosa culture and custom.[73] Increasing numbers of Xhosa entered the Cape in search of work, while social relations, living conditions and the African economy came under pressure as a result of the extension of colonial power and expansion of settlement.[74]

Smith had also launched the Cape into conflict beyond its northern boundaries in the region north of the Orange River, where Boer trekkers were engaged in increasingly tense struggles over land with Griqua and African groups. In the early 1840s, the Griqua leader Adam Kok and Sotho king Moshoeshoe had, with the support of the veteran John Philip, secured treaties with the Cape authorities.[75] However, over the course of the decade tensions increased, fuelled by calls for the formal annexation of the territory by Cape land speculators. In 1848, Smith obliged, and proclaimed British control in what became, briefly, the Orange River Sovereignty. In a remarkably short period, Smith had mapped out – at least in draft form – some of the main contours of the future political map of South Africa.[76] Smith's autocratic empire-building enterprise was, however, at odds with the ideas of representative government being promoted by both officials in the Colonial Office in London and settler elites in the Cape. Popular support for elected political institutions was aroused, suffused (worryingly for colonial officials) with radical ideas as a result of the revolutionary ferment in Europe in 1848. Popular agitation against colonial authorities took hold in response to a proposal to establish a penal settlement at the Cape, which convinced officials in London that the oligarchy under Smith was unsustainable, and in 1850 the Colonial Secretary, Earl Grey, drafted proposals for new constitutional arrangements. Before the political crisis could be resolved, however, a new conflict in the Eastern Cape had broken out.[77]

The renewed campaign was inspired by the young prophet, Mlanjeni, whose message of purification served to re-energize the amaXhosa in the face of Smith's continuing efforts to break the power of the ruling lineages.[78] In late 1850, amaXhosa forces launched a series of attacks on British military outposts in the Eastern Cape; at the same time, the Khoisan of the Kat River Community, a centre of LMS missionary activity and long-standing allies of the Cape, joined the wider rebellion against British rule. After the initial attacks were thwarted, the fighters withdrew into bush and forest territory that severely hampered British forces. In the Waterkloof, north of Fort Beaufort, Xhosa fighters under Maqoma, along with Khoisan led by Hans Brander, held off thousands of British troops for eighteen months.[79] In the face of the ongoing black resistance, Smith was recalled in something like disgrace in late 1851, while the British military under Lieutenant-Colonel William Eyre turned to ruthless and brutal tactics and the systematic destruction of Xhosa crops and livestock. The fighting finally concluded in 1853, when Sandile surrendered to Smith's replacement, Lord Cathcart. The eighth and most brutal frontier war between the Xhosa and the Cape Colony signalled, perhaps more than anything else, that coercion had displaced philanthropic humanitarianism, and colonial agendas began to settle on a consensus that centred on the suppression of African power beyond colonial boundaries.

The brutal wars in the Eastern Cape reinforced British notions of essential difference between themselves and indigenous 'Others' around the world. Specifically, British attitudes towards colonial peoples were increasingly marked by a sense of immutable, biological differences between themselves and the 'native' races of Africa and Asia. Theories of racial difference, which were applied as much to the social strata of urban Britain as they were to the peoples of the wider world, were often informed by personal experience of colonial society. Pioneer of scientific racism, Robert Knox, drew on his time as an army surgeon in the Cape when developing his model of the various groups of humankind that were elaborated in his book *The Races of Men* (1850).[80] And the image of the South African 'Native' continued to shape popular conceptions of empire and nation. In mid-1851, as Harry Smith's troops struggled to contain the Xhosa, the Great Exhibition in London celebrated – and proclaimed – Britain's central place in the new world order of free trade. The model of globalization presented at the exhibition was one that dispassionately embraced the eradication of indigenous peoples unable or unwilling to participate in the civilizing process.[81] As an *Economist* article put it, where 'we have savages for our neighbours in Caffreland, we seem to have no alternative than to keep them at bay or to exterminate them'.[82] The expensive war at the Cape was contrasted, in the *Times*, with the approach to indigenous groups in the United States, where, without the interference of missionary societies, the 'rifle did its work, and the savages disappeared'.[83] In South Africa, Smith asserted that 'extermination is now the only word and principle to guide us', but was thwarted in his expansionist efforts by both black resistance and lack of Boer support.[84] Early-nineteenth-century humanitarianism was in retreat, but nor was this entirely a triumph for settler ideologies.

In the aftermath of the 1853 rebellion, the social and ecological destruction of the war was compounded by an epidemic of cattle disease and crop failure, the consequences of which were to push colonial settlement ever further eastward towards the Kei River. In 1856 a young woman, Nongqawuse, prophesied the salvation of the amaXhosa, on the condition that they slaughtered their cattle and destroyed crops. A number of Xhosa leaders, notably the paramount Sarhili, were convinced by the prophecy, with the result that as many as 50,000 amaXhosa died.[85] Many migrated into the Cape seeking work, and the independence of what would later become known as the Ciskei was brought to an end as Africans were drawn into the social, economic and cultural orbit of the Cape. The area became a zone of white settlement, particularly around the urban centres of East London and King William's Town.[86] In a move reminiscent of the experience of the 1820 Settlers in Albany, British Kaffraria saw the influx of thousands of German settlers in the aftermath of the Crimean War, members of the German Legion who had volunteered to fight for the British under Richard von Stutterheim.[87]

The environmental and social disaster of the Cattle Killing was exacerbated by the actions of Cathcart's successor, George Grey, who did all he could to turn the disaster to the advantage of the Cape, steering refugees from British Kaffraria into the Colony's labour pool and crushing the power of African chiefs by despatching their leaders to Robben Island.[88] Grey was a fervent imperialist and believer in the 'civilizing mission', and he had come to the Cape with a reputation as adept colonial administrator, having served as a Governor in Australia and New Zealand. His was, in fact, the epitome of the mid-nineteenth-century colonial career. Soon after his arrival in 1854, Grey quickly set upon a more interventionist mode of colonial administration than his predecessors, launching a programme of major public works and a system of 'industrial' education in British Kaffraria. At the heart of his plan to 'civilize' the Xhosa, however, was the imposition of a British system of law, overseen by magistrates. Colonial policy and cattle disease combined to destabilize African political power in the region. But, even before the prophecies of Nongqawuse, millenarian responses began to develop. News of Cathcart's death at the hands of Russian forces in Crimea sparked anticipation of the arrival of a 'black army' from overseas. Similar stories about salvation at the hands of an Indian army began to circulate in 1857, when news of the Indian Mutiny reached South Africa. This was no inward-looking and atavistic movement, then, but a rational attempt to make sense of – and control – complex local disasters within the connected worlds of the Victorian British Empire.

The interconnectedness of imperial sites and colonial careers meant that the struggles for ideological and material dominance in South Africa were played out with reference to the comparable experiences of settlers and humanitarians in Australia, New Zealand, India and the Caribbean, all of which intersected with metropolitan images of and attitudes towards subordinate groups, not least women and the working classes.[89]

The worldwide networks fostered by colonialism also enabled the emergence, in nascent form, of global networks that connected the subordinate classes of empire. As with Jan Tzatzoe, missionaries provided the primary opportunities for black South Africans to establish connections with the wider Victorian world. Alumni of one of the foremost mission centres of the Eastern Cape, Lovedale School, Tiyo Soga embodied the ambivalence associated with the transnational identities imbued by mission education. After travelling to Scotland to study Theology, Soga became a Presbyterian minister in 1856, then returned to South Africa the following year to establish, with his Scottish wife, a Presbyterian mission with the Ngqika Xhosa. Although in many ways an 'unusual example of a cultural broker', his life provides a South African counterpart to contemporary pioneers of pan-African identity such as Edward Blyden.[90]

To the north in Transorangia, the retreat of British forces brought the Boer settlers into the ascendancy, and their rights to self-government were recognized in the Sand River (1852) and Bloemfontein (1854) conventions. The British had effectively discarded their agreements with African chiefs and underwritten the political power of the trekkers on the Highveld. The new states recognized in the conventions of the early 1850s – the

South African Republic (Zuid Afrikaansche Republiek: ZAR) to the north of the Vaal River and the Orange Free State were to become a focus of European colonialism beyond the boundaries of British imperialism. By 1855, then, two new colonial states had been created in the southern African interior, although initially the actual institutions of statehood were undeveloped. Constitutions were adopted, and forms of governance established, based upon the commando system of collective protection that had existed at the Cape. In both the new republics, and in the ZAR particularly, subsistence farming was the dominant mode of social and economic activity. But the constitutions of the new states suggested the germ of republican identities was beginning to take hold. In the ZAR, the break with the ideologies of the Cape was underlined in its 1858 constitution, which denied the 'equality of the non-white with the white inhabitants, either in the Church or the State'. The position in the Orange Free State was more ambivalent, however, and there continued to be a reference to the Cape as the 'intellectual and spiritual heartland of South Africa'.[91]

In the Cape, the 1850s saw significant changes in the organization of the colonial state, not least the granting of representative government in 1853. The new parliament was elected under a nominally colour-blind franchise, giving Africans – and poorer Afrikaners – voting power in a system that came to be regarded as the cornerstone of 'Cape Liberalism'. The new constitution was, however, as much a defensive measure as it was a positive expression of liberalism; it sought to reassert the authority that had begun to breakdown and was being imposed (at least on the eastern boundaries of the colony) by military, rather than civic means.[92] The establishment of self-rule in the Cape was rooted in the political and economic transformations that had taken place since the start of the century. These changes coincided with, and were often driven by, the perceived moral and physical needs of industrial society in Britain itself.

Self-governance at the Cape coincided with what James Belich has described as a 'hidden boom' in nineteenth-century South Africa, stimulated by the continuing development of public works and resurgence of investment from London. As had been the case throughout the first half of the nineteenth-century, the economy of the Cape was also buttressed by imperial military endeavours. The metropolitan government spent £3 million on the 1850–53 Xhosa Wars alone, which boosted the settler economy in the Eastern Cape. The imperial connection would continue to be of vital material importance, not least in terms of access to investment and capital via the City of London. Nevertheless, the self-governing colony at the Cape was founded when its place in the imperial economy was secure enough to sustain its independent existence.

The emerging racial order of the Cape was also shaped by the emergence of a colonial middle-class, whose desire for 'respectability' invariably made reference to metropolitan culture and resulted in the development of public institutions, including the South African Library and South African Museum in Cape Town, both established in the 1820s.[93] The collections housed in these buildings constituted a body of knowledge that embodied the assertion of power over the lives and bodies of the indigenous occupants of the territory and established claims for recognition of the rights of colonial citizens to determine their own political destinies. An emergent colonial bourgeois discourse came to displace the social and political debates of the early nineteenth century. By the 1850s, the egalitarianism that had characterized missionary institutions twenty years earlier had declined in the face of a new bourgeois and respectable evangelicalism.[94]

Summary

During the first half of the nineteenth century there was hardly any concept of 'South Africa' as a discrete identity, and where larger territorial formations were defined (e.g. 'The Cape'), these were by and large constructs of colonial knowledge and imagination. By 1860, the political map of southern Africa comprised a patchwork of colonies situated alongside a series of independent African polities. Groups such as the amaZulu, BaPedi and amaXhosa maintained control over parcels of land in between settler-controlled zones, or were – as in the case of the Griqua and Sotho – under the nominal 'protection' of the British Empire.[95] However, for many Africans, an independent existence was becoming tenuous. In January 1866, what had been British Kaffraria was formally annexed as the Ciskei and incorporated into the Cape, adding over 60,000 Xhosa to the African population of the colony. The incorporation of these new colonial subjects into the political and social life of the Cape highlighted a dilemma that marked settler colonialism across the British Empire in the second half of the nineteenth century, namely how reformism and the mission to 'civilize' might be made compatible with the desire to secure settler interests. Race, it seemed, lay at the heart of the solution – a way of encoding inequality without apparently betraying the principles of self-government.

As it expanded to the north and east of the Cape, colonial society, measuring distinctions of status via categories of respectability, 'civilization' and above all racial appearance, set in chain the transformation of African societies. But the history of African societies cannot simple be framed with references to colonial dominance or indigenous resistance; instead the process of interaction between Africans and Europeans in the region might be understood as a 'conversation', in which indigenous groups gradually became conscious of the meaning of colonization and its ramifications for their lives.[96] Thus, while historians can still state confidently that, after 1800, 'the growing British presence profoundly shaped South Africa', they have also acknowledged that British power 'although pervasive, was not straightforward'.[97] The cultural impact of mission Christianity and European technologies played a critical role in reshaping African society and culture. But it was settler expansion, and the alienation of the land itself, that arguably had the greatest impact of all. The first half of the nineteenth century saw the beginnings of a process of dispossession across South Africa that would accelerate with the development of industrialization in the latter part of the century. The process began, however, with the construction of a pattern of land rights and legal entitlements, repeated across the colonial world that 'strengthened the power of landholders and allowed them to encroach on the lands of African peasants and pastoralists'.[98]

These transformations in southern African societies in the first half of the nineteenth century were shaped by local contingencies but at the same time reflected global developments, as European imperialism emerged alongside industrialization and a decisive shift in the centre of gravity of the world economy.[99] The world was increasingly characterized by a split between the manufacturing economies of Europe and commodity-producing economies elsewhere, and southern Africa sat uneasily on the imaginary frontier between the two. Conflicts over the control of land, between European settler populations and the indigenous peoples desperate to maintain sovereignty wherever possible, became a fundamental feature of the social and political history of South Africa from the late nineteenth century.

Further reading

Bayly, C. A. *The Birth of the Modern World, 1780–1914: Global Connections and Comparisons*. Oxford: Blackwell, 2004.

Comaroff, Jean and John L. Comaroff. *Of Revelation and Revolution*. Vol. 1: *Christianity, Colonialism, and Consciousness in South Africa*. London: University of Chicago Press, 1991.

Crais, Clifton C. and Pamela Scully. *Sara Baartman and the Hottentot Venus: A Ghost Story and a Biography*. Princeton, NJ: Princeton University Press, 2009.

Crais, Clifton C. *White Supremacy and Black Resistance in Pre-Industrial South Africa: The Making of the Colonial Order in the Eastern Cape, 1770–1865*. Cambridge: Cambridge University Press, 1992.

Daunton, Martin and Rick Halpern, eds. *Empire and Others: British Encounters with Indigenous Peoples, 1600–1850*. London: UCL Press, 1999.

Elbourne, Elizabeth. *Blood Ground: Colonialism, Missions, and the Contest for Christianity in the Cape Colony and Britain, 1799–1853*. Montreal: McGill-Queen's University Press, 2002.

Etherington, Norman. *The Great Treks: The Transformation of Southern Africa, 1815–1854*. Harlow: Longman, 2001.

Hyam, Ronald. *Britain's Imperial Century, 1815–1914: A Study of Empire and Expansion*. 3rd edn. Houndmills, Basingstoke, Hampshire: Palgrave Macmillan, 2002.

Keegan, Timothy J. *Colonial South Africa and the Origins of the Racial Order*. Cape Town: David Philip Publishers, 1996.

Lambert, David and Alan Lester, eds. *Colonial Lives across the British Empire: Imperial Careering in the Long Nineteenth Century*. New York: Cambridge University Press, 2006.

Lester, Alan. *Imperial Networks: Creating Identities in Nineteenth-Century South Africa and Britain*. New York: Routledge, 2001.

Magubane, Zine. *Bringing the Empire Home: Race, Class, and Gender in Britain and Colonial South Africa*. Chicago: University of Chicago Press, 2004.

Ross, Robert. *Status and Respectability in the Cape Colony, 1750–1870: A Tragedy of Manners*. Cambridge: Cambridge University Press, 1999.

Worden, Nigel and Clifton C. Crais. *Breaking the Chains: Slavery and Its Legacy in the Nineteenth-Century Cape Colony*. Johannesburg, South Africa: Witwatersrand University Press, 1994.

CHAPTER 3
MINERALS AND MODERNITY

In 1850, colonial South Africa was a minor, if strategically significant, outpost of empire. Over the next six decades it would be transformed into one of the most important centres of the imperial world, the focus of struggles rooted in the complexities of local political as well as global socio-economic forces. For black South Africans, the period saw alienation and loss of political independence at an accelerated pace, with the impact of European systems of economic exchange and political organization discernible almost everywhere. The second half of the nineteenth century saw the high point of British imperialism in South Africa, but throughout the period other forces and influences, both local and global, shaped the political and social worlds occupied by South Africans. Beyond formal systems of power, South African societies were transformed by the expansion of industrial capitalism in the nineteenth-century world. Thus, while the foundations of a new colonial South Africa under British imperial hegemony had been built in the first half of the nineteenth century, it was in the second half of the century that much of the actual occupation of imperial spaces took place. In the process, South Africa became part of, but was not completely subsumed by, the British world.

South Africa was distinctive in many ways, however. Between 1860 and 1914 increasing numbers of migrants were drawn by the opportunities offered by a new industrial economy, although South Africa attracted smaller levels of immigration from Britain relative to territories such as Australia and Canada.[1] Other colonial territories saw a doubling of the settler population every decade over the course of the century, but this occurred in southern Africa only in the final years of the nineteenth century, a result of the gold mining boom. It was a 'non-explosive Anglo-owned new land', which bore greater similarities to Quebec or New Mexico than Australia or California.[2] Nevertheless, the economic transformation of southern Africa in the late nineteenth century cannot be separated from contemporary transformations in Europe and North America.[3] The formation of a modern South Africa was shaped not just by British imperialism, but by global developments and transnational processes associated with industrialization.

Labour before the mineral revolution

The establishment of European control over labour was a critical foundation of the racially defined social order that characterized modern South Africa. Securing access to labour was, of course, intimately bound up with the appropriation of land, and both processes lay at the heart of nineteenth-century colonialism. As we have seen, one of the consequences of the expansion of colonial authority into the Eastern Cape in the 1850s was to draw large numbers of Africans into the Cape labour market, while similar processes were underway in Natal. Colonial administration sought to secure African labour through a number of practices, including various forms of taxation.[4] The introduction of a 'hut tax' in Natal in 1849 was one of the first examples of such a venture, designed both to secure Africans into the labour market and to raise revenue. More than a crude instrument of coercion, these taxes provided a means of social control, seeking to diminish the status of cattle as a definition of wealth and thereby suppress the practice of polygamy.[5]

The Natal tax was an integral part of the system of 'native administration' established by the colonial administrator Theophilus Shepstone. It was a model of indirect governance that operated through supposedly 'traditional' political and social institutions, centred on the figure of the 'chief'.[6] Arguably, it provided a historical foundation for later systems of segregation, but Shepstone was determined, like Grey in the Eastern Cape, to focus on sociocultural transformation and the 'civilizing process'.[7] He had worked as an interpreter during the 1834–35 war on the Xhosa, before being appointed as diplomatic agent with the amaZulu in 1845. For Shepstone, ongoing moves to regulate African lives, such as control over marriage practices, were driven by a belief that policy should integrate economic efficiency and cultural imperialism.[8]

In addition to its role as a testing ground for colonial administration, Natal was the site of significant new expansion of the colonial population in the latter half of the century. The territory had seen the arrival of thousands of British and Irish settlers between 1849 and 1852, but most significantly, over 150,000 indentured workers from India, from 1860 to 1911, part of a global movement of labour to Africa and the Caribbean.[9] The majority of Indian indentured workers in Natal were assigned to developing sugar plantations around Durban and the Natal coast. Indenture schemes after 1874 continued to be focused on the coastal plantation sector, but workers could increasingly find work elsewhere in Natal, from railway construction to the coal mining industry, and by 1910 made up around 40 per cent of the total labour force.[10] By the end of the 1860s, Natal had developed into a second major British colony in South Africa, and was granted self-government in 1893. Economically, it remained centred around the port of Durban, which served both the rapidly expanding sugar industry and, from the 1880s, the gold-mining centred on the Rand.

Imperialism, confederation and war

The focus of British imperial power in southern Africa remained rooted in the basic strategies of the eastern British Empire – control at the southern tip of Africa was meant to secure British hold over a strategic point in the Indian Ocean world. Efforts to establish control at the imperial 'bridgeheads' of the Eastern Cape and Natal served these basic imperatives. However, the costs of securing control and the relative weakness of the colonial economy meant that concerted efforts to establish British supremacy in South

Africa remained in abeyance for much of the 1860s.[11] By the end of the decade, however, new directions in imperial policy would intersect with major economic developments and transform the politics of South Africa.

In 1867, alluvial diamonds were discovered close to the Harts River west of Bloemfontein, within the territory of Griqualand West. Within three years, thousands of hopeful prospectors had travelled to the district, setting in motion profound social and economic transformations. The site of the 'New Rush' – soon known as Kimberley – was revealed as one of the world's richest deposits of diamondiferous rock. Initially claimed by the Boers of the South African Republic, then briefly an independent 'Diggers Republic', the territory became a British colony in 1871 and was eventually incorporated into the Cape in 1880.[12] Although rooted in a particular set of economic and political circumstances, the annexation of Griqualand West in order to secure the diamond fields, together with the extension of imperial control over Moshoeshoe's Basotho kingdom in 1868, represented the first moves in renewed expansionary imperialism in South Africa. In 1874, the new Colonial Secretary in London, Lord Carnarvon, began to shape a plan for a South African confederation along the lines of the Canadian federation that he had helped to establish in 1867.[13] Again, the colonial politics of South Africa would have a significant impact on the development of British imperial policy.

Thus, while confederation revived the 'Imperial Factor' in South African political history, there were also significant local influences on the increased expansionism of the 1870s and after.[14] Strongly opposed by the Cape Prime Minister, J. C. Molteno, it was Shepstone, the 'unrelenting Natal sub-imperialist', who steered Carnarvon's efforts to establish imperial hegemony in South Africa.[15] Shepstone was not without his critics, however, notably the Anglican Bishop John Colenso, who had protested at Shepstone's capture and trial of the amaHlubi leader Langalibalele in 1874. A former ally of Shepstone, Colenso had become a figure of some notoriety in London in the 1860s, as metropolitan intellectuals including Matthew Arnold poured scorn on his attempts to understand Christian doctrine from the perspective of his Zulu translator, William Ngidi.[16] Another view of local conditions was provided by the historian James Anthony Froude, who had been despatched to South Africa in 1874–75 to report on the feasibility of confederation. Impressed by the attitudes of white settlers, particularly those of Dutch descent, Froude regarded South Africa as a space in which a new, purer form of Englishness was being established.[17] As a consequence, he was contemptuous of Shepstone's policy of indirect rule, and declared that Natal was the 'powder magazine of South Africa'.[18] Nonetheless, Carnarvon found Shepstone's vision persuasive, and set him the task of brokering a deal to bring the South African Republic under British control. Shepstone subsequently negotiated an agreement in 1877 to annex the Transvaal, heavily in debt, politically divided and recovering from a failed attempt to conquer the Pedi kingdom on its eastern border.[19]

Confederation therefore entangled metropolitan ideas of imperial policy alongside local conceptions of cultural and intellectual unification.[20] But confederation was also a manifestation of broader imperialist visions that began to coalesce in Britain in the late nineteenth century. It was not merely a political strategy, but a feature of an ideology that entwined the extension of colonial power with the expansion of knowledge. Its two leading advocates in the Cape, Sir George Grey and Sir Bartle Frere, were both patrons of intellectual endeavour, supporting institutions such as the South African Museum and the South African Philosophical Society. British confederation policy was as much an exercise in intellectual and cultural colonialism – the attempt to achieve 'cognitive mastery over the subcontinent' – as it was a political and strategic impulse directed by shifting material circumstances.[21]

Social and political transformations in the Eastern Cape continued to be shaped by the processes of colonial expansion and appropriation of territory that had been underway since the 1850s. Following the formal incorporation of the Ciskei (British Kaffraria) into the Cape in 1866, Thembu and Mfengu migration across the Kei River intensified the interconnections between the Cape and nominally independent Xhosa territories. These 'black frontiersmen' fostered the emergence of market-oriented, small-scale farming and further undermined the political independence of the amaXhosa.[22] The process accelerated further following a final frontier war in 1877–78, prompted by a rebellion on the part of the Gcaleka and Ngqika, which was followed by increased white settlement and the gradual incorporation of the Transkeian territories into the Cape.[23]

The war in the Eastern Cape coincided with a series of events across southern Africa that, taken together, might be characterized as a general British war of unification.[24] In 1878 in the Transvaal, the Pedi kingdom under Sekhukhune reignited its conflict with settlers, resisting colonial forces until defeated by a combined British and Swazi assault in late 1879.[25] At the start of that year, the High Commissioner, Sir Bartle Frere had focused his attention on the Zulu kingdom, after an ultimatum to disband the Zulu military was ignored by Cetshwayo. Despite defeat at Isandhlwana, when the amaZulu overwhelmed a third of the British forces, the Zulu kingdom was defeated, fragmented and its population drawn into the orbit of colonial economic and administrative power. The process of 'destruction and reconstruction' of the Zulu kingdom would be protracted, and would ultimately lead to the formal incorporation of the territory into Natal in 1887.[26] Boer resistance thwarted plans for confederation, however. Led by Paul Kruger, who had been elected as President of the South African Republic in 1877, rebel burghers declared the restoration of the republic in December 1880. The armed revolt that followed established the effectiveness of Boer forces in combat against the British, particularly after the overwhelming victory at Majuba in February 1881. British forces were withdrawn and the entire federation scheme was shelved.[27]

The mineral revolution(s)

The most significant factor in the social and economic transformation of southern Africa was the discovery of significant deposits of diamonds and gold in the 1860s and 1880s. Before the 1870s, South African trade was in essence an exchange of wool and wine for guns, tools and blankets, little 'different from other pieces of colonial real-estate'.[28] After the discovery of diamonds, the South African economy was transformed, taking a distinctive and significant position in the emerging imperial/world economy. Wool exports had fostered greater integration with British trading networks; minerals, and more specifically gold, launched export-led economic growth.[29] Mineral extraction quickly came to dominate the region's economy, drew in ever-greater numbers of migrants, and had become a primary political concern. The establishment of mining industry at Kimberley resulted in the development of structures for the organization, recruitment and disciplinary control of labour that have been seen as a model for the entire system of segregation that became routinized in law and practice in twentieth-century South Africa.[30]

While South African racism cannot be explained in material terms alone, the establishment of diamond-mining industry around Kimberley established precedents for the divisions of labour along lines of race and class that would underpin South African experiences of modernity. Moreover, the mining centres at Kimberley and on the Rand became centres of cultural interchange, which fostered the creation of hybrid forms of music and performance. Coloured *oorlams* music, rooted in the Cape farms, or dance forms brought by amaTsonga migrants from Mozambique, together with 'respectable' cultural forms associated with Christian churches combined to create new performance styles.[31] By the end of the century, urban African music was beginning to reflect the struggles of black workers within constraints of the racial hierarchies of industrial South Africa; none more so, perhaps, than Enoch Sontonga's *Nkosi Sikelel' iAfrika*, adopted by the African National Congress as its anthem in 1925.[32]

The development of diamond mining at Kimberley also demonstrates the global contingencies that shaped the development of the mineral economy. The 'share-working' practices employed in the early years of the diamond economy were rooted in the Cornish 'tribute' system, replicated around the Anglophone world in the nineteenth century.[33] But the system could not meet the needs of the costly enterprise, and a process of amalgamation began, with an increasing reliance upon manual labour. Tensions between small-scale 'diggers', merchant interests and the colonial state resulted in the 'Black Flag' revolt of 1875, suppressed by the British army. At the same time grievances became increasingly defined by the fault lines of race, as white workers began to articulate collective rights through a racially exclusive trade unionism. Branches of overseas unions were formed, such as the Cape branch of the Amalgamated Society of Carpenters and Joiners in 1882.[34] Following the 1876 Labour Commission report, formal control over labour recruitment was established, based on the regulation of migrant labour in the Indian Ocean world, from India itself to Natal and Mauritius.[35] While the early stages of the migrant labour system drew in Bapedi and Basotho workers keen to purchase guns and other commodities, from the 1880s, long-distance Tsonga migrant workers from Mozambique came to predominate.[36]

In the 1880s, small-scale diggers were gradually making way for larger mining operations. The process of amalgamation was exacerbated by the collapse of diamond prices, following the onset of the Great Depression in the mid-1870s, combined with the increasing costs of extracting diamonds from ever-deeper layers of rock. In an effort to ensure profitability, controls over the market in diamonds were developed, affecting both the working conditions of miners, who were subject to ever-greater scrutiny, and the formation of joint-stock companies as small groups of claim holders began to accumulate rights to abandoned claims. In 1888, the two major mining concerns, operated by Cecil Rhodes and Barney Barnato, merged into De Beers Consolidated Mines, effectively establishing a cartel, which came to control diamond production worldwide.[37] By the turn of the century, the company was alone responsible for half of the total exports from the Cape.[38] The consolidation of South African industrial capital on the diamond fields laid foundations that enabled the rapid exploitation of new discoveries of gold to the north.

In 1886, the discovery of an outcrop of gold on the Witwatersrand in the Transvaal set in motion yet another shift in the centre of gravity of the South African economy. From a relatively minor position in the 1880s, by 1914 South Africa became the source of around 40 per cent of global gold production. The income and foreign investment that accrued from the mining industry would come to dominate the South African economy for the first half of the twentieth century, and remained a powerful influence thereafter. From the outset, mining on the Rand favoured large-scale, capital-intensive operations, and encouraged the development of amalgamated companies able to exploit economies of scale. Deeper-level mining from the mid-1890s led to further consolidation of production and the emergence of a small and influential set of operations, led by Wehrner Beit and Company and Rhodes' Consolidated Gold Fields.[39] Together, these 'Randlords' began to exert control over social and political life in Johannesburg, as the more complex deep-level mining drew in ever increasing numbers of workers. In the twenty years between 1890 and Union, Johannesburg became the focal point of South Africa, both economically and politically, and as the crucible of social transformations that would shape South African modernity. Johannesburg witnessed a rapid metamorphosis from diggers' camp to urban sprawl, from rural backwater to a cosmopolitan centre remarkable, even by the standards of the period, for its culture of materialism. It was, as an Australian visitor remarked in 1910, 'a city of unbridled squander and unfathomable squalor'.[40] In many ways, the South African experience replicated that which had characterized the mineral booms of Australia and the American West. The radicalization of economic and social rivalry in the cosmopolitan milieu of the mines, the gradual 'civilization' of the social world of the miners could be seen in southern California in the 1850s just as clearly as the gold fields of the Transvaal in the 1880s and 1890s.[41]

By the end of the century, South Africa provided a quarter of the world output of gold, and the South African mining was a major site of international investment, much of it originating in Britain.[42] South Africa's mining revolutions – in diamonds and then in gold – galvanized the colonial economies in the subcontinent. In the Transvaal, the Kruger administration sought to exploit the burgeoning mining industry as a means to build a state powerful enough to protect its independence from Britain. Efforts to capitalize on the wealth created by the Witwatersrand, through the establishment of a monopoly over dynamite and plans to complete the rail link with Delagoa Bay were, however, a greater source of political tension than they were of economic benefit.[43]

Similarly, in the Cape, the mineral economy was intended to establish a security and self-sufficiency in colonial administration.

In both cases, the 'gentlemanly capitalism' of the London money market continued to play a critical role in securing – and constraining – the success of the South African economies. As the primary conduit of international trade, shipping played a key role in the development of the South African economy, as the introduction of steam cut the costs of long-distance transport.[44] After persuading the Cape parliament to share the vital mail contract between the USSC and his own Castle line, the Scottish shipowner Donald Currie became a highly influential figure in South African and British politics during the 1870s. He was a close friend of John Molteno, but also supported Kruger in his attempt to lobby Carnarvon in 1877. Currie was an embodiment of Victorian imperialism, in which personal interests were in alignment with those of Britain's expanding empire.[45]

The rising influence of Currie reflected the importance of imperial networks of exchange that connected South Africa to the wider world in the nineteenth century. But industrialization also brought increasing contact with the world beyond the British Empire. The US government had established diplomatic contacts with the Boer Republics by 1870, and large numbers of American miners were attracted to work on the diamond fields. Trade between the United States and South Africa was, however, insignificant until the 1880s. Gradually, though, Americans began to see South Africa as a potential market and took an increasing interest in developments in the region. The Republican tradition encouraged some Boer leaders to appeal to the United States for support, but until the 1880s the State Department operated a policy of 'passive neutrality', which, by the end of the century, had moved towards support for a stable and unified South Africa under British control.[46]

Expanding global networks of trade and transport accelerated the circulation of microbial life, with significant impact on the societies of southern Africa. Transoceanic trade routes had long been a conduit for the importation of disease into the region, but their impact was heightened as a consequence of the expansion of internal movements and labour migration in the nineteenth century. Attempts to suppress the outbreak of smallpox in Kimberley in 1883–85, which originated with African migrant workers from Mozambique, had economic impacts on the costs of labour and supplies that contributed to the major strike by white workers in 1884.[47] Even greater social and demographic impact was felt by the spread of the rinderpest epizootic virus in southern Africa in the 1890s, which originated in the horn of Africa in the late 1880s, imported into the continent via Asian cattle brought as supplies by Italian forces to serve imperial endeavours in Somalia.[48] The loss of cattle as a consequence of the disease had a significant impact on rural African communities. It brought impoverishment and starvation, and compounded the pressures forcing Africans into migrant labour within the colonial economy.[49] Industrialization and urbanization in the late nineteenth century sparked a greater prevalence of diseases, such as tuberculosis, that had been present in African societies since at least the eighteenth century.[50] By the end of the century, public health responses to contagious diseases, especially syphilis and plague, had begun to intersect with colonial racial discourse, resulting in the development of a 'sanitation syndrome'

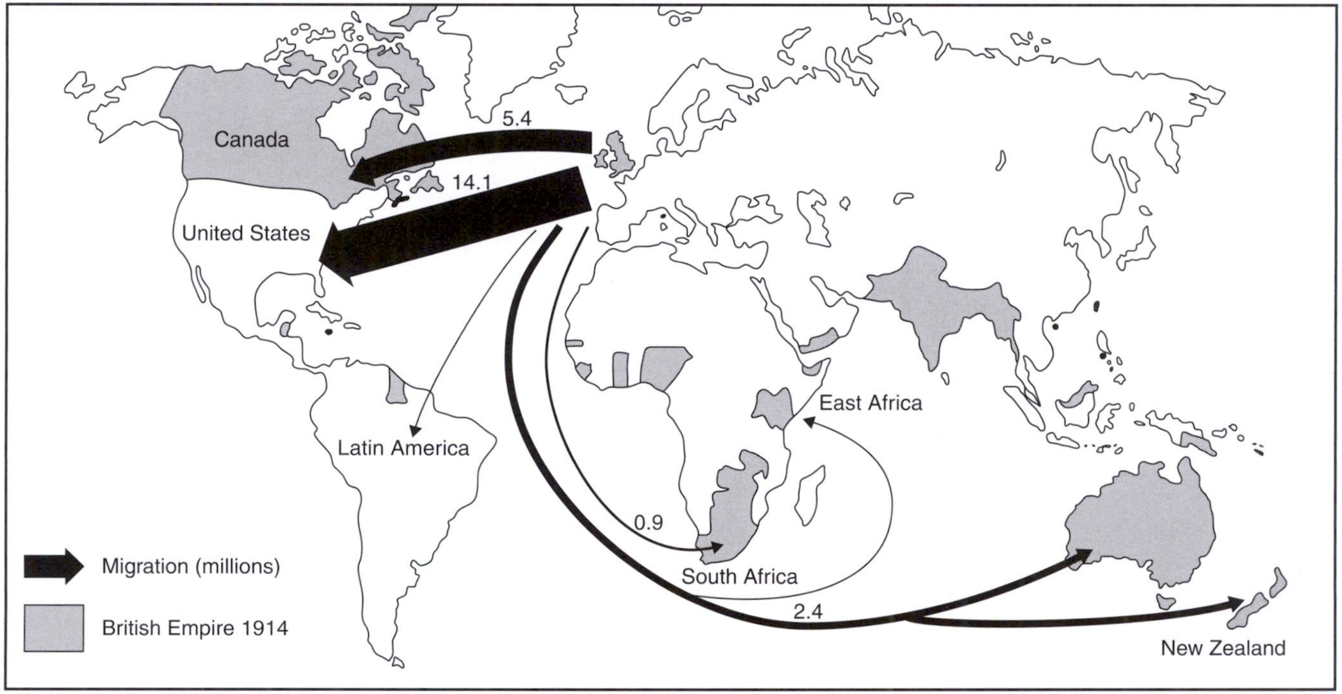

Map 2 Migration in the British Empire, 1815–1914.

Source: 'British emigration, 1815–1914': A. J. Christopher. *The Atlas of Changing South Africa*. London: Routledge, 2001, p. 10.

that justified the enforced removal of Africans from urban centres and set a precedent for segregationist practices of the twentieth century.[51]

During the late nineteenth century, international influences had an increasingly visible – and audible – affect on the formation and transformation of South African culture. In the Cape, indigenous music had integrated Western forms and instruments by the eighteenth century. Industrialization and urbanization during the nineteenth century provided cultural interchanges that established the foundations of an integrated and hybrid South African music culture. In Kimberley and thereafter on the Rand, the traditional oral form of African praise-songs became marked by narratives that described the struggles of migrant labourers on the mines. Cape Town became an entry port for African-American musical influences, as minstrel companies such as the American Jubilee Singers toured the country at the end of the century, establishing a route for new musical forms, such as jazz, that would shape black South African popular culture in the twentieth century. Mission Christians saw performance as an integral part of the process of proselytization and attempted to bolt African linguistic forms onto Western religious hymns. By the latter part of the century, African converts began to respond to these forms of acculturation by composing hymns blending European church music with African oral culture. The Eastern Cape provided fertile ground for these endeavours, exemplified by the music composed by black Christians such as Tiyo Soga and John Knoz Bokwe, whose ‘Plea from Africa’ gave expression to an emergent cultural nationalism that sat alongside its political counterpart.[52] As the new urban centres developed around gold mining, mission Christians brought this hybrid culture into the ‘locations’ that had begun to house the black population of the city. In 1897, at one of these locations, Nancefield, a Xhosa teacher Eric Sontonga composed what would become the anthem of African nationalism, *Nkosi Sikelel’ iAfrika*.

Transnational connections were significant, too, in the everyday experience of workers in the rapidly developing industrial centres of South Africa. The burgeoning workforce on the Rand in particular drew on the comforts and vices that coloured urban life around the world. Johannesburg was connected to transnational networks of crime that, for example, brought ‘Russian’ women to the country following a clampdown on vice in New York.[53] Alcohol was a particular focus of concern shaped, as elsewhere, by emerging conflict around class, but also of race.[54] While local enterprises, such as the Hatherley distillery near Pretoria, exploited local agricultural surpluses in profitable ways, the demand for alcohol, often in the guise of low quality counterfeits of well-known brands, again linked southern Africa to an emerging global network of production and supply, bringing potato spirit from Germany, via East African ports, to the drinking dens of the Rand.[55]

There was much more to the burgeoning German relationship with South Africa than schnapps, however. The development of German imperial ambitions in southern Africa was one of the most important external factors that framed late-nineteenth-century British imperial policy in South Africa. The idea that southern Africa might provide Germany with an empire to rival that of Britain’s Indian Raj was mooted just a few years after unification, and the possibility of a German–Boer alliance was viewed as desirable, both in strategic terms and also as an expression of 'Teutonic' racial solidarity.[56] Moreover, familial and cultural links between the South African settler population and Germany ran deep. Alongside Dutch and French Huguenot, a significant proportion of colonial families could claim German ancestry.[57] Germany positioned itself as a leading imperial power, most notably at the Berlin Conference of 1884–85, when claims in South-West Africa (Namibia), where a settlement had been established at Angra Pequena (renamed Lüderitz) in 1883, were confirmed.

German colonialism in southern Africa added a new 'imperial factor' in regional politics that Republican leaders in the Transvaal were glad to exploit. Kruger made concerted public efforts to emphasize the German connection in ways designed – whether intentionally or not – to arouse maximum frustration among officials in the Cape and London. In 1894, the creation of a National Bank of the South African Republic was made possible by German capital, an obvious deployment of financial power that powered speculation over whether Germany was preparing major investments in southern Africa. By the mid-1890s, then, British officials feared that the Boer Republics were becoming 'outriders of German expansion', a threat both in the region itself, but with potential impact on the balance of power in Europe.[58] At the same time, the increasing power and influence of mining capital in both South Africa and London made the Rand a focus of imperial politics, bringing renewed calls for the extension of British control over the subcontinent.

Imperial tensions and transnational crisis

In 1880, as he was establishing himself as the colossus of the diamond fields, Cecil Rhodes was elected MP for Barkly West in the Cape. Fifteen years later, he had played a significant role in the expansion of British colonial interests, the reconfiguration of race politics in the Cape – and had brought South Africa on the verge of war. Assessments of Rhodes's life and achievements tend to reflect on the divisive and controversial nature of his rapid ascent to unprecedented personal power – he can be equally regarded as the archetype of an imperial patriot and the embodiment of the ruthlessness and corruption of colonialism.[59] Even before his election as an MP in the Cape legislature, Rhodes had developed close connections with South African political figures in the ferment of Kimberley. But it was the formation of the De Beers Company, with its extraordinary political as well as commercial power, that enabled Rhodes to extend his influence as the leading representative of diamond interests in the Cape parliament.

Rhodes's imperial vision overlapped with the 'official mind' of British imperialism, but was driven by a powerful personal ambition. In 1884–85, he brokered British control over supply routes to the north of Kimberley and the establishment of the Bechuanaland Protectorate, driving a wedge between the Transvaal and the new German colony on the Atlantic coast. His attention then moved further north, towards the territories controlled by Matabele and Mashona rulers beyond the Limpopo River. In 1889, following the extraction of a concession treaty from the Matabele king Lobengula, the British South Africa Company was granted a Royal Charter, giving Rhodes and his associates the capacity to create a 'grand, ambiguous outreach of empire'.[60] Rhodes's imperialism was itself ambiguous however: while he supported the extension of imperial control he was a firm advocate of white interests and the maintenance of local power in the hands of white settlers. In 1890, with the support of the Afrikaner Bond, Rhodes was elected Prime Minister in the Cape.

As Prime Minister, Rhodes also began to grapple with task of incorporating Africans into the colonial system without diluting the white supremacy that he saw as a natural right. Informed by the experiences of colonial administrators in other parts of the British Empire, namely the example of Maori enfranchisement in New Zealand, Rhodes introduced legislation that raised the bar for qualification to vote. He went further in 1894, with laws that removed the connection between individual land ownership and voting rights for Africans in the Glen Grey area of the Eastern Cape. Rhodes saw the legislation as a 'Native Bill for Africa' that, he hoped, would establish a blueprint for colonial administration throughout southern Africa.[61] Rhodes' efforts as Prime Minister at the Cape and his empire-building adventures to the north of the Transvaal embodied the process by which South Africa became stitched together as an economic unit during the 1890s.

Two issues, in particular, were critical for the development of regional unity and relations between the Cape and the Boer Republics in the early 1890s: the construction of communications links from the coast to the industrial heartland and formation of customs unions to regulate transport and trade across internal borders. While Rhodes sought to push the railway north from Kimberley along the border of Bechuanaland, Kruger sought backing for a rail connection between the Rand and the Portuguese port at Lourenco Marques on Delagoa Bay. The financial power of the City of London provided the British government a degree of leverage over Kruger, but he sought instead to attract German capital, stoking the fire of imperial rivalries in the cause of South African republicanism.[62] The gold discoveries on the Rand had provided the Transvaal with the means to cement its independence, while the shift in the economic centre of gravity towards the Rand attracted increased levels of foreign investment and provided a major market for farmers in the Orange Free State.[63] In short, the discovery of gold created a potential rival to British regional hegemony.

Meanwhile, Rhodes's imperial ambitions were increasingly entangled with his personal commercial interests. With Rhodes offering financial backing to major British enterprises, it appeared, by 1895, that 'power and initiative lay with Rhodes upon one hand with Kruger on the other, not with the Colonial Office'.[64] Other international interests were nevertheless significant, particularly as gold production on the Rand moved to the more capital-intensive deep-level mining in the 1890s. Alongside the machinations of powerful individuals and the grindstone of Great Power tensions, US interests began to exert increasingly important influence through the presence of mining experts, such as John Hays Hammond, Rhodes's chief engineer and the 'virtual czar of South African mining'. Hammond sought preference for American companies, such as

Fraser & Chalmers, which accounted for nearly half of the mining machinery supplied to the Rand by 1893.[65]

By 1895, the interests of deep-level mining favoured a change of regime in the Transvaal. Foreign mineworkers (or Uitlanders) cited administrative inefficiency and disenfranchisement as major causes of unrest on the Rand. In an attempt to steer Uitlander discontent down the path into outright rebellion, Rhodes began to organize an armed insurrectionary force on the Rand. However, the Uitlanders were by no means united in their desire for the Transvaal to come under British imperial control directed from the Cape. Thus, when Rhodes's lieutenant, Leander Starr Jameson, led a small military force into the Transvaal in December 1895, there was no uprising in Johannesburg. Within days, Jameson and his force were in Pretoria prison. Rhodes lost the premiership of the Cape and his directorship of the South Africa Company, his reputation shaken, particularly amongst his former Afrikaner allies, for whom he would be remembered as little more than a self-serving imperialist.

International responses to the Raid expressed significant sympathy for the Transvaal. Launched at a moment of crisis in Anglo-American relations resulting from a border dispute between Venezuela and British Guiana, many Americans felt that the Raid was a further example of British imperial aggression; the *New York Times* suggested both were examples of 'the immemorial British manner' of imperial adventures.[66] Despite this, the rapid growth in the value of US exports to South Africa, which reached over $16 million per year by 1899, prompted others to conclude that US interests were best served by British predominance.[67] Thus, despite public opposition to British imperialism, American official responses to the Raid were muted. German officials, in contrast, were assiduous in their support for Kruger. Kaiser Wilhelm sent a telegram of congratulations to Kruger, which provoked a storm of xenophobic reaction in London, during which, it was alleged, German and Dutch sailors were attacked by angry Londoners.[68] As the Boer Republics began to strengthen their military forces, Germany also provided practical assistance, supplying new Mauser rifles and training a 'Europeanized' artillery force that began to see themselves as the 'distinctive heirs of the Prussian fighting tradition'.[69]

British officials, such as Chamberlain and the new Governor and High Commissioner in the Cape, Alfred Milner, regarded the Transvaal as the key to British imperial ambitions in Southern Africa.[70] A new imperial confederacy would, in their eyes, be built upon the mineral wealth of the Rand, which required the kind of efficient, modern administration that British imperialism could secure. In fact, throughout the 1890s, the Transvaal had, under Kruger's guidance, begun to recognize the significance of the Rand mineral economy and moved – albeit slowly – to accommodate the interests of the mining magnates.[71] The Cape Afrikaners, meanwhile, considered themselves simultaneously loyal subjects of the British Empire and bound by ethnic ties to the Boer Republics. They supported the concept of a loosely bound empire, rather than formal federation.[72] The loyalty of Cape Afrikaners was, however, ignored by Milner, who like others was fearful of the creation of a unified settler republic centred on the Transvaal – a 'United States of South Africa'. The British government sought to reassert authority, and provoked a war that was, as much as anything else, a struggle to dictate the terms of South African modernization.

The South African War

Explanations for the 1899–1902 South African War point to the strategic concerns that appear to have underpinned British officials' reasoning: fear of the shifting balance of power in the subcontinent towards the Boer Republics, and the consequent loss of control over a critical strategic node of empire. Other interpretations of the crisis focus attention on the material interests of the Transvaal mining magnates. In the years following the Jameson Raid, these influences converged, leading to what has been described as 'Britain's last great expansionist imperial war'.[73] In recent years, the international dimension of the war has risen to prominence, and it seems almost as if the South African conflict has been partly undocked from the country's history and is now primarily a subject of comparative imperial, international or global history. There have been benefits from this change of emphasis, not least in the priority now given to the impact and legacies of the war, in contrast to the overploughed furrow of its causes.[74] We look now for the ways in which events taking place in South Africa were significant for various European powers, for the United States, and for the broader 'British world'. We might even discern attempts to address the impact of the war for India. What follows, though, is an attempt to reframe the war in a transnational history, in which the main aim is to examine how the war prompted changes within, and reflected the shape of, late-nineteenth-century global society.

The South African War was a struggle to define South Africa, to unite the disparate territories south of the Limpopo into a modern state, and thus the beginning of a ten-year process that ended with Union in 1910. It was, if not a 'world war', then certainly a pan-imperial conflict that had repercussions far beyond southern Africa. It helped shape a sense of imperial unity, fostered local identities in the 'British world' and mobilized popular nationalism in Europe. Moreover, the conflict in South Africa became entangled with the imperial ambitions and rivalries of the major powers. German responses reflected the desire of its ruling elite to consolidate power in Africa, while Russian efforts to intervene might be seen as an attempt to weaken Anglo-German relations to their own advantage.[75] In addition, this was a war fought in the direct gaze of global news services, utilizing modern technologies to communicate reports on the fighting to readers around the world.[76] The extended reach of newspaper reporting made it possible to set the conflict in South Africa alongside contemporaneous examples of imperialist endeavour, notably the suppression of the Boxer Rebellion in China, the US war in the Philippines, and German and Russian imperial adventures in China in the late 1890s.[77] Taken together, these developments demonstrated that European imperial rivalries were global in scope, and ultimately set limits on British policymakers' designs for southern Africa. The South African War thus came at a critical juncture for European diplomacy and the 'international system'.

The unexpected success of the Boer advance in the first weeks of the war prompted Germany, France and Russia to exploit the conflict in the hope of enhancing national power and status.[78] In Germany, popular Anglophobia and the history of public support for the Boer Republics was balanced by the obvious advantage that was to be gained by acting in accord with British interests – or at least not acting to intervene in the war. In fact, the pro-Boer policy of the mid-1890s had already been sacrificed when an agreement in 1898 established German recognition of southern Mozambique as a British sphere of interest, effectively ruling out any intervention in any conflict between Britain and the Boer Republics. The 'high politics' that shaped the war were conducted within the confines of cosmopolitan political classes, but the impact of the war was felt more widely, as popular support for the Boer cause gripped the public in Europe and the United States. The makers of foreign policy had little respect for the views of the masses, but the Boer War demonstrated that the pressure of public opinion would have a direct impact on the politics of European states.[79]

An international conflict?

Although ultimately their efforts were of little military significance, several thousand foreign volunteers from across the globe fought alongside Republican forces, including American Rough-Riders, Italian veterans of the Abyssinian War, and French nobility. A number of international brigades were formed, the largest being the Dutch, German and Scandinavian contingents.[80] The majority of international pro-Boer fighters were Uitlanders, already part of the cosmopolitan population of South Africa before the start of the war. There was an element of adventurism in these endeavours, and some fighters moved seamlessly between the various international crises of the early twentieth century, notably the Russian, Alexander Guchkov, who was a member of Jan Smuts' commando during the war, but would go on to become the Minister of War for the Provisional Government following the February Revolution of 1917.[81]

Support for the Republican cause was particularly significant for Irish nationalists, who found an obvious parallel with their own struggle against British imperialism. A significant number of Irish and Irish-American volunteers joined the Irish Transvaal Brigade, organized by the Irish Republican, John MacBride, which bolstered the defences of the Orange Free State in 1900.[82] MacBride and other volunteers would go on to participate in the Easter Rising in Dublin in 1916, but even where they had no direct experience of the South African War, the efforts and tactics of Boer fighters inspired nationalists as they launched their own armed struggle for independence. In the Irish Republic, though, the war was remembered as a symbol of anti-colonial nationalism, helping to cement an alliance of discontented Dominions during the interwar years under the Prime Minister of South Africa, J. B. Hertzog and his counterpart in the Irish Free State, Eamon de Valera.[83] Irish participation in the war cut both ways, though, and a number of leading post-war Unionists were also shaped by their experiences of the war, including Sir James Craig, the first Prime Minister of Northern Ireland in the 1920s.[84]

Similarly, the British army in South Africa was an imperial force that comprised contingents from across the Anglo-world, primarily Australia, New Zealand and Canada. This was not necessarily a testament to widespread imperial loyalism, as exemplified by the initial difficulties in securing Australian volunteers and protests against the war by French-speaking Canadians.[85] Despite these protests, and wider calls for greater Canadian independence, the war helped to foster popular visions of a liberal empire of self-governing Dominions.[86] The First World War would form the primary reference-point for these Dominion nationalisms (as indeed it would for a particular kind of white South African masculinity), but these ideas of Australian, New Zealand and Canadian blood sacrifice were initially framed in the context of the South African War. In contrast with the anxieties felt in Britain over the frailties of military planning and organization revealed in the disastrous early weeks of the war, the public imagination in settler dominions shaped the war as evidence of the virility and bright prospects for the emerging nations.[87] The success of Australian mounted troops in South Africa turned the bush from a site of refuge for criminal gangs into a testing ground for Australian masculinity, just as Australia was itself unified as a federation in 1901.

Once British forces had established control by mid-1900, the majority of foreign volunteers who had fought for the Boer cause were sent back to Europe and the United States, but popular sympathies for the Boer cause were maintained throughout the war, sharpened by the British conduct in its latter stages.[88] In the Netherlands, popular support for the Republics was underpinned by a sense of ethnic affiliation and the importance of South Africa for Dutch nationalism.[89] In Germany, nationalist and anti-British sentiment was stimulated by a raft of petitions, fund-raising appeals and political lobbying in support of the Boer cause, organized by protest groups such as the German Centre for the Struggle to End the War.[90] The strength of public sentiment in Europe persuaded some Boer leaders to seek assistance from the continent as British forces began to establish control over the military situation, in the hope that external influences might yet persuade Britain to enter into negotiations. After the capture of Bloemfontein, delegations were despatched to Europe to seek aid and diplomatic assistance. In the Netherlands, the delegates found enormous public support and sympathy, but while political leaders were unstinting in their pro-Boer sentiments, they would offer no practical support against Britain.[91] When Kruger arrived in Europe in late 1900, he was feted by the public and received with ceremonial honours befitting a visiting Head of State. The Boers became a symbol of popular Anglophobia across Europe at the turn of the century, literally embodied in the tattoos of Kruger found on Parisian gang-members.[92] Support for the Boer cause in Europe thus seemed vociferous, if fleeting, strongest where close ethnic or familial links existed, or where strong nationalist sentiment engendered affinity with South African republicanism.

In the United States, similar distinctions between official and popular attitudes to the war were evident. Officially, the United States adopted a neutral but largely pro-British stance, a reciprocal response to British neutrality during the Spanish-American War, a mutual understanding between imperial powers whose global ambitions and spheres of interest did not substantially overlap. Although leading Americans, including the family of President Theodore Roosevelt, saw Boers as 'kith and kin', official policy veered towards a 'great rapprochement' in official relations between the United States and the British Empire.[93] Pro-Boers nevertheless found support within the anti-imperialist movement that had opposed US action in the Philippines and who saw British imperialism as a similarly exploitative endeavour. At the same time, there existed a powerful pro-British lobby that included missionary and business interests, who developed an overconfident belief that Britain had 'fought a war for American interests', only to discover that British officials regarded US business with increasing concern in the aftermath of the war.[94]

Race and war

At the turn of the twentieth century, many saw the race struggle in South Africa as that between Boer and Briton, rather than between black and white, 'Native' and 'European'. But the conflict was by no means a 'white man's war'. The war was fought by a 'pan-imperial' force, but one shaped by race. British officials, mindful of the sensitivities of the local white political elite, agreed that in contrast to the expansionist wars of the previous century, the imperial force would comprise only white combatants. Thus, while Indian cavalry forces were deployed in South Africa, they were restricted to non-combatant duties. Officers of the Indian Army complained that some of their best mounted troops, as well as trusted Sikh and Gurkha infantry, were unavailable. Offers of military assistance from Indian 'Princely States' were declined, although the same forces were deemed acceptable in the campaign against the Boxer Rebellion, later in 1900.[95] Similarly, in order to appease opposition from the Cape Parliament, a company of Maori scouts was barred by the Cape Prime Minister Gordon Sprigg.[96] Like the British, Boer leaders were reluctant to supply Africans with weapons due to fears of uprisings within the Republics.[97]

Black South Africans were nevertheless active participants on both sides of the conflict. It is estimated that over 10,000 African and coloured fighters took part in the fighting. Barolong fighters participated in the defence of Mafeking, while Kgatla and Ngwato forces were tasked to protect the border between the Transvaal and Basutoland, securing the communication links between the Cape and Rhodesia. In Natal and Zululand, amaZulu military units were involved in fighting, while Bapedi groups aligned themselves with the British and supported efforts to suppress Boer guerrilla operations in the eastern Transvaal in the latter part of the war.[98] In many cases, Africans saw the conflict as a chance to regain political power and territorial control that had been lost. Stories of black involvement in the war, such as those of Abraham Esau in the north-western Cape, suggest that the war offered opportunities for black South Africans. African participation in the war would, it was believed, bring possibilities for cultural and social self-determination.[99] The nascent black middle class responded to the war in diverse ways. Some African political leaders such as A. K. Soga offered loyalist support for the British war effort, while future Congress leader Sol Plaatje, a court interpreter in Mafeking, continued to work as a colonial civil servant throughout the siege of the city.[100] Other black leaders were, however, implacably opposed to the conflict. Under the editorship of John Tengu Jabavu, for whom the war was 'the very quintessence of unfairness', the newspaper *Imvo Zabantsundu* took a critical stance throughout the war.[101] Jabavu's stance reflected political loyalties in the Cape, where the South African Party leaders John X. Merriman and J. W. Sauer were equally vociferous in their opposition to the war. Jabavu, in line with 'respectable' African opinion, nonetheless remained an empire loyalist and hoped that Britain would secure and extend political rights of Africans in the aftermath of the war.[102]

Like their African counterparts, the Indian National Congress supported the war insofar as it seemed to raise expectations that principles of justice and equality might be applied across the empire. Indian nationalists were calling, in essence, for a greater proportion of the 'benefits of empire'. Many in India, including leaders of the emerging nationalist movement, saw support for the war as expressions of their sense of themselves as 'imperial subjects', part of a transnational community. But both African and Indian political leaders were equally frustrated by the failure to reward their loyalty, in contrast to the apparent prioritization of Boer agendas in the period of reconstruction after 1902.[103] For Indians (and for Africans), the South African War was the moment at which the idea of an 'imperial subject' began to disintegrate, generating ambivalence towards the Raj.[104] For Africans, the hope that had been vested in the declared values of British imperialism did not survive long past the cessation of hostilities in 1902. In the following year, a Commission of Enquiry appointed by Lord Milner began to investigate methods of 'Native Administration', thus helping to lay some of the foundations of the system of segregation that was gradually imposed by the Union governments after 1910.

British responses to the war

The war also had a significant political impact in Britain. The public euphoria on the streets of London that greeted the relief of Mafeking in May 1900 was real, even if unrepresentative of working-class feelings beyond the capital.[105] Despite the efforts of W. T. Stead's Stop The War Committee, which attracted significant support from nonconformists and leading socialists, opposition to the war was limited during the first phase of the conflict.[106] How far popular enthusiasm for the war brought victory for the Conservative Party in the so-called Khaki election in 1900 remains a matter of debate, but the conflict was clearly presented as the primary issue in the Conservative campaign.[107] But whatever public enthusiasm did exist began to ebb as it became clear that that the capture of Pretoria had not signalled the end of the war. As efforts to pacify intransigent Boer commandos came to be recognized as 'methods of barbarism', public opinion began to turn against the war.[108] Of particular importance were the revelations of the plight of Boer women and children in concentration camps set up by the British military to house the families of Boer Commandos evicted from the countryside. The levels of disease, malnutrition and starvation in the camps shocked the British public and further hardened popular Anglophobia elsewhere in Europe. Female activists were particularly prominent in the campaign against the camps, notably Emily Hobhouse, who toured the camps on behalf of the liberal South African Conciliation Committee in 1900. Her reports eventually prompted the government to set up a commission of investigation headed by the suffragist, Millicent Garrett Fawcett.[109] Other campaigners, such as Olive Schreiner and Jane Cobden Unwin, had close ties with Cape liberals and humanitarian networks, and might be regarded as successors to the Exeter Hall movement of the 1820s and 1830s.[110]

Others opposed the war on ideological grounds, seeing it as representative of a capitalist imperialism. Leading socialist and British Labour Party founder, James Kier Hardie – a member of Stead's Stop the War Committee – declared that the conflict was a 'capitalist war' in the service of commercial interests:

> The British merchant hopes to secure markets for his goods, the investor an outlet for his capital, the speculator more fools out of whom to make money, and the mining companies cheaper labour and increased dividends.[111]

Another member of the Committee, the economist J. A. Hobson, whose assessment of the crisis was shaped by his experience in Johannesburg as a correspondent for the *Manchester Guardian* in 1899, had provided the framework of this argument. His book, *The War in South Africa: Its Causes and Effects* (1900) sketched out his analysis of empire that would be more fully detailed in his *Imperialism: a Study* published two years later. Hobson's perceptive insights on the distrust between Boer and British leaders, antagonized by Milner, were allied with a polemical against the conspiracy 'of international mine-owners and speculators holding the treasures of South Africa in the hollow of their hands'.[112] This was ultimately a reductionist view of the war that, as historians now suggest, overplayed the influence of mining magnates and was shot through with a seam of anti-Semitism.[113] Nevertheless, Hobson's vision of the war as an asymmetrical conflict, a global hegemon imposing its will on a small and weaker nation in order to secure its economic interests, has resonated throughout the intervening years. For the Left, the South African War thus became a paradigm example of the fundamental relationship between empire and capitalism.[114]

The South African War has been regarded as the embodiment of an imperial war, but it should be considered much more than a war fought to secure imperial objectives. It stimulated nationalist sentiment in southern Africa and Europe, in Britain itself and in other parts of the British world. It sharpened perceptions of collective identity for Afrikaners, Australians and Africans, and was a stimulus to popular nationalism in Germany and the Netherlands. Moreover, the war demonstrated that imperialism itself was a 'global' phenomenon at the turn of the twentieth century. During the South African War, the overlap between imperial and global politics, always significant, became such that imperial struggle played out in a global context. As such, the South African War presaged aspects of the 'world' wars of the twentieth century, in terms of the configuration of rival powers that shaped the geopolitics of the conflict, but also in light of the sheer scale of the mobilization of human, animal and material resources in order to secure control of South Africa.

Summary

The South African War clearly demonstrated the extent to which the region had been drawn into global networks of exchange, and not merely in terms of goods and capital. By the turn of the twentieth century, South Africa was entangled by global communications networks that extended deep into the interior; by 1900, British forces were able to utilize over 4,000 miles of railway lines that connected the country's sea ports to the industries on the Rand.[115] By the end of the nineteenth century, South African societies had undergone dramatic transformation, due in large part to the combined effects of imperialism and industrial capitalism. The South African War was in many ways the epitome of this process, but it by no means captured the full impact of the transnational influences that began to shape the unified country that emerged in its aftermath. Over the course of the nineteenth century, global circuits had stimulated a process by which the region's social and political structures gradually became integrated so that South Africa was, in 1902, in all practical terms an economic and political reality rather than a geographical expression. Colonialism and imperialism had played a major role in this process, but the transnational influences that had come to bear on South Africa also included those – such as the impact of continental European political and intellectual thought, or American capital, or the ill-fated notion of 'imperial citizenship' embraced by Indian nationalists – that moved beyond British imperialism.

Further reading

Cain, P. J. and A. G Hopkins. *British Imperialism, 1688–2000.* London: Longman, 2001.

Clarke, Colin G., Ceri Peach and Steven Vertovec, eds. *South Asians Overseas : Migration and Ethnicity*. Cambridge: Cambridge University Press, 1990.

Evans, Julie, Patricia Grimshaw, David Phillips and Shurlee Swain. *Equal Subjects, Unequal Rights: Indigenous Peoples in British Settler Colonies, 1830–1910*. Manchester: Manchester University Press, 2003.

Giliomee, Hermann. *The Afrikaners : Biography of a People*. London: Hurst, 2011.

Guy, Jeff. *The View across the River : Harriette Colenso and the Zulu Struggle against Imperialism*. Charlottesville, VA: University Press of Virginia, 2002.

Levine, Roger S. *A Living Man from Africa : Jan Tzatzoe, Xhosa Chief and Missionary, and the Making of Nineteenth-Century South Africa*. New Haven, CT: Yale University Press, 2011.

Lowry, Donal, ed. *The South African War Reappraised*. Manchester: Manchester University Press, 2000.

Marks, Shula and Richard Rathbone, eds. *Industrialisation and Social Change in South Africa : African Class Formation, Culture, and Consciousness, 1870–1930*. Harlow: Longman, 1982.

Metcalf, Thomas R. *Imperial Connections: India in the Indian Ocean Arena, 1860–1920*. The California World History Library; 4. University of California Press, 2007.

Moodie, T. Dunbar and Vivienne Ndatshe. *Going for Gold: Men, Mines, and Migration*. Berkeley, CA: University of California Press, 1994.
Nasson, Bill. *The South African War, 1899–1902*. London: Arnold, 1999.
Omissi, David E. and Andrew Thompson, eds. *The Impact of the South African War*. New York: Palgrave, 2002.
Peires, J. B. *The Dead Will Arise: Nongqawuse and the Great Xhosa Cattle-Killing Movement of 1856–7*. Johannesburg: Jonathan Ball, 2003.
Wilson, Keith M., ed. *The International Impact of the Boer War*. Chesham: Acumen, 2001.

CHAPTER 4
RACE AND SEGREGATION

Alongside the Spanish-American War and the Boxer Rebellion in China, the war in South Africa formed part of a grand imperial crisis rooted in the rapid expansion of continental European powers in the latter decades of the nineteenth century. The growth of industrial capitalism, state modernization and nation-building had led to a global technological and economic dominance by European powers not only in Africa, but also in North America and central Asia. Only the rise of a modernized industrial economy in Japan challenged the notion of 'natural' European supremacy on the world stage. The unitary South African state that came into being in 1910 formalized the political and economic dominance of Europeans, but the construction of a strict racial hierarchy took place alongside contests over political representation, the formation of new collective identities and definitions of belonging. For both blacks and whites, the relationship between national and imperial identities, between the politics of the nation and the politics of empire, became a primary political point of reference.

Empire, race and class

In the aftermath of war, the British authorities under Milner determined that rebuilding the Witwatersrand mining industry was critical to a stable South African economy and prospects for a unified state under imperial control. Productivity and profit remained closely linked to the costs of labour, but sources of African workers, even from the main labour pool in Portuguese East Africa, had begun to dry up.[1] Milner turned instead to China, and between 1904 and 1908, over 63,000 Chinese indentured workers were brought to South Africa.[2] Many of these workers had travelled from rural parts of present-day Hebei and Shandong provinces in northern China, areas affected by environmental crisis, population pressure as well as social and political instability in the aftermath of the Boxer Rebellion.[3] The so-called Chinese labour question quickly became a political controversy that affected both the development of South African labour politics and shaped the course of (another) British general election.

In South Africa, attempts to secure public support for the Chinese migrant scheme played on assumptions of racial inferiority and the need to protect white workers from 'uncivilized' forms of labour.[4] On the Rand, opposition was somewhat weakly led by trade unionists, drawing on a pan-imperial vision of white workers' solidarity. In Britain, however, the campaign against 'Chinese slavery' galvanized politics within and outside parliament. Trades Union Congress officials protested that the scheme was a 'return to slavery and the insulting injustice of capitalism', while humanitarians spoke of 'Chinese slavery' as a moral admonition against untrammelled capitalist exploitation in Africa.[5] At a mass rally in London's Trafalgar Square in March 1904, a succession of labour leaders denounced the Chinese labour scheme as a betrayal of the sacrifice of British forces during the South African War.[6] For Liberal MPs, the talk of 'slavery' exposed a perceived weakness in the Conservative government that was ruthlessly exploited during their successful 1906 general election campaign, when images of Chinese labourers became 'provocative symbols of the Conservatives' commitment to capitalist interests at the expense of the average British citizen'.[7]

The new Liberal government moved quickly to disperse responsibility for South African labour policies by granting responsible government to the Transvaal. It was no 'magnanimous gesture', but a political expediency designed to secure imperial loyalty.[8] As part of the peace settlement signed at the Treaty of Vereeniging, English and Dutch languages were granted equal and plans for a 'colour-blind' franchise were quietly omitted. In 1907, the Het Volk party under former Boer generals Louis Botha and Jan Smuts won a clear majority in elections in the Transvaal, which allowed them a leading role in the development of proposals for the Union of South Africa in the following year. Union in 1910 therefore formalized a political rapprochement between British and Boers, creating an 'inclusive white nation' that smoothed out the formerly significant distinctions between white 'races' in South Africa, entrenched white supremacy and excluded black South Africans from full citizenship.[9] The presence of a unified South Africa at the 1911 Imperial conference marked the high point of Britain's colonial initiatives, symbolized by a series of independent settler states employing broadly similar forms of legislation to impose racially defined limits on property rights, labour and the franchise.[10]

Beyond the 'high' politics of empire inaugurated at the 1911 conference, the first decade of the twentieth century also witnessed the emergence of a pan-imperial politics of labour, built on middle- and working-class imperial networks. Between the end of the war and Union, South Africa played a particularly important role in the private economy of empire, accounting for 20 per cent of the total remittances sent to the UK from overseas.[11] By 1912 over 40 per cent of miners in the Transvaal were either married or sending remittances to families, and as such were a more settled constituency, characterized both by strong transnational links with other parts of the British world, but also a burgeoning sense of rootedness in South Africa itself.[12] It was from this population that labour politics emerged in the aftermath of the South African War. Representative bodies of urban industrial workers, such as the Witwatersrand Trades and Labour Council, became centres of emergent white working-class power. Leaders in these groups, such as the Scottish activist Alexander Raitt, exhibited both paternalist concern for the conditions of black workers and supremacist determination to protect white political privilege.[13]

The birth of organized labour in South Africa was bound up with the creation of a white oligarchy that characterized political cultures across the British settler Dominions. Major strikes in South Africa in 1907 and 1913, although primarily focused on working conditions, also made claims for what might be described as the 'wages of whiteness',

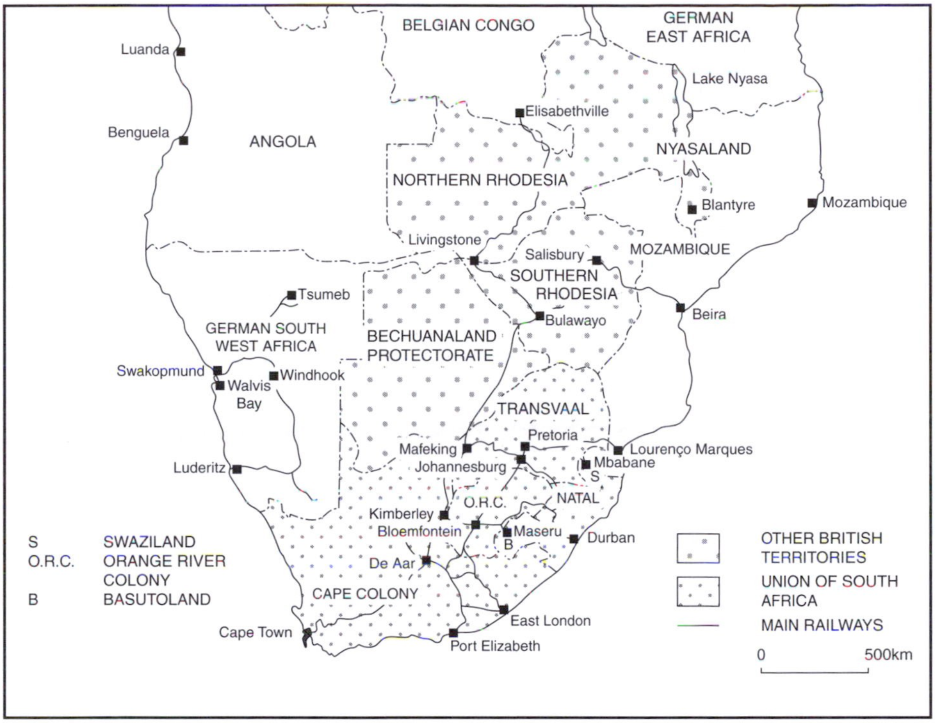

Map 3 Southern Africa in 1910.

Source: 'Southern Africa in 1910': A. J. Christopher. *The Atlas of Changing South Africa*. London: Routledge, 2001, p. 12.

as workers sought to carve out their own spaces within a racialized global economy.[14] Concerns around the importation of Chinese labour in South Africa were echoed in the labour politics of the emergent Dominions of Australia, New Zealand and Canada, as white workers sought to restrict the use of Asian labour.[15] In the first decade of the twentieth century, 'whiteness' became an integral force in the transnational working-class politics of the British world. Of central importance was the formal division of labour by race – or 'civilization', sanctioned in the Mines and Works Act of 1911. South Africa was a pivotal point for a loose worldwide network of white working-class activists, a 'British Empire of Labour' that incorporated a shared white working-class ideology, centred on a blend of militant anti-capitalism and racism.[16] This was a multifaceted phenomenon, as illustrated by the complex responses to the venerated British Labour leader James Keir Hardie during his imperial tour in 1907–8, where his support for the Indian nationalist *swadeshi* movement and criticism of South African race policies exposed the contradictions between loyalty to the ideals of the labour movement and the racially defined character of colonial working-class identities.[17]

In 1913 and 1914, a series of general strikes on the Witwatersrand culminated in a bloody confrontation between strikers and police and the imposition of martial law.[18]

They came at a conjuncture of international labour unrest across the Dominions and in the United States. In South Africa, the strikes on the Rand coincided with protests by indentured Indian workers in Natal (see the next section). The strikes were led by workers with close connections to the transnational networks of the British world, such as Tom Mann, the syndicalist leader who had organized strikes in Australia before visiting South Africa in 1910 on his return to Britain.[19] When nine leaders of the strikes, including the Scottish-born socialist J. T. Bain, were deported to Britain in early 1914, hundreds of thousands of British workers marched in London to express their solidarity. South Africa had become a focal point for an imperial working class and one, moreover, that had 'made itself white'.[20]

There were, at the same time, indications of a nascent anti-racist radicalism within the imperial working class. In particular, the formation of the small breakaway International Socialist League (ISL) in Johannesburg in 1915, under the leadership of W. H. Andrews, demonstrated that labour politics in South Africa was not destined to be purely centred on white supremacist notions of solidarity. Global influences were also to be found through connections to groups such as the International Workers of the Worlds (IWW), a South African branch of which was formed in 1910. Although short-lived, the tenets of non-racial workers' unity were found in the ISL, which established links with African political leaders and campaigned in support of black workers.[21] Alongside Africans such as T. W. Thibedi and Fred Cetiwe, ISL recruits included Indian activists R. K. Moodley and Bernard Sigamoney, who helped establish a union along IWW lines in Durban in 1917. The first South African black trade union, the Industrial Workers of Africa, was organized in 1918, and Clements Kadalie's Industrial and Commercial Union (ICU), formed in the Cape Town docks in 1919. IWW influences might also be discerned in efforts to unify African labour in the early post-war years, the most important being the federation launched under the name of the Industrial and Commercial Workers Union of South Africa in 1920.[22]

Gandhi and South African Indians

Between 1860 and 1911, around 140,000 people migrated to South Africa from India, but the Indian population was not a homogenous group.[23] Religious differences were apparent, between largely Hindu indentured labourers and the Muslim traders, or 'passenger Indians' from Gujarat that followed. There were obvious socio-economic distinctions, between the poorer indentured group and the relatively wealthier traders, with greater accumulations of both financial and social capital. For Indian women, whose presence was often deemed both unnecessary and threatening by the settler population, constraints were felt both in terms of the gender relations that emerged in colonial society as a whole, and the particular relations that developed within the Indian population. One of the most prominent of the early 'passenger' Indians was Abdullah Haji Adam, who became the first president of the Natal Indian Congress when it was founded in 1894. He was a leading partner in Dada Abdullah and Company, a Durban-based trading enterprise that controlled a network of stores in Natal and a steamship line between Durban and Mumbai. Adam, along with the Coovadia brothers and Ahmed Cachalia, established a web of business interests that connected South Africa with the South Asian economy.

The issue of voting rights for South African Indians became a subject of imperial debate when, in 1894, a draft Franchise Law proposed that registration of new Indian voters in Natal should be barred, on the grounds that the achievement of political rights were 'a race privilege'.[24] Concerned by their implications for British rule in India, Chamberlain objected, noting that Indian MPs had been elected in London. He did not object, however, when the Natal government set up a language test for immigrants, with the implicit aim of setting racial limits on political rights, and the approach was replicated in the machinery of the immigrant legislation that laid the basis for the 'White Australia' policy in 1901. The privileges of race had become a key factor in South African policies by the end of the nineteenth century, but they were by no means uniquely South African in form or intent.

In the years leading up to, and immediately after Union, South African Indian politics was embodied by the future figurehead of Indian nationalism, Mohandas K. Gandhi. He arrived in South Africa in 1893 as a young lawyer; when he left two decades later, Gandhi had laid the foundations for the tactics of non-violent resistance employed in India in the interwar years. In the last decade of the nineteenth century, however, Gandhi's agitation on behalf of Indians in South Africa was expressed in terms of the moral framework of empire and its justification of racial equality. With an emphasis on both tradition and civilization, Gandhi's vision differentiated between Indian and European populations of South Africa, on the one hand, and Africans on the other – he was, in effect, seeking a privileged political space for Indians. More crudely, Indian political campaigners complained vigorously about segregationist practices that placed Indians at the same level of social status as Africans.[25]

His campaigns in South Africa provided Gandhi with a political platform that bridged the Indian Ocean and imperial worlds. In his 'Green Pamphlet' on the conditions of Indians in South Africa, Gandhi chronicled the racial abuses and maltreatment suffered by Indians, but concluded, in an embryonic form of his later political philosophy, that political leaders should seek 'to conquer this hatred by love'.[26] The pamphlet spoke to the question of the status of Indians throughout the empire, was widely disseminated in India, and communicated via telegram to London and Natal. In 1896, Gandhi addressed a public meeting in Mumbai organized by the Bombay Presidency Association, where he argued that the grievances of a million Indians in South Africa should be a political question for India itself, as it spoke to the wider question of Indians' place within the empire.[27] In many respects, though, Gandhi remained an empire loyalist, and like many other elite Indians supported the British cause during the South African War, organizing the Indian Ambulance Corps, and declaring that 'Indians too are ready to do duty for their Sovereign on the battlefield'.[28] An inter-communal organization, the Corps comprised over 1,000 volunteers drawn from a cross section of the Natal Indian Community.[29] In India, the contingent was seen as a contribution to a 'test of empire', a struggle that raised the possibility that Indians might play a role in a more racially inclusive imperial body politic.

Following the war, more radical nationalists in India, began to see the treatment of Indians in South Africa as evidence of the failure of the Government of India and its weakness in the imperial context.[30] At the same time, Gandhi continued to frame his campaign around the concept of imperial citizenship. In 1901, styling himself as a 'petitioner on behalf of the hundred thousand British Indians in South Africa' (and encouraged by supporters in Britain), Gandhi persuaded the Indian National Congress in Kolkata to pass a resolution highlighting the conditions in South Africa.[31] This was a transnational politics of empire that paralleled the threads of white solidarity that crossed the 'British world'. It conjured visions of multiracial imperial citizenship, within which the peoples of India, wherever they found themselves across the empire, could 'claim the privileges of British subjects'.[32] Indian and African nationalists' Edwardian empire loyalism was not simple devotion to Britain, but a desire to engage more fully in its declared ideals.

Gandhi's South African campaigns were at the same time a reflection of local circumstances, and his political vision in many ways represented the aspirations and agendas of a commercial elite as much as the claims of workers. It was a 'merchant politics', suffused with an empire loyalism, rather than a unifying Indian nationalism that Gandhi embodied in his early years in South Africa.[33] But, as Gandhi's efforts to promote Indian rights within a framework of imperial citizenship failed to bear fruit, he began to construct a politics that gave primacy to a shared Indian identity and a romantic notion of a 'motherland' across the ocean, despite the lack of direct connections between many Indian South Africans and the subcontinent.[34]

Gandhi would be most widely remembered for the passive resistance strategy of *satyagraha* or 'truth force', in which South Africa provided a testing ground for anti-colonial campaigns in India. The catalyst for the campaigns was the 1906 Black Act in the Transvaal, requiring Indians to be officially registered. After becoming one of the first protestors jailed for refusing to abide by the terms of the new law, Gandhi secured a compromise agreement with influential Het Volk leader Jan Smuts. Then, in 1913, Gandhi widened the focus of Indian campaigns, moving beyond immigration issues to include the grievances of indentured workers themselves. The passive resistance protests of October 1913 were a critical shift in Gandhi's tactical thinking, but also (perhaps primarily) represented the emergence of a working-class movement among Indian South Africans.[35] Bringing together Indian miners and over 15,000 sugar plantations workers, the campaign again brought Gandhi into negotiations and a compromise with Smuts. As the legislation was making its way through Parliament in 1914, Gandhi left South Africa, to return to India the following year, having secured a reputation both in India and in Britain as a highly effective political figure.

The emergence of African nationalism

In 1911, Pixley ka Izaka Seme returned to South Africa after studying in the United States and Britain, having established a reputation as an eloquent political speaker and early exponent of African nationalism. He called for the formation of a 'Native Union' that would enable Africans to 'make their grievances properly known and considered both by the government and by the people of South Africa at large'.[36] In the following January, a meeting of representatives from across South Africa met in Bloemfontein to inaugurate a national movement, the South African Natives National Congress (SANNC). In its initial stages, African nationalism largely represented a nascent mission-educated middle class. As such, it reflected the political consciousness that emerged from the class of Africans most closely bound up with colonial public affairs, including church ministers, school teachers, clerks and farmers.

During the last two decades of the nineteenth century, African political consciousness had developed particular strength in the Eastern Cape, where the black electorate had reached close to 50 per cent in some districts.[37] Although some colonial officials saw the African vote as little more than a 'safety valve' for indigenous dissent, the last two decades of the nineteenth century saw the development of political organizations and channels of public communication that would lay the foundations for the emergence of a nationalist movement.[38] In 1882, the Imbumba Yama Nyama (South African Aborigines' Association) was formed in Port Elizabeth, which aimed to unite Africans in a campaign for 'national rights'.[39] Influenced by the establishment of the Afrikaner Bond, the Association highlighted similarities between African and Afrikaner nationalist programmes, both of which centred on farming and religious interests, with activities focused on 'cultural movements' and journalism, expressing grievances that stemmed from a perceived marginalization within the colonial state.[40]

The African political elite that emerged in the Eastern Cape in the 1880s was powerfully influenced by the mission schools that had been established in the area in the years of conflict and the expansion of the colonial frontier. In particular, Lovedale College, opened by the Glasgow Missionary Society in 1841, provided a foundation for key figures involved in late-nineteenth-century African political activity, including the journalist John Tengu Jabavu. With close links to Cape liberals including Saul Solomon, Jabavu also maintained contact with the Aborigines' Protection Society in London. He was a contributor to the black newspaper *Isigidimi Sama Xosa* (The Xhosa Messenger), and became the founding editor of *Imvo Zabantsundu* (African Opinion) in 1884. Under Jabavu, *Imvo* developed into one of the most influential channels of black political views in South Africa.[41] By the late 1890s, however, divisions began to emerge in black politics in the Cape, particularly around a rival newspaper, *Izwi Labantu* (Voice of the People), edited by A. K. Soga, the son of the pioneer African missionary Tiyo Soga. By the turn of the twentieth century a number of leading African writers and activists were associated with *Izwi* and the SANC, including Walter Rubusana, who was to become Jabavu's leading political rival in the years leading up to Union.

On all sides, the emerging nationalist politics of the Eastern Cape was markedly loyalist in its approach. Nascent nationalism shared – and extended – the belief in loyal deputation that had marked the approach of African rulers and 'chiefs' to imperial authority throughout southern Africa in the late nineteenth century.[42] To a significant extent, the development of political consciousness in the late nineteenth century was predicated upon the increasing economic interdependence of African and colonial societies.[43] But the persistent reality of white domination persuaded many Africans that independence was preferable to white paternalism. African separatism first emerged in mission churches during the 1880s, as black Christians began to argue that colonialism had delivered dispossession and discrimination rather than salvation.[44] Many African Christians rejected European denominations and mission societies and established their own independent 'Ethiopian' churches along similar lines to those emerging in the Caribbean, North America and elsewhere in Africa.[45] By the early twentieth century, colonial anxieties had been intensified by the emergence of a pan-African dimension to Ethiopianism, embodied in 1896 by the formal affiliation between the Ethiopian Church led by former Wesleyan Methodist James Dwane, and the African Methodist Episcopal (AME) Church in the United States. Within two years, the influential African-American leader of the AME Church, Bishop Henry Turner, toured South Africa, where the new church had gained over ten thousand members. As a pioneer of pan-Africanism, Turner helped to set South African independent churches within a set of wider influences drawn from the African diaspora.[46] Ethiopianism provided a spiritual focus for black resistance, notably the Bambatha Rebellion in Natal in 1906.[47]

The African-American influence on black nationalist identities and agendas took two connected, but contradictory, forms. A strand of liberal humanitarianism, embodied in the self-help ethos of Booker T. Washington, was central to the development of institutions including the Native College at Fort Hare in the Eastern Cape. Washingtonian principles of 'Industrial Education' had shaped the thinking of a number of African nationalists, including the founding President of the SANNC, John L. Dube, who had met Washington as a student in the United States in 1897. He went on to establish the Zulu Christian Industrial School at Ohlange in Natal, modelled on Washington's Tuskegee Institute.[48] At the same time, the AME Church fostered a more radical version of African-American political identity, and Bishop Turner's slogan of 'Africa for the Africans' represented an influential body of opinion that rejected the Washingtonian vision and also cast doubt on the benefits of British imperialism.[49] Black politics at the turn of the twentieth century drew, therefore, on international influences communicated by individuals with transnational connections that bridged South Africa and the African diaspora in North America. The Trinidadian lawyer, Henry Sylvester Williams, a moving force behind the first Pan-Africanist Conference in London in 1900, practised law in Cape Town from 1903–5 and worked closely with the Coloured political leader Abdul Abdurahman.[50] The perceived threat of African-American influence resulted in restrictions on the work and movements of black missionaries, while the American experience after the Civil War became a point of reference for segregationist arguments for restrictions on black political rights in South Africa.[51]

Britain nevertheless remained the principal touchstone when access to political rights was curtailed in South Africa, and Africans tended to blame local, rather than metropolitan, agents for their lack of success.[52] Just as their mid-twentieth-century compatriots would view the tenets of the Atlantic Charter as a validation of their claims to democratic rights, Edwardian African leaders defined the principles of liberal imperialism on their own terms. African leaders aligned themselves with Cape liberals and sought assistance from the imperial parliament, in part because of ideological affinities, but also in the hope of protecting the Cape franchise.[53] These efforts intensified following the National Convention in 1908, which set out the terms of Union. In March 1909 a 'counter convention' was held in Bloemfontein that brought together a representative body of African leaders from across the country, who declared their dismay at the 'absence … of the principle of equal rights for all the races in the South African Colonies' in the draft Act. The African leaders who attended the conference clearly considered themselves as 'loyal citizens' of an imperial polity that had 'specific obligations towards the natives and coloured races of South Africa'.[54]

Empire loyalism was put to the test in 1909 when a South African delegation set out for London seeking amendments to the plans for Union. The representatives included the Cape Liberal W. P. Schreiner, the increasingly bitter rivals Jabavu and Rubusana, and Abdurahman, while an Indian delegation, including Gandhi, also set out for London.[55] Although the public sympathies were aroused and the delegation found support from Labour and Liberal MPs, British ministers opted to accept the proposals for Union 'without outside interference from a distance'.[56] Despite their lack of success, African leaders continued with this strategy in the ultimately vain hope that efforts to raise the conscience of the British public and metropolitan political elites might, eventually, prove successful. Their faith was founded upon the notion that the imperial connection with Britain provided a degree of protection for colonized peoples, in that it exposed colonial administration to a higher authority. As with Gandhi, African elites felt that empire offered a possibility of universal citizenship, articulated by metropolitan supporters as a commonwealth 'founded on unity, toleration, justice and liberty'.[57] The loyalism of the early nationalists was neither 'collaborationist' nor naive, but 'deeply African in nature and outlook' based on profound recognition of the realities of colonialism.[58]

In 1914, another delegation of African Congress leaders travelled to London to protest against the segregationist provisions of Natives Land Act of 1913. However, despite attracting a significant degree of public sympathy, the delegates found it difficult to make any impression on British officials. Within a few weeks of their arrival, they found themselves caught up with the outbreak of the First World War in Europe. In South Africa, the SANNC met and declared its support for the war and announced the suspension of its political activities.[59] The delegation returned to South Africa, save for Sol Plaatje, who remained in Britain until 1917, during which time he published a polemical account of the effects of the Land Act, *Native Life in South Africa* (1916), an appeal to the British public 'on behalf of five million loyal British subjects'.[60]

Colour, class and war

In South Africa, responses to the war were complex and multifaceted. Popular enthusiasm was evident among the white populations, reflecting a nascent South Africanism. Similarly, black loyalism prompted support for the war and offers by both African and Coloured political leaders to recruit military volunteers (an offer declined by Smuts).[61] These efforts were, in part, political calculation: participation in the war effort might bolster claims to citizenship. Not all black South Africans embraced the war, however. Congress member J. T. Gumede argued in 1915 that 'idle talk of war' had distracted African political leaders from their primary purpose. Whether manifest as empire loyalism or rebellious anti-white sentiment, African responses were broadly united in the belief that the war would be a catalyst for social change.[62]

Afrikaner reactions to the war were more ambiguous, and many felt a stronger affinity with Germany than Britain. The despatch of South African forces to German South-West Africa triggered armed rebellion in the western Transvaal and Orange Free State, but Union forces commanded by Botha remained loyal and the rebellion was suppressed by February 1915. On the surface, the rebellion was a straightforward rejection of the new South African state: a 'civil war between Afrikaners' and a stimulus to the ethnic nationalism that would come to dominate white politics by the middle of the century.[63] But the revolt was stimulated by multiple factors that included rural impoverishment, general concerns over the Anglicization of state institutions, and in particular, the imposition of British disciplinary codes and hierarchy in the military.[64]

Working-class opposition to the war, inspired by internationalist and anti-capitalist ideologies, set South African labour somewhat apart from its compatriots in Australia, New Zealand and in Europe itself.[65] However, moderate figures in the South African Labour Party steered the labour movement towards a loyalist line, leaving socialists such as Sidney Bunting, Bill Andrews and David Ivon Jones and others associated with groups including the War on War League, became increasingly detached from mainstream labour leaders. These disaffected figures would, in late 1915, split away from the Labour Party to form the International Socialist League.[66] Despite these divisions, many white South Africans undertook military service in South-West and South-East Africa as well as the European western front. Around 150,000 South African troops were engaged in all three campaigns, while about half that number of black recruits were enlisted as non-combatant servicemen.

Although engaged in in non-combatant roles, members of the black Labour Contingents were exposed to dangers of attack and capture. In East Africa, mortality rates from malaria and other diseases, exacerbated by inadequate medical facilities, led Botha to halt the recruitment of workers in 1917. In Europe, some 21,000 black volunteers were engaged with the South African Native Labour Contingent (SANLC) during 1916–18, engaged as dockworkers in French ports as well in in road-building, forestry and other labouring duties. It has been estimated that the South African contingent made up nearly a quarter of the non-combatant labour force on the western front.[67] Subjected to segregated conditions organized 'along South African lines', the experiences of SANLC volunteers nevertheless indicated a significant degree of multiracial interaction. Tragedy struck the contingent in February 1917, when over 600 volunteers died when their transport ship, the SS *Mendi*, sank in the English Channel.[68] For African leaders, the work and sacrifices of the SANLC demonstrated the legitimacy of claims to the rights of citizenship and full participation in social and political life.

The war extended and deepened South African integration within global networks, the significance of which was further underlined with the impact of the worldwide influenza epidemic in late 1918. By the end of the year, around 300,000 South Africans had died, the vast majority of them black. Facilitated by rail networks and migrant labour, it was an unprecedented human disaster.[69] South African leaders also played a significant role in negotiations at the Paris Peace Conference, where Smuts established a reputation as a major figure in international and imperial relations. A leading advocate for the formation of a League of Nations and wartime member of the Imperial War Cabinet, Smuts proposed an informal and decentralized approach to relations across the British Empire, laying the groundwork for the system of imperial governance that emerged in the Statute of Westminster in 1931.[70]

Within South Africa, the war had transformed the relationship between white labour, their employers and government. In the gold industry, depletion of the workforce due to military service meant that large numbers of new workers, many poor white Afrikaners, joined the labour force on the mines. The economic importance of mining prompted the South African government to encourage employers to accede to workers' demands, or at least seek negotiation rather than confrontation as a solution to disputes.[71] Simultaneously, the mines entered a 'profitability crisis', with the price of gold fixed at 1914 levels just as wartime conditions contributed to rising costs.[72] As a consequence, the war left white workers feeling greater confidence in their capacity to protect their interests, while mine owners were less willing to resort to authoritarian means to control militancy – although this did not stop the authorities from brutally suppressing a strike by black workers in 1919. The end of the war saw an upsurge in worker militancy, which culminated in 1922 in a full-scale revolt.

The Rand Revolt of 1922 was an unprecedented episode of white working-class rebellion in South Africa. It began as a dispute over the renegotiation of contracts for underground workers that resulted in a strike in January. The conflict escalated until, in early March, it burst into full-blown insurrection, with armed militants fighting police for control of parts of the city. The South African defence force, including the air force, was enlisted to suppress the uprising. In many ways a proletarian struggle, the Revolt shared many of the characteristics of the wave of strikes that took place across the industrialized world in the aftermath of the October Revolution in Russia. In South Africa though, race was the defining characteristic of the rebellion – this was, arguably, a struggle to save the *white* working class from a perceived existential threat.[73] The slogan of Rand strikers in 1922, 'Workers of the World Unite for a White South Africa', was not a parody of solidarity, but a reflection of the particular white working-class ideologies in

South Africa, and an indication of its divergence from contemporary worker militancy elsewhere.[74]

Segregation and the 'Native Question'

For Smuts, the political consequence of the Rand Revolt was defeat, in the 1924 election, by an alliance between the South African Labour Party and the National Party led by J. B. M. Hertzog. While Smuts was himself a segregationist, it was under Hertzog that key legislation designed to establish a wide-ranging system of racial segregation was enacted. The policies aimed to address the so-called Native Question – how to secure African labour without compromising the concerns and interests of whites. This had been the subject of intense debate since the end of the South African War, and between 1903 and 1905, the South African Native Affairs Commission explored ways to harmonize the variety of approaches to 'Native Affairs' in the run up to Union.[75] Among the Commission's recommendations were the formal separation of land between Europeans and Africans and a separate system of political representation.[76] Principles of segregation focused on the creation of 'reserved' territories for Africans, in order, it was argued, to preserve indigenous systems of social control and discipline in the face of industrialization.[77] This would be the basis of the Natives Land Act of 1913, which set in place the basic outline of a series of reserves, initially comprising only 7.3 per cent of the total area of South Africa. Deeper historical roots of South African 'native policy' have been cited, from the Shepstone 'system' of the mid-nineteenth century through to the policies of the Rhodes administration in the Cape in the early 1890s.[78] It was, however, in the first decades of the twentieth century that racial segregation emerged from the connected processes of industrialization and the integration of South African societies as a consequence of political union.[79]

By 1924, segregationist legislation had been introduced with the aim of regulating employment, land rights and rights of residence in urban areas.[80] The ideological rationale that lay behind segregation at the same time exhibited a significant degree of ambiguity, however. It offered something for both liberal paternalists keen to emphasize their 'protectionist' attitude towards Africans, and those, like Hertzog, whose concerns were focused on exclusionary labour policies and the political separation of races. After Hertzog came to power, the latter began to take centre stage. Taking advice from intellectuals such as Edgar Brookes and Charles Templeman Loram, Hertzog began to elaborate a plan to complete the piecemeal segregationist legislation that had been established since Union, including the abolition of 'colour blind' voting rights in the Cape.[81] The Representation of Natives Act eventually passed in 1936, after Hertzog's nationalists had formally 'fused' with Smuts' South African Party and were thus able to secure the two-thirds majority of parliament required to abolish the Cape franchise. The Act offered a 'compromise' whereby African voters would vote on a separate roll for a handful of 'Native Representatives' in parliament, very similar to the proposals made by the Native Affairs Commission thirty years earlier.

Segregation in the 1920s was both uniquely South African and deeply inscribed with transnational influences, drawn from the US South and the administrative ideologies of British colonialism.[82] Insofar as it was rooted in a concept of 'reserved' land, segregation in South Africa resembled the policies of the federal government in the United States towards the indigenous populations of North America. The conquest of indigenous nations in the United States that had begun in the 1820s, established forms of differentiated sovereignty that fixed Native Americans in a relation 'of a ward to his guardian'.[83] This concept of 'trusteeship', grounded in a sense of sacred duty, also shaped British colonial administration based on systems of indirect rule.[84] Moreover, the notion of trusteeship was embedded in the principles of the League of Nations Mandates established during the Versailles Peace Conference.[85] In both cases, relativist notions of 'adaptation' informed by the development of anthropological concepts of 'culture' – ideas that also shaped segregationist thought in South Africa.[86] Parallels might also be drawn with the segregationist practices that developed in the American South in the latter years of the nineteenth century, where political disenfranchisement, separate provision of amenities, education and housing, along with everyday racism reinforced with casual violence showed a marked similarity to the experiences of black South Africans. For many observers, it was the United States, not South Africa, that provided the most egregious example of racial inequalities in the first half of the twentieth century.[87]

Segregationist ideologies were also shaped in the nineteenth and twentieth centuries by networks of intellectuals that collectively formed a transnational 'Commonwealth of Knowledge'.[88] These included figures such as the Australian-born and British-educated Raymond Dart, whose interwar study of the hominid *Australopithecus* helped promote the view that South Africa formed the 'Cradle of Humanity'.[89] Segregation drew heavily on eugenics and scientific racism in identifying the fundamental differences between Europeans and 'Natives', while notions of biological determinism underpinned popular fears of a 'Black Peril'.[90] As race science extended its focus from the external features of difference to methods of assessing the mental capacities of Africans and Europeans, it contributed to the development of segregationist thought. The educationalist Charles Templeman Loram, for example, employed intelligence tests first developed in the United States for his *Education of the South African Native* (1917), impressed by the models of adapted education pioneered at the Tuskegee Institute in Alabama.[91] An advisor to Hertzog during the 1920s, Loram was an influential contributor to debates around segregation.[92]

African responses to segregation

Two broad strands of African responses to segregation developed during the interwar period. Industrial centres, such as the Rand and the port cities of Cape Town and Durban saw the beginnings of a black labour movement, while established political figures clung on to loyalism and the hope that segregated institutions might provide a viable outlet for political grievances. Thus, despite a wave of black militancy that began in the latter months of the First World War, Congress leaders maintained that 'we respect the Union

Jack and are loyal to the British Government'.[93] Yet again they looked overseas for support, with another Congress delegation to Britain in 1919. Their experience reinforced the impression that the British government lacked the power, means or desire to intercede on behalf of black South Africans; the Prime Minister, David Lloyd George, refused to formally meet the Congress deputation on the grounds that it would give the impression that he was 'mixing up South African politics with British politics'.[94] Congress leaders also appealed to the wider body of international opinion. Like many other representatives of 'dependent peoples', they had interpreted US President Woodrow Wilson's rhetoric of self-determination as a framework for their own demands and ambitions.[95] Petitioning King George in 1918, the SANNC called for former German colonial territories to 'be developed in the interests of African inhabitants until they become sufficiently advanced for their own civilised government'.[96] Congress leaders thus espoused a form of liberal internationalism that was compatible with their empire loyalism.

Some leading members of Congress were, however, coming into contact with more radical forms of internationalism. When he visited the United States during 1921–22, Plaatje met with John E. Bruce, an editor of the United Negro Improvement Association (UNIA) newspaper, *Negro World*. Under the charismatic leadership of Marcus Garvey, the UNIA mobilized a mass movement among African-Americans, enthused by Garvey's vision of African unity and power. By the start of the 1920s, the UNIA had established branches worldwide, including South Africa. Plaatje addressed a number of UNIA meetings, sharing a platform with Garvey himself. While in the United States, he also met W. E. B. Du Bois, who subsequently delivered a message from Plaatje to the Pan-African Congress in 1921.[97] He returned to South Africa in November 1923, having spent four years campaigning in Britain and North America. But, despite coming into contact with radical Africanists, much of his efforts were dedicated to the development of the religious Brotherhood movement, 'a vision that no longer had any relevance to the realities of South Africa'.[98]

Plaatje's mixed success overseas matched the fortunes of the renamed African National Congress (from 1923) in South Africa. In the years after the First World War, the movement struggled to respond to the extension of segregationist legislation under the Smuts and Hertzog governments. Congress continued to register protest against restrictions and threats to African political and civil rights through deputation, rather than confrontation. By the mid-1930s, fissures in the ANC leadership resulted in the near-cessation of activities. At this point, the ANC was a movement in abeyance, the result of a failure to develop effective ways of communicating with a segregationist state, or forge links and alliances with either the rural mass of the population or the emerging urban African proletariat. While Congress politics became increasingly moribund, there were, however, indications that a popular politics of resistance was possible. In the aftermath of the war, a wave of strikes by black workers on the Rand seemed evidence of a nascent working-class consciousness. For a brief period between the end of the war and 1920, the leadership of the Transvaal Natives Congress took up a radical stance in support of working-class grievances, extending from demands for higher wages to protests against pass laws.[99]

Some movements brokered connections between rural and urban resistance, often characterized by millenarianism and charismatic religion, drawing on and reframing international influences. Enoch Mgijima's Israelite sect, initially formed as a breakaway from Wesleyan Methodists, had affiliated to the American-based Church of God and Saints of Christ in 1912, although the ties were severed after the war when Church leaders questioned Mgijima's militant prophetic vision. Tensions between the sect and the authorities escalated in 1921 after Mgijima led his followers to occupy government land near Ntabelanga in the Eastern Cape. When negotiations broke down, armed police were despatched to evict the Israelites, leaving over 160 dead and many more wounded.[100] The movement seemed to embody a new, overtly dissident form of popular resistance that threatened direct rebellion against the state. And for some white observers, it represented the chilling influence of the doctrine of 'Africa for the Africans', revitalized under the influence of Garveyism.[101]

Garveyism had a potent influence on popular politics and cultural resistance in interwar South Africa and provided a reference point for millenarian visions that influenced the form of rural political consciousness. Garveyite ideologies shaped the campaign of Wellington Buthelezi, who launched a movement in the Transkei in the mid-1920s that blended references to the Xhosa cattle killing with black American separatism.[102] Garveyite ideas were viewed with sufficient seriousness that white observers, although dismissive of ideas of a 'black republic', increasingly expressed concerns about the influence of African-Americans. As a consequence, black visitors from the United States were treated with extreme caution. The newly appointed AME Church head, Bishop William T. Vernon, was subject to 'a great deal of inconvenience and delay' when arriving in South Africa in 1920, while the YMCA Secretary Max Yergan found many white liberals anxious about 'Marcus Garvie [*sic*] propaganda from New York'.[103] Yergan's treatment in South Africa was cited by Du Bois as evidence of the encroaching interference of white liberals in African-American affairs.[104]

By the latter part of the 1920s, Garveyism had also established an important influence on the ANC itself. In Cape Town, the regional Congress leader, James Thaele, had studied at Lincoln University and the University of Pennsylvania and headed the Cape UNIA branch. Through Thaele, a thread of Garveyite discourse was injected into the thinking of the Western Cape Congress, inspiring activists such as Bransby Ndobe, who coordinated a campaign amongst rural farmworkers during 1929–30.[105] By the end of the 1920s, more radical elements within the ANC had come to articulate their own struggles against South African race policies in terms that made explicit reference to key transnational influences. Garveyite ideals could act as a unifying discourse that spoke to educated bourgeois supporters as well as rural peasants and workers.[106]

Garveyism also helped to shape the politics and ideology of the Industrial and Commercial Workers' Union (ICU), perhaps the first genuine example of a mass political movement in South Africa, that came to rival the ANC as the centre of black popular politics during the 1920s. Formed in 1919 as a trade union for African and Coloured dockworkers in Cape Town, the ICU was transformed into a general trades union after 1922, when its founder, Clements Kadalie, gained control of an emergent national trades union movement. Claiming a mass membership across South Africa, the national ICU rapidly gained remarkable levels of support, particularly in the countryside. For many rural followers of the ICU, the Garveyite slogan of 'Africa for the Africans' offered the hope of liberation, and the launch of the UNIA Black Star shipping line in 1919 prompted rumours of the imminent arrival of a force of African-Americans who would deliver South Africa from white dominance.[107] As news of Garvey's campaigns in the United States began to penetrate popular consciousness, the 'coming of the American Negroes' had become a consistent strand in popular protest.[108]

Kadalie personified the transnational character of the migrant labour system that underpinned South Africa's industrial society and drew African workers from across the subcontinent. Born in 1896 in Nyasaland (Malawi), he moved to South Africa during the First World War and established himself as a prominent activist amongst dock workers in Cape Town. Kadalie's rhetoric blurred Africanism and vaguely defined socialism, and drew on Biblical language to underscore declarations of racial and workers' unity. 'We are now at the brink of the River Jordan', he wrote in 1923, declaring the African worker to be 'a new man … quite different from his forefathers'.[109] The ICU under Kadalie developed little in the way of a clear ideological framework in the mid-1920s, and his support for Hertzog's Nationalist alliance with the South African Labour Party in 1924 seemed at odds with the cause of black workers. However, as the segregationist agenda of the Hertzog government became clear, Kadalie steered the ICU towards more active opposition to South African Native policy.[110]

The strength of the ICU lay not in its ideological coherence, but its ability to mobilize large numbers of supporters, which began to attract international attention. The movement impressed British writer Winifred Holtby, who met Kadalie during her tour of South Africa as a League of Nations representative in 1926, although paternalist liberals raised concerns that he had become a 'useful catspaw to men of the Moscow type'.[111] When, under Kadalie's direction, the ICU began to expel communist members, the movement began to attract the attention of moderate labour leaders in Britain and Europe. In June 1927, Kadalie travelled to Geneva to attend the International Labour Conference; as the first African representative to attend an international labour conference, Kadalie attracted significant public attention, which continued when he undertook a tour of Britain under the auspices of the British Independent Labour Party (ILP). Presented as the representative of the 'Native workers of South Africa', he worked closely with the ILP's Fenner Brockway, but also made connections with figures from the Labour Party, trade unions and churches.[112]

With the support of moderate trades unionists and liberal activists, Kadalie appealed to British workers in his campaign against the Native Administration Act (1927), which entrenched a segregated system of African law centred on 'traditional' authorities embodied in the power of 'chiefs'. He argued that the Act was 'a declaration of martial law' intended to suppress the nascent black labour movement.[113] But the network of British supporters ultimately contributed to the fracture of the ICU within two years of Kadalie's return to South Africa in 1928. Sponsored by the group of supporters around Holtby, the Scottish trade unionist William Ballinger was despatched to advise Kadalie, but instead,

Ballinger's presence exacerbated tensions, which split the union into rival factions.[114] The decline of the ICU was predicated on its lack of capacity to create a stable link between the national movement and local grievances, particularly in the countryside. Its millenarianism and Garveyism provided a powerful appeal to rural supporters, but was a weak foundation for sustainable protest against segregation.[115] International support for Kadalie drew largely on a paternalist desire to direct an emergent African labour movement, but, hampered by antipathy of white trade unionists, European supporters failed to develop a realistic view of Kadalie's own position, let alone the character of the movement he represented.

The Communist Party and black politics

From its formation in 1921, the Communist Party of South Africa (CPSA) provided a 'radicalizing influence' for both black and white political protest.[116] While its role in the 1922 Rand Revolt underlined the relationship between socialist ideology and racialized white labourism, the CPSA gravitated towards a black politics by the end of the 1920s. The shift reflected increasing black working-class support, and by the end of the decade the majority of its (relatively small) membership were African. The CPSA provided an organizational focus for radical black politics that, moreover, fostered international connections. Under direction from the Comintern, and backed by a younger group of activists, the CPSA adopted in 1928 its 'native republic' policy, aligning itself with nationalist groups. Black members began to take increasingly prominent roles in the party, and in 1929 Albert Nzula became its first black secretary-general.[117]

The newly found communist interest struck a chord with those in the ANC leadership who had become disillusioned with traditional strategies based on white political institutions and officials. One of these was Josiah Gumede, elected as ANC president in 1927, who visited the Soviet Union that same year and returned reportedly impressed by what he had seen of Soviet communism.[118] Gumede, whose political influences included a strong seam of Garveyite Africanism, became alienated from the more established nationalist leadership, notably Pixley Seme, who saw his radicalism, and the more assertive protest methods he espoused, as a threat. In 1930, he challenged Gumede for the ANC leadership and won, pushing the ANC away from communist influences for the best part of a decade.[119] The idea of a 'black republic' nevertheless established a relationship between communism and nationalism that would become a fundamental part of the make-up of South African liberation movements in the years after the Second World War. Influenced by the Comintern, South African Communists shared the outlook of others, notably in the United States, where industrialization had seen the convergence of race and class as factors shaping the lives of the black working class. However, as was also the case elsewhere, the relationship between communism and nationalism was at the same time subject to local contingencies and inconsistencies.[120]

The conditions of life for black South Africans had the capacity to radicalize international observers. During the 1920s, YMCA Secretary Max Yergan established himself at the Native College at Fort Hare in the Eastern Cape, where he developed a programme of religious education and built a Christian centre funded by US donors. Connected with international missionary networks, Yergan played a key role in the organization of the multiracial 'Bantu-European Conference' at Fort Hare in 1930. By the mid-1930s, however, Yergan had begun to develop a more radical view of South African race relations. When he returned to the United States in 1937, he joined with the actor, singer and political activist Paul Robeson to form the Committee on African Affairs in New York. For Yergan, the experience of a decade and a half in South Africa resulted in a fundamental shift in ideological viewpoint.

Urbanization

Underlying much of the debate around the so-called Native Question in the interwar period was the influence of the ongoing process of urbanization. This was a development that affected lives across divides of colour, as conditions in rural areas had resulted in a dramatic movement towards towns by white South Africans, 65 per cent of which could be defined as urban by the mid-1930s.[121] Urban growth in the mid-twentieth century was by no means isolated to South Africa, although industrial development, urban growth and modern infrastructure was of a greater density there than most other parts of the continent throughout the twentieth century. Nevertheless, the 1930s and 1940s saw the growth of urban African populations in major mining centres such as the Copperbelt in present-day Zambia, as well as key cities on the Atlantic and Indian Ocean coasts.[122] Aside from the growth in the urban population itself, concerns over the impact of urbanization on Africans were widely expressed across colonial Africa by anthropologists and administrators, in the main focused on the mystical threat of 'detribalization'. Colonial policymakers thus began to pay serious attention to the question of urbanization in the interwar years, as the focus of colonial administration itself began to turn from systems of rule to systems of development.

Almost everywhere, the expansion of colonial cities resulted in the segregation of urban space. In older cities, the distinctions between European and African quarters were becoming more sharply defined, while in the new industrial centres like Johannesburg, as in Nairobi or more particularly on the Copperbelt of Northern Rhodesia, cities became marked by the emergence of an often-marginalized class of African urbanites. At the very least, lack of planning and provision for black workers meant that African housing, in contrast to the carefully planned white suburbs, was characterized by a lack of infrastructure, minimal provision of services or, as was often the case, the entirely unplanned growth of informal shack dwellings in marginal zones. In these liminal spaces, new forms of culture and group identity began to form.

For contemporary white observers, the development of urban African culture posed a dilemma – how to administer a stable urban workforce within an intellectual landscape that assumed Africans to be 'naturally' rooted in rural societies? In the 1930s, studies of industrial cities in South Africa, on the central African Copperbelt, and elsewhere became a key concern of a new generation of social scientists.[123] In South Africa, the key research institution of the interwar years was the Institute for Race Relations (SAIRR), a liberal offshoot of the Joint Council Movement that had been founded in 1929. Along with its annual *Race Relations Survey*, researchers associated with the SAIRR pioneered the social study of urban Africans, most notably the social anthropologist Ellen Hellman, whose study *Rooiyard: A Sociology Survey of an Urban Native Slum* was first published in 1948. Despite echoing the widely held concerns around 'detribalization' and the loss of connection to rural social structures and cultural practices, Hellman ended her study on a positive note, suggesting that contemporary observers were witness to a transitional stage in African development, and that out of that would 'emerge a people who will adopt such elements of European culture as may enable them to attain to an ordered and economically secure social life'.[124]

Again, these conclusions were in accord with observers of African migrants elsewhere in Africa. Anthropologists associated with the Rhodes-Livingstone Institute felt, like their South African counterparts, that they were witnesses to a new industrial revolution, a process of 'modernization' that was placing intense pressure on African patterns of social life. What was characterized as the transformation of 'tribesmen' into 'townsmen' was therefore a continent-wide phenomenon that became a key concern for social scientists and administrators in the post-war period. South African urban experiences were therefore highly compatible with those in cities elsewhere in Africa.[125] Migrancy fostered relationships between town and countryside that, despite fears of 'detribalization' created individuals who straddled the worlds of rural and city life, of 'tradition' and 'modernity'.

In South Africa, where segregationist policies imposed a particularly rigid form of labour migrancy, the experience of workers, especially those in the mining industry, shaped new forms of collective identities and social relations. Living in male-only mine compounds and working in the harsh conditions deep underground affected the definition and performance of masculinity, while the movement of African women to cities (until the 1950s uncontrolled by pass laws) fostered the emergence of independent 'town women'.[126] The transformations of social relations and reworking of identities that were the consequences of urbanization resembled the changes that had been – and were continuing to be – shaped by transnational migration, not least because migrancy in South Africa continued to draw on a pool of labour from beyond the country's borders. This 'internal transnationalism' saw the construction of hybrid identities – Africans did not metamorphose cleanly from 'tribesmen' to 'townsmen', but instead maintained a sense of themselves as workers, as Africans, and as part of ethnic communities.[127]

Urban growth brought with it the transformation of social relations, customs and practices in a new urban culture. Urban youth were a particular barometer of social change, disconnected from the intergenerational structures of social control encountered in rural society. This urban youth culture adapted the structures of rural social organizations and combined them with cosmopolitan influences into new forms. Stick fighting amongst groups associated with rural initiation rituals became transplanted in cities in new forms. The rural age set shaded into urban gangs, whose allegiances were at times determined by ethnicity, as was the case with the largely migrant Sotho-speaking 'Russians'. The Russians, who blended modern fashion with 'traditional' rural blankets (which were transnational artefacts in themselves), were commonly regarded as the most threatening and violent of South Africa's urban gangs in the 1950s, whose 'strongly tribal' identity set them aside from other groups in the eyes of observers.[128] In fact, contrary to the vision of 'detribalization' expressed by white commentators during the interwar period, the Russians provided an illustration of the extent to which urbanization created, rather than broke down, ethnic identities and interethnic conflict. In South Africa, as it was elsewhere, the city became a crucible of African ethnicities.[129] Ethnic identities were also fostered by the insecure and heterogeneous crowded space encountered by migrants in the cities, with certain forms of employment (such as Xhosa building-workers) and geographical locations taking on a particular ethnic character.[130]

While the cities fostered the construction of exclusivist ethnic identities, urban culture reflected and drew more extensively upon global influences. Youth – and particularly *tsotsi* – styles were strongly influenced by an American 'gangster' forms of clothing and demeanour. The 'Americans' in one contemporary account, wore 'expensive "American" clothes ... straw hats, elegant cardigans, brown and white shoes and narrow blue trousers called "Bogarts" because Humphrey Bogart once wore them'.[131] In this context, cinema was a key reference point in the culture of *tsostis* and youth gangs, and a channel for transnational cultural influences. As such, townships were touched by the globalization of American culture.

Urban African culture was also expressed through popular music, which again exhibited strong transnational influences. From the late nineteenth century, South African ports – and Cape Town in particular – provided a point of entry for African-American cultural forms. Minstrel band the Jubilee Singers, who first toured South Africa in 1887, was enjoyed by both black and white audiences, and inspired the formation of a number of similar troupes within Cape Town's Coloured working class. The 'Cape Coon Carnival' that emerged as a yearly event saw competitive displays by groups that reflected the disparate and hybrid reference points that characterized Cape Coloured urban culture. American musical influences permeated South Africa.

During the interwar years, the popular cultural style known as *marabi* came to epitomize the music and lifestyle of the black urban working class. A syncretic mix of African and Western influences, *marabi* was an indigenous form of modern popular culture that centred on sociability, sexuality and drinking.[132] It shaped the American-influenced jazz bands as well as street-music, but was always more than a simple matter of cultural style, for it 'served as both a setting and a symbolic expression of the birth of an urban community'.[133] As such, *marabi* represented a threat to 'respectability' in the eyes of both white observers, especially missionaries, and middle-class Africans. Efforts to preserve, and simultaneously 'modernize' African culture could be harnessed to the task of creating a nationalist consciousness, and songs such as J. P. Mohapeloa's 'U Ea Kae' ('Where Are You Going') have continued to resonate as expressions of African solidarity.

Nor were cultural influences one-way, even if the work of South African artists was not always given the recognition it deserved. The interwar period saw major recording companies establish offices and distribution networks in South Africa, and local recording studios were set up in the 1930s, pioneered by the Gallo studio in Johannesburg. The studio's most successful recording and 'the greatest South African hit of all time' also provided the starkest example of the ways in which racial inequality powerfully marked commercial music production. In 1939, Zulu performer Solomon Linda and his band the Evening Birds recorded the song 'Mbube'; after becoming a major hit in South Africa, it was 'discovered' in the late 1940s by the US musicologist Alan Lomax and recorded by folk musician Pete Seegar as 'Wimoweh' in 1952. By the end of the 1950s, the song had transformed into 'The Lion Sleeps Tonight', eventually to be recorded by scores of artists.[134] Although Seegar sent Linda payments in recognition of his composition, the rights to the song eventually fell to US songwriter George Weiss, who adapted Linda's original version in 1961. It was not until 2006 that the family of Solomon Linda (who had died in 1962) began to receive royalties for his composition from the Disney Corporation, who had used the song in the global cinema and musical hit, *Lion King*.[135]

Summary

In 1936, J. B. M. Hertzog introduced two new laws that entrenched the segregationist policies of the interwar period. First proposed in 1926, Hertzog's 'Native Bills' comprised a Native Trust and Land Act, which extended the terms of the 1913 Land Act and, most significantly, a Native Representation Act that abolished the 'colour-blind' Cape franchise and instead created four white 'Native Representatives' in the Senate, elected by African voters. The 1936 Acts represented the pinnacle of Hertzog's power, although their passage relied in part on the formal alliance between the National Party and the South African Party under Smuts in 1934. The Pact government which brought Hertzog's 'Native Bills' into being thus represented a consensus in white politics around the principles of segregation and the desire to maintain white supremacy. While it voiced opposition to the Bills, the weakened Congress under Seme had little impact on African responses to the political debate in the late 1930s. While independent figures D.D.T. Jabavu (son of John Tengo Jabavu) and the US-trained medic (and later ANC President) Dr Alfred Xuma led the defence of the 'Cape Tradition' in the face of the Bills at gatherings such as the 1935 All-African Convention, black responses were largely disorganized and limited to discussions within and between those same moderate elites that had again sought to mobilize the politics of delegation in the hope of securing advancement within a unified, but ultimately Eurocentric political system.

Between 1920 and 1936, black politics was marked by increasing disconnection from the South African state. While movements such as the ICU had demonstrated that popular mobilization was possible, this was not channelled into a direct challenge to the institutions of government or state authorities. The development of black politics in the interwar period thus reveals something of the developing nature of the state itself, determined increasingly along racial lines, with segregation as the dominant discourse of administration. Relations between the state and black individuals and groups were predicated upon patron–client style arrangements, but these relationships were continually destabilized by the foundational reality of South African politics: white supremacy.[136] As segregation developed as the primary tool of social control in the modern industrialized economy, stable relationships between the state and black clients became harder to maintain. The 1936 Bills marked the final triumph of segregationism over older liberal traditions, but it also drove home – to some black leaders at least – the pointlessness of a political strategy based upon moral persuasion and loyal alliance with white 'friends of the native'.

Further reading

Beinart, William and Saul Dubow, eds. *Segregation and Apartheid in Twentieth-Century South Africa*. London: Routledge, 1995.

Coombes, Annie E., ed. *Rethinking Settler Colonialism: History and Memory in Australia, Canada, Aotearoa New Zealand and South Africa*. Manchester: Manchester University Press, 2006.

Crush, Jonathan, Alan H. Jeeves and David Yudelman. *South Africa's Labor Empire: A History of Black Migrancy to the Gold Mines*. Boulder, CO: Westview Press, 1991.

Drew, Allison. *Between Empire and Revolution: A Life of Sidney Bunting, 1873–1936*. London: Pickering & Chatto, 2007.

Elkins, Caroline and Susan Pedersen, eds. *Settler Colonialism in the Twentieth Century: Projects, Practices, Legacies*. New York: Routledge, 2005.

Elphick, Richard. 'The Benevolent Empire and the Social Gospel: Missionaries and South African Christians in the Age of Segregation'. In *Christianity in South Africa: A Political, Social and Cultural History*, ed. Richard Elphick and Rodney Davenport, 347–69. Cape Town: David Phillip, 1997.

Evans, Ivan Thomas. *Bureaucracy and Race: Native Administration in South Africa*. Berkeley, CA: University of California Press, 1997.

Grant, Kevin, Philippa Levine and Frank Trentmann, eds. *Beyond Sovereignty: Britain, Empire and Transnationalism, C. 1860–1950*. Basingstoke: Palgrave Macmillan, 2007.

Krikler, Jeremy. *White Rising: The 1922 Insurrection and Racial Killing in South Africa*. Manchester: Manchester University Press, 2005.

Moodie, T. Dunbar and Vivienne Ndatshe. *Going for Gold: Men, Mines, and Migration*. Berkeley, CA: University of California Press, 1994.

Odendaal, André. *The Founders: The Origins of the ANC and the Struggle for Democracy in South Africa*. Auckland Park, South Africa: Jacana Media, 2012.

Rich, Paul B. *State Power and Black Politics in South Africa, 1912–51*. Basingstoke: Macmillan, 1996.

Walker, Cherryl, ed. *Women and Gender in Southern Africa to 1945*. London: J. Currey, 1990.

CHAPTER 5
EMPIRE, NATION AND WAR

The Great Depression of the 1930s had significant economic, political and social repercussions for South Africa. The collapse in world commodity prices at the start of the decade resulted in a 50 per cent decline in prices for agricultural products, accelerating the shift towards large-scale commercial farming. Poorer white farmers and black sharecroppers, already under pressure from the structural constraints imposed by segregation, left the countryside in increasing numbers in search of work in urban areas. Despite the fixed price of gold on the world market, a fluctuating exchange rate meant that the price of gold in sterling dramatically increased when South Africa belatedly abandoned the gold standard in 1932.[1] Gold mining therefore retained its importance to the South African economy, although the formerly dominant De Beers Company was taken over by Ernest Oppenheimer's Anglo-American Corporation in 1929.[2] While agriculture still employed a larger number of workers and contributed a greater proportion of GDP, gold mining was a particularly significant source of foreign earnings, inward investment and tax receipts. Gold (and diamonds) thus continued to provide the primary engine of economic growth.

The Hertzog administration had, however, sought to promote the development of manufacturing industries, introducing tariff protections and reorganizing the national Board of Trade and Industries. The state also took an active role in industrial development, through the formation of public utilities, including the Electricity Supply Commission (1923) and the Iron and Steel Industrial Corporation (1928).[3] With government support, secondary industries expanded rapidly from the mid-1930s, and in particular during the Second World War, when local production replaced imports affected by wartime restrictions. Between 1924 and 1948, the number of private manufacturing companies more than doubled, and by the end of the 1940s the value of industrial output was four times higher than at the start of the 1930s. However, expansion masked key structural weaknesses, which included relatively low levels of productivity, artificially restricted levels of wages and a deficit in the skills and training of the workforce.[4] Moreover, the imperial connection remained a dominant force in the economy through to the 1940s, not only in terms of trade (Britain continued to be South Africa's major trading partner) but also via firm financial links to the City of London, notably through Barclays and Standard banks.[5]

The interwar period also saw the emergence of new international partners and sources of inward investment, with the United States emerging as a particularly significant international partner beyond the British Empire. American car manufacturers Ford and General Motors set up South African factories in 1923 and 1926, with the former setting up a factory in Port Elizabeth. From Coca Cola to Metro Goldwyn Mayer, US corporations established operations in South Africa, exploiting an expanding market for US manufactures and cultural products.[6] But the 1930s were largely a period in which the processes of globalization fostered by imperialism were in retreat, superseded by an unstable 'fractured world order'.[7] In South Africa, as elsewhere, the two decades after the Great Depression saw nationalist consciousness playing an increasingly important role in politics.

Benevolent empire and the 'friends of the Native'

As the experience of Plaatje and the SANNC delegation in 1914 had shown, metropolitan Quaker and Missionary networks, centred on the Anti-Slavery and Aborigines' Protection Society, were reluctant to offer support for black nationalism, however moderate its politics. The imperial networks that had fostered and sustained humanitarian interventions in colonial South Africa in the nineteenth century were geared more towards 'protection of the Native' rather than the advancement of African political agendas. The interwar period saw the influence of these established liberal networks diminish, just as new activists connected with trades unions and Fabian Socialism began to take a more central role in British expressions of concern over the impact of segregation.[8] Nevertheless, there were continuities, as traditional humanitarian networks and missionary organizations maintained their important – and often central – role in transnational interactions between South Africa and the West.

Of particular concern in the years after the First World War were the potentially deleterious effects of industrialization that emerged from a new cultural evaluation of the process of 'detribalization' that liberal observers saw at work in South African cities.[9] Although they rejected crude racial essentialism, humanitarians in urban missions worked particularly assiduously to 'protect' black workers from the influence of radical 'agitators'. The American Board missionary, Ray Phillips, notably screened Charlie Chaplin films in order to divert the attention of black workers during the Rand Revolt in 1922. The architects of the new urban missions, including Phillips and his predecessor Frederick Bridgman, were firm advocates of an approach rooted in Social Gospel ideas that rose to prominence in industrial centres of the United States – an approach that redefined missionary activities as 'the task of capturing the whole African – the whole man and all his activities'.[10] The ethos of urban missionary work was epitomized by the Bantu Men's Social Centre founded by Phillips in 1924, a multipurpose institution that sought to provide for 'religious, athletic, musical, theatrical and academic activities for the black Johannesburg elite'.[11] It was a physical manifestation of liberal-Christian ideologies in the mid-twentieth century, whose welfarism was rooted in the paternalist desire to 'guide' Africans towards social and spiritual redemption without questioning the political economy of racial inequality.

Further from the centre of gravity of white liberalism, another important institution of interwar mission humanitarianism was established by the Anglican Community of the

Resurrection in the racially mixed north-western Johannesburg suburb of Sophiatown. The Community, formed in late-nineteenth-century Britain by figures connected to the Oxford Movement, brought an Anglo-Catholic emphasis on collective well-being to the urban mission in South Africa.[12] Under the leadership of Raymond Raynes, the mission became a central institution of Johannesburg social life and helped to foster a working-class 'culture of respectability' that would underpin community identity and political resistance movements in the 1940s and 1950s.[13]

Sophiatown, which lay around four miles north and west of the Johannesburg city centre, was established as a racially mixed area in the years immediately following the South African War. As a consequence of its location, and not least the proximity of the municipal sewage works, it had become difficult to attract buyers for plots, and by Union sales of plots were taking place without racial restrictions. Exempted from the provisions of the 1923 Urban Areas act, during the interwar period the suburb became a hub of Johannesburg's black culture, a racially mixed (but predominantly African) urban space that was home to a number of leading figures, including the ANC President in the 1940s, Alfred Xuma. By that point, though, the expansion of Johannesburg's suburbs had brought white working class districts to the very edge of Sophiatown and increased political agitation for the removal of this 'black spot'. It was only with the advent of the apartheid state, however, that political will and legislative apparatus was brought together to facilitate the destruction of what had become a vibrant and creative centre that black South Africans in other cities saw as 'a symbol as well as a partial realisation of their aspirations'.[14]

Beyond these groups, with their close connections with South African liberals and the mission-humanitarian heirs of Exeter Hall, the emerging ecumenical movement also shaped interwar Christian internationalism. Organizations such as the International Missionary Council (IMC) embraced anthropological notions of difference and cultural relativism; its head, Joseph Oldham, criticized Smuts's segregationist ideas in his 1930 book *White and Black in South Africa*. Oldham argued that, contrary to Smuts's contention, segregationist South Africa did not offer a model for 'Native Policy' in southern and East Africa more generally, and that efforts should instead focus on social and economic development.[15]

Alongside its classical missionary components, mid-twentieth-century philanthropy in South Africa was also shaped by the efforts of international organizations concerned with new forms of scientific research and, by the end of the 1930s, plans for social and economic development. The Carnegie Corporation, representative of the 'American liberal developmentalism' of the new century, began to take an interest in Africa in the late 1920s. Its Commission of Investigation into the Poor White Problem investigated conditions in South Africa in 1929 and 1930, and published its findings in 1932, in a report that would have a significant impact upon Afrikaner nationalist ideologies. As such, the Commission's work in South Africa reflected the multilateral influences that went into the making of international perspectives on South Africa. The normative role of South African intellectuals and institutions in the design and planning of the Carnegie Commission research reveals more ambiguous channels of power beyond the dominance of North over South.[16] While these new forms of intervention reflected an international intellectual culture largely shared by South Africans, nationalist ideologies were resilient.

Internationalist notions of 'development' had a significant impact on ideas of colonial administration during the interwar years. By the late 1930s, social and economic development was beginning to challenge the orthodoxy of Indirect Rule in British colonial policy, and in turn shaped perceptions of South African policies of segregation. Liberals and missionaries, concerned to divert African attention from the seductive attractions of communism, saw development schemes as a method of protecting African interests. The IMC-sponsored study of industrialization on the Northern Rhodesian copper belt in 1932 included South African liberal Leo Marquard alongside Ray Phillips in its commission. Oldham himself sat on the committee set up to examine the issues raised by Smuts's 1929 lectures, which resulted in Lord Hailey's highly influential *Africa Survey*. From an internationalist perspective, South Africa was as a primary focus for those concerned with issues of race relations, even to the extent of being considered as a central site of 'world race conflict' in the 1930s.[17]

Internationalism was not only a 'perspective' on South African affairs, but also an ideological position in itself that tied together liberal and radical visions of South African segregation within a singular framework marked by a liberal developmentalist 'worldview'. For Bush, the efforts of international liberal networks in the 1930s to fight on behalf of the 'underdog' in southern Africa were hampered by their reluctance – or inability – to critique the structural foundations of the inequalities experienced by Africans.

The politics of Afrikaner nationalism

The 1930s saw South Africa drawn more closely into the political structures of the British 'Empire State'.[18] The principle of Dominion equality, enshrined in the 1931 Statute of Westminster, envisaged an imperial system that saw Britain as the centre of a community of states, in control of their own political destinies, but tied together by a sense of shared values and interests. Under Hertzog, the South African approach to imperial relations steered a course between nationalist independence and pragmatic desire for unity. While notions of the 'British bogeyman' informed nationalist politics in the interwar period, Hertzog managed the imperial relationship, in ways not dissimilar to the Irish Free State in the same period.[19]

The economic pressures of the Depression were the source of crisis in Afrikaner nationalist politics. After Britain left the gold standard in 1931, nationalists were initially determined not to follow, seeing South African retention of the gold standard as a symbol of the country's independence.[20] As South African agriculture saw diminishing incomes and the gold-mining industry found it increasingly difficult to secure adequate financial investment, Hertzog was faced with revolt within the National Party. In order to secure the passage of legislation to allow South Africa to come off the gold standard and sign up to the provisions of the Statute of Westminster, Hertzog made a coalition agreement with Smuts's South African Party. The 'Fusion' agreed by Hertzog and Smuts in February 1933 prompted the breakaway of Afrikaner nationalists led by Daniel Francois Malan, a Dutch-Reformed Minister, who went on to form a 'Purified' Nationalist Party. The creation of the United Party secured Dominion status and appeared to diminish the hopes of republicanism for the foreseeable future. However, the way was open for the assertive form of Afrikaner nationalist politics of Malan and his followers to become the main opposition to the Hertzog-Smuts alliance, and to forge a new Afrikaner political – and historical – narrative.[21]

At the heart of this narrative lay the plight of 'poor whites'. In the interwar years, the African continent became the focus of a number of studies concerned with the social impact of modernity.[22] From the late 1920s, the nascent discipline of social science turned its attention to the 'Poor White problem' in South Africa. In 1929, following a tour of South Africa by its president two years before, the US Carnegie Corporation launched a commission to investigate white poverty in South Africa. Its five-volume report set out in stark terms the nature of white poverty, estimating that around 17 per cent of the white population could be defined as poor. A large proportion of this number, both in rural areas and recent migrants to cities, were considered to be of 'Afrikaans-speaking' descent, adding an ethnopolitical dimension to the debates around the commission findings, which provided the focus for a national conference sponsored by the Dutch Reformed Churches (DRC) in 1934.[23] The Carnegie Commission report acknowledged the significance of black poverty in South Africa and indeed that it was a 'problem of greater magnitude and complexity'.[24] Notwithstanding such concerns, the commission report gave intellectual support to advocates of state-directed support and 'uplift' for the white minority in South Africa – and particularly for those who could be defined as Afrikaners.

Afrikaner identity was rooted in colonial social and cultural history, and the term, as a general description of South African-born settlers, had been in use since the nineteenth century. From Union in 1910, Afrikaner identities began to take on new, politicized meanings in the context of the new unified state. The importation of British models of administration and governance on the Westminster model thus deepened social divisions.[25] Afrikaner political identities emerged from contests over the definition of a South African nation and struggles for cultural hegemony within the white population. A critical point of tension developed around the status of the Afrikaans language, which had become the prime characteristic of the new Afrikaner nationalist consciousness.

Afrikaans was systematically reconstructed into a 'respectable' form through the work of cultural entrepreneurs such as Gustav Preller, who worked to create a publishing industry that would establish Afrikaans as a serious language. While nationalist programmes often tend towards introspection, the Afrikaans language movement sought inspiration from around the world. The model for Afrikaans-language magazines was based on American examples, while the Afrikaans language movement was set alongside campaigns to promote the Welsh, Quebecois or Flemish languages.[26] Preller sought to construct a respectable language, cleansing Afrikaans of any taint of African influence, and in the process distancing white Afrikaners from Coloured Afrikaans speakers. As such, two ethnicities were forged from the process of building an Afrikaner nation, as Coloured identity became more sharply defined through its exclusion.

Gender was a key element of Afrikaner nationalist rhetoric – at least in its foundation. The Afrikaans literature that emerged from the language movement often emphasized the *volksmoeder*, the 'mother of the nation', and women were seen both as a driving force in the formation of a more assertive Afrikaner identity at the same time that they found themselves objects of its pity. The *volksmoeder* was an ambiguous figure, emblematic both of the assertive rural traditions but also in need of protection from the dangers of racially mixed towns and cities.[27] The centrality of the *volksmoeder* to Afrikaner identity in the mid-twentieth century is embodied in the ways in which she was deployed as an iconic symbol of the nation during the 1938 *eufees* celebrations to mark the centenary of the 'Great Trek'. And yet, even here, the figure was not entirely unambiguous. In a creative repositioning of the core nationalist vision, the Garment Workers' Union (GWU) organized a 'Kappie Kommando' of 400 women who paid homage to nineteenth-century Voortrekkers as symbols, not of Afrikaner freedom per se, but a broader struggle for liberation from capitalism.[28]

The development of Afrikaner nationalism was, perhaps, most deeply connected to the formation of class identities in an urbanizing and industrializing South Africa. The celebrations of 1938 crystallized the burgeoning national myth of Afrikanerdom, centred around a struggle for independence from British imperialism. The event captured the imagination of white South Africa, but signalled in the clearest terms that the more inclusive nationalism of Hertzog was quickly being supplanted by the divisive ethnic nationalism of a new generation of Afrikaner leaders. At the centre was Malan, who oversaw the patriotic fervour at the ceremony to mark the anniversary of the Trekkers' victory over the amaZulu at Ncome River. Hertzog was absent, dismissive of the exclusive nationalism of Malan, and it seemed that the leadership of Afrikaner nationalism 'was passing into the hands of the Cape predikant'.[29]

Overseas commentators viewed the celebrations in 1938 as a critical moment for Afrikaner nationalism. An editorial comment in the *Times* in London cast the foundational myth of the Great Trek in terms of two contrasting claims of liberty; one centred on individual freedom, one on the freedom of groups to determine their own destiny. The authority of the descendants of the Trekkers had 'come to outweigh that of the Cape Colony through whose boundaries their ancestors broke'. With that freedom, however, came the responsibility to provide a solution to 'the problem of the interpretation of liberty for the aboriginal population of the land'.[30] In a further reminder of South Africa's status within the Commonwealth, a message from King George VI, read out (in Afrikaans) at the ceremony to lay the foundation-stone of the new Voortrekker Monument overlooking Pretoria, stated that commemoration of the Great Trek 'must appeal to the hearts of all South Africans'.[31] The *eufees* celebrations were a moment of high political theatre with international significance. The threat of Republican, separatist nationalism was recognizable, but not yet dominant, and the more inclusive 'South Africanist' nationalism of Smuts and Hertzog prevailed within the urban middle- classes.[32]

Fascism and apartheid

The Afrikaner nationalism that began to assert itself in the 1930s was republican, anti-imperial and staunch in its support of the white supremacist status quo, and had the appearance of an inward-looking, parochial and defensive movement. An international dimension of Afrikaner nationalism was nevertheless present in its formation, its emergence as a popular force and in the ideological foundations of its politics. A crude account of Afrikaner nationalism would thus envision it as an attempt to reject modernity and erect a political *laager*. But, until the outbreak of war, nationalist politics was fluid and pluralist rather than monolithic.[33] During the 1930s, following Hitler's rise to power in Germany, Nazi sympathies and ideological affinities facilitated the rise of ultra-right movements within South Africa. The most important of the 'shirt movements' of the 1930s was the Greyshirts, formed in 1933 in the Western Cape and led by a former hairdresser, Louis Weichardt, who developed an ambiguous relationship with Malan's 'Purified' nationalists. It was these Purified Nationalists that most resembled the German Nazi Party in its base of support, although direct connections between Malan's party and European fascist movements are difficult to discern.

The ideological foundations of the radical nationalism that emerged in the 1930s were varied. Many of the patterns of thinking that shaped the gestation of apartheid in this same period were rooted in ideological influences imported from overseas, particularly from continental Europe. A wide range of Afrikaners, including those within Hertzog's party as well as intellectuals from Stellenbosch University, supported popular protests against Jewish immigration, which rose significantly in the mid-1930s, prompting calls for legal restrictions, supported in Parliament by Malan himself and his later Cabinet Minister, Eric Louw.[34] Protests in 1936 against the arrival of *The Stuttgart*, a German ship carrying over 500 German-Jewish emigrants, drew radical Afrikaner support away from the nascent fascist movements represented by the Greyshirts.

Alongside fears around immigration, populist Nationalist media drew upon racial stereotypes that had been mobilized by fascist movements in Europe when condemning the Jewish businessman, via the crude image of 'Hoggenheimer', representative of a British imperial and Jewish capitalist oligarchy.[35] But the rise of anti-Semitism in interwar South Africa had deeper roots in negative stereotypes of eastern European Jews, contrasted with the supposedly more 'loyal' and enterprising Jews of Anglo-German background.[36] Interwar radical nationalism borrowed from a 'vocabulary of concepts' associated with European fascism and included an attraction to authoritarian government, suspicion of democracy and a desire to promote a politics rooted in an organic sense of the 'volk'.[37] It was this latter aspect that secured the greatest appeal to Afrikaners amidst the process of cultural reclamation that took place in the aftermath of the 1938 Great Trek celebrations.[38]

The fluidity of Afrikaner nationalism during the interwar period was also evident in the developing intellectual framework that began to shape both Afrikaner politics but, more significantly, the developing idea of *apartheid* that came to embody a nationalist solution to the 'Native Question'. European intellectual influences again played an important role in the shaping of theological frameworks and social thought that informed the elaboration of apartheid ideas. The DRCs in South Africa had not remained aloof from the debates around the Social Gospel that had underpinned much of the Anglophone missionary activity in the first half of the century, even if their support was conditional. Those DRC leaders that had shown a willingness to work with white liberal and African mission-Christians in the 1920s certainly did not countenance any visions of racial integration, and by the early 1930s, DRC councils began couching social Christian concerns with agricultural and industrial issues in terms of more assertive policies of racial separation.[39] The central theological basis of DRC policy was drawn from the neo-Calvinist teachings of the Dutch religious thinker Abraham Kuyper, who had a vision of a world divinely divided into distinct social and cultural spheres.[40] Kuyperian ideas, introduced to Afrikaner students attending the Free University of Amsterdam returned to South Africa, where it was taken up in particular by Reformed ministers, including Malan himself, who were increasingly committed to the 'civil religion' of Afrikaner nationalism.[41]

Aside from Dutch neo-Calvinism, the ideology of apartheid drew on German Romantic notions of an organic cultural basis for nationhood, which fed not only the self-conception of Afrikaner nationalists, but also their sense of the natural cultural order of southern Africa more broadly. Like neo-Calvinism, volksnationalist ideas were injected into Afrikaner nationalist thought as a consequence of the experience of Afrikaner students in Europe in the first half of the twentieth century. Very much like their black counterparts, this was a formative experience for many Afrikaner intellectuals, including figures who would go on to play prominent roles in the apartheid government, such as Nico Diederichs (who studied at the University of Leiden) and most notably the future prime minister widely regarded as the architect of apartheid, Hendrik Verwoerd (who studied psychology as a graduate in Germany during the 1920s). The 'volksnationalist' ideas that figures such as Diederichs and Verwoerd brought back to South Africa placed more emphasis, however, on a secular and authoritarian model of the nation.[42] Their vision of the nation, which helped to infuse Afrikaner nationalism with ideas that bore some similarity with Nazi ideology, was compatible with neo-Calvinism but also led to ideological tensions, specifically where the idea of the nation was elevated above all other things – the 'civil religion' did not play well with those who believed in God's primacy in all spheres.[43]

The volksnationalist influence might also be seen in the tendency of the post-war apartheid state to idealize a nostalgic and romanticized vision of nineteenth-century Republicanism. 'Krugerism' formed a core characteristic of the apartheid state, which was not simply a version of authoritarianism modelled on European fascism, but 'reactionary in its determination to recreate the simpler world of the old Boer republics'.[44] A similar blend of modern and anti-modern tendencies might also be discerned in the influence of European eugenicist ideas on apartheid ideologues. During the 1930s, Afrikaner academics such as the geneticist Gerrie Eloff and the criminologist Geoffrey Cronjé sought to graft scientific racist ideas to South African volksnationalism. As with its influence on more liberal segregationist ideas, race science and eugenics tended to provide more of a rationalization for widely held racist sentiment – and most importantly, the fear of miscegenation – than a programme for administration.

Nonetheless, these transnational ideological influences came to shape – in outline form – the race policy espoused by the National Party. After 1943 when, despite Smuts's election victory, Malan's position as leader of the opposition was secured, he began to make regular references to a policy of racial separation, or *apartheid*, in his political speeches.[45] First used in the mid-1930s, the slogan appeared more frequently during the 1940s as an expression of National Party race policies. While the racism associated with the far-right groups of Europe had formed an important element of Afrikaner nationalist discourse in the first half of the war, the subsidence of support for groups such as the OB (Ossewabrandwag ('Ox-wagon sentinel')) after the end of the war meant that a more nuanced set of racial policies, rooted in South African social realities was required. While the policy of race separation integral to *apartheid* was seen as a product of the historical experiences of the Afrikaner volk, it nevertheless drew upon ideas circulated via transnational networks of intellectuals.

War and reconstruction

On 4 September 1939, Smuts's argument for South African participation in the war against Germany prevailed over Hertzog's desire for South African neutrality. It was a close vote, and the subsequent departure of Hertzog and his supporters from the United Party was a blow that meant the global conflict would be fought, for South Africa, on the battleground of domestic politics as well as the fields of Africa and Europe. For Hertzog, the war in Europe had no direct impact on South Africa, save for the effect it would have on national unity. Smuts, on the other hand, located South African national interests in a larger Commonwealth context.[46] The war was, for Smuts, entirely compatible with the 'politics of international holism' that had informed his support for the League of Nations during the interwar period.[47] Moreover, the threat to South African interests in the region, given Hitler's stated intention to reclaim South-West Africa as German territory was real.

Following the outbreak of war, Malanite Nationalists such as Oswald Pirow became outspoken in their support of the German cause, while more radical groups developed plans for more active pro-Nazi endeavours. Most prominent of the wartime paramilitary organizations was the OB, formed during the *eufees* celebrations. The OB claimed a membership over 150,000 and, led after 1941 by the former nationalist student leader J. F. J. Van Rensburg, developed close links with German agents in southern Africa, while its armed wing, the *Stormjaers,* engaged in a series of militant operations in the early years of the war, blowing up power and telephone cables. Moreover, the OB had connections with the Broederbond, including members who would go on to hold office during the apartheid era, notably the future prime minister, B. J. Vorster, who was interned for his OB activities in 1942.

Under Smuts, the South African government quickly established plans for the defence of South Africa and the expansion of its military forces. Union Defence Force volunteers, especially those who signed up for service outside South Africa were a potent symbol of support for Smuts's imperial loyalism within South Africa. Smuts himself became an embodiment of the imperial war effort, whose words of support were broadcast to the British people in 1940 and again at the start of 1941.[48] In 1940, Smuts persuaded Churchill of the necessity of establishing Allied control in East Africa, in order to protect against the extension of Axis power, particularly in the Middle East. After a short and successful campaign in the Horn of Africa, South African forces were engaged in North Africa by mid-1941, where in 1942 they faced the disaster of defeat at Tobruk. During that same year, faced with the increasing threat from the Japanese navy in the Indian Ocean, Durban was used as the assembly point for forces involved in the invasion of Madagascar. For the remainder of the war, South African forces continued to play an important role in Allied offensives – a South African armoured division was incorporated into the Allied forces that took part in the Italian campaign from 1944, marking a decisive break from Smuts's earlier declaration that South African forces would not be committed to fight outside of the continent of Africa.

The decision to take South Africa into the war played a considerable part in sharpening divisions in the white population; the recruitment of black volunteers, and the suggestion that African soldiers might be armed, intensified debate around the nature of South African citizenship. Smuts and his supporters aimed to co-opt Africans into the war effort, playing on vestiges of African loyalism – although it seems that opportunities for personal advancement rather than loyalty motivated the majority of black volunteers.[49] The attempt to promote black participation in the war, although it bore similarities to recruitment to the Native Labour Contingent during the First World War, appeared as an acknowledgement of the impact that war was having on existing political and social taboos. This went, or so it seemed, to the very heart of South African race policies. The idea that 'segregation had fallen on evil days', as Smuts put it in 1942, came at the height of the wartime threat from both Axis powers and Afrikaner militancy, but seemed to presage a dramatic policy shift as key tenets of the interwar policy were brought into question by the exigencies of war. Alternatively, the apparent change of direction might be interpreted as a superficial flourish, and that Smuts remained reluctant to address the social transformations that were being exacerbated by war.[50]

The apparent shift in the tone of government policy – away from hard-line segregation and towards a version of 'common society' liberalism – came as a consequence of a complex mix of wartime opportunities and imperatives, both domestic and international in origin. War necessitated an interventionist state and a 'developmentalist' approach to social and economic reform. Similarly, while calls for social reform have been most often linked to Smuts's liberal supporters, notably his wartime Finance Minister, J. H. Hofmeyr, leading Afrikaner nationalists also began to incorporate plans for state interventions, including social security provision, into policy. For the National Party from the early 1940s, it was 'the duty of the State to provide for better and more equitable distribution of goods and products' and plans were set out for contributory pensions, social housing and a form of national health services.[51] The ubiquity of welfarist policies in the 1940s reflected global discourses on development, reform and the interventionist state, most obviously illustrated by the federal initiatives implemented by the Roosevelt administration in the United States in the 1930s, and British plans for welfare reform embodied in the Beveridge Report of 1942. For South Africa, promises of reform and reconstruction provided a vision of a 'future worth fighting for', just as it did elsewhere.[52]

Plans for post-war reconstruction were given moral backing by a report commissioned in 1943 by the Anglican Bishop of Johannesburg, Geoffrey Clayton. While it favoured a narrative of individual redemption over collectivism, the report nonetheless captured some of the flavour of the reformist impulse evident across the Anglican Communion, notably in Archbishop William Temple's popular thesis of Christian social reform, *Christianity and the Social Order*.[53] At the same time, the South African Army Education Service provided a secular space in which utopian ideas of democracy and social reform were diffused through officers such as Leo Marquard, who would go on to play important roles in post-war liberal politics.[54] Wartime idealism also stimulated the emergence of political movements, such as the Campaign for Right and Justice, that brought together a wide spectrum of left-liberal opinion in efforts to promote social welfarist and democratic reforms. Efforts to mobilize support for a more inclusive definition of South African identity were boosted during the early war years, and were seemingly secured by the success of the United Party in the 1943 election.[55] However, the victory did not signal any moral or ideological shift towards greater racial inclusivity; for Smuts, attempts to improve the social and economic position of black South Africans did not signal a desire to create an inclusive 'common society', even if his wartime policies did appear to implicitly accept a permanent black urban population. His 1942 speech was as much concerned with territorial ambitions – the need to establish South Africa as the predominant power in an interconnected region that was fully integrated into the world economy.[56]

Organizational and administrative changes during the war were often, therefore, in advance of popular appetites for change. Nevertheless, the war was a catalyst for the establishment of a series of national bodies aimed at centralized planning of economic and social development, building on the interventionist moves of the Pact government in the 1930s. Clayton's Church Commission was an ecclesiastic counterpart to a series of government commissions, on social welfare, on industry and agriculture, on African social and working conditions and on African urbanization. The focus on development ushered in with the establishment of the Social and Economic Planning Council in 1942 followed the direction of government planning across the British Empire, not least the overarching colonial policy indicated by the British Colonial Development and Welfare Acts of 1940 and 1945.[57] Labour reforms and welfare provision were designed to increase economic efficiency, but were also a response to protests in Asia and the Caribbean during the 1930s.[58] Unlike many other colonial states, however, the process of social and economic planning in South Africa was subject to the politics of the settler state, instinctively antipathetic towards proposals that ran counter to segregationist principles. South Africa's situation was closer to that prevailing in Kenya and Southern Rhodesia, where 'protection' of and support for the 'traditional' agrarian peasantry was preferred over large-scale welfare policies.

South African social and economic policies in the 1940s were therefore subject to liberal internationalist visions of post-war reconstruction. The language of churches, newly formed official bodies tasked with economic planning, and non-governmental organizations was suffused with talk of common society and social welfare that reflected imperial and international trends. Government policy in South Africa was, however, geared towards a 'war on two fronts': international and domestic; this was particularly the case up to the point at which Malan secured his leadership of Afrikaner opposition in 1943. United Party policies were, as Nattrass suggests, subject to limits imposed by deep-seated European support for racial discrimination in the political and social arenas.[59] Beyond that, it is unclear how far South African politicians were convinced of the need for significant reforms of race policy. To a great extent, the Smutsian vision remained rooted in a racialized view of the world, despite the superficial retreat from hard-line segregationist thought apparently signalled by his speech of 1942. For black South Africans, however, the war was a catalyst for new, radical, political and cultural visions.

The politics of urbanization and African rights

In the mid-1940s, South African politics was marked by a number of interrelated developments: the emergence of a powerful Afrikaner ethnic nationalist political opposition, liberal concerns over welfare and development, and scepticism over the long-term viability of urban segregation. The latter would provide the ultimate point of conflict between liberal and nationalist views on the eve of the fateful 1948 election. African city dwellers had been a historical fact of life, but the urban African population had expanded significantly over the first half of the twentieth century. The war saw this process accelerate, spurred on by the wartime growth of manufacturing industry. Throughout the war, black employment in manufacturing grew, attracting workers away from mining and agriculture, and making it harder to find recruits for military service.[60] Moreover, the deterioration of conditions in the Reserves and on white farms, compounded by severe drought, meant that many rural Africans moved to the cities out of desperation as much as aspiration. At the crisis point of the war, between 1942 and 1943, formal relaxation of segregationist controls facilitated this process, which resulted in the virtual doubling of the black urban population during the decade.[61]

Rapid urban growth in the 1940s was at times characterized by chaotic and unplanned development that sparked political protest in the form of squatter movements that developed large informal settlements on the borders of municipal locations. Charismatic individuals such as James Mpanza provided a focus for these movements, independent of nationalist leaders in the ANC. Similarly, community protests, such as the bus boycotts launched by residents of Alexandra township to the north of Johannesburg in 1945, were detached from established black political movements, despite support from radical activists including the former Communist Party member Hyman Basner. Grassroots level protest and activism did, however, begin to prompt municipal authorities and central government to consider more active intervention in the management and control of the African urban population.[62]

Along with a settled urban population came more organized working-class politics. The growth of trades unions was a wartime phenomenon seen across Africa, as the need to mobilize civilian labour enhanced the power of some groups of urban workers.[63] In South Africa, black trade unions played a central role in the development of wartime political campaigns, with the Campaign for Right and Justice working closely with individual unions such as the Transvaal Teachers' Association and larger conglomerations such as the Council of Non-European Trade Unions.[64] This new black working-class emerged as a consequence of wartime economic growth, and its underlying strength and confidence was belied by the suppression of worker militancy by the Smuts government.[65] Instigated by the African Mine Workers' Union led by J. B. Marks (who had received training in the Soviet Union during the interwar years), a major strike in August 1946 saw over 60,000 workers on the Rand withdraw their labour. Police succeeded in violently breaking the strike within days, but it nevertheless marked a significant moment in the development of African politics. While it may have been a 'plebeian' protest rooted in a moral economy, rather than evidence of a burgeoning 'proletarian' consciousness, the strike signalled the possibilities for mass, urban-based black protest.[66]

The Second World War reinvigorated African politics in ways that would have a lasting impact, creating a foundation for the national campaigns against apartheid in the 1950s and beyond. At the start of the war the ANC had virtually ceased to be a relevant organization, but a new generation of younger activists began to assert calls to transform Congress into a more radical movement oriented towards the mass of the black population. From 1943, the ANC Youth League (ANCYL) became the centre of a new radicalism within the organization, urging its leaders to adopt a more populist and mass-oriented approach. The Youth League was one of a range of more assertive civil society organizations that developed in urban areas in the early 1940s. African ex-servicemen and teachers' unions joined movements such as the Campaign for Right and Justice, which called for large-scale efforts to improve living conditions and rights for urban Africans in a period of wartime reconstruction. Across Africa, wartime military service and transformations in colonial economies were a spur to nationalist politics, which often focused on the material interests of urban elites and emerging working-classes.[67] Alongside the new generation of radicals in the ANCYL, the Communist Party and the Non-European Unity Movement began to mobilize supporters during the 1940s.

The Youth League would ultimately become a cornerstone of the ANC, whose members would continue to shape – and challenge – the leadership of the movement. During the 1940s, it played a particularly influential role in reorienting Congress away from its traditional base of an intellectual elite and towards a populist politics that aimed to enlist mass support. Under the leadership of Anton Lembede, the ANCYL adopted a powerful Africanist rhetoric that fed a deep distrust of communist influence within Congress. As Lodge suggests, the Youth League were motivated by the strategic 'political opportunity' represented by tactics of popular protest, including boycotts and other forms of civil disobedience, as much as they were driven by a clear ideological programme.[68] Over the course of the 1940s, black politics in South Africa began to develop a more radical and assertive agenda, driven by the emergence of a younger generation of activists influenced by international discussions of democratic rights.

Official attempts to nurture domestic public support for a war fought for democracy, both by Smuts and the United Party within South Africa, and by leaders on the international stage, provided an ideological justification for renewed calls for African political and social rights, The Allied war aims set out in the Atlantic Charter of 1942, and particularly its reassertion of the rights to self-determination, had inspired nationalist movements throughout the colonized world. In 1943 the ANC published 'African Claims in South Africa', which provided an explicit statement of the new orientation of Congress politics. Bearing the hallmarks of Youth League influence, it laid out a response to the Charter, asserting that 'a just and permanent peace will be possible only if the claims of all classes, colours and races ... are granted and recognised'.[69] Cast as a global struggle against fascism and for democracy, the war provided catalyst for citizenship demands by the ANC, as African leaders began to exploit the language of internationalism in the service of their own agenda.[70]

The same claims to democratic and citizenship rights resonated with groups of activists in the United States, who began to look to developments in South Africa as a representation of a global struggle against racial injustice. In New York, Max Yergan continued to work with the Council on African Affairs (CAA), as it campaigned assiduously to connect the struggle against fascism with the subordination of African peoples under colonialism and the marginalization of African-Americans within the United States.[71] Race policies in South Africa thus became a focus of international attention as radical groups such as the CAA increasingly turned to South Africa as a primary example of colonial injustice that set American racial struggles within a global context. Discourses of democracy and rights provided anti-colonial nationalists around the world with a shared language that legitimized their own local efforts.

Civil disobedience and Indian identities

Black politics in South Africa also began to look towards India and the evidently successfully anti-colonial movement centred on the Indian National Congress. From 1946, Indian politics in South Africa would also enter a new and more radical phase. Although not formally incorporated into South African race legislation until the advent of apartheid, efforts to draw South African Indians within systems of segregation were intensified in the aftermath of the war – just as India itself was moving rapidly towards independence. Although Indians in South Africa had been subject to differential treatment and legal restrictions throughout the twentieth century, the interwar years saw increased levels of anti-Indian sentiment. As successful Indian merchants and traders extended their activities to 'white' areas in Natal and the Transvaal, calls for the formal segregation of the so-called Asiatic population grew.[72]

At the same time, the influence of activists from India, such as Sarojini Naidu, who visited South Africa in the early 1920s, prompted the South Asian community leaders to think in nationalist terms, discarding pre-1918 notions of 'imperial citizenship'. By the end of the 1930s, narrower ethnic interests were dissolving and Indian activists were coming to see themselves as part of a wider struggle against white domination.[73] While it became marked by debates over political status and citizenship that drew on wider black nationalism within South Africa, as well as trans-Indian Ocean political networks, Indian politics emerged primarily out of struggles for control of space within South Africa's expanding cities.

In Durban, increasing numbers of South African Indians came to live in the city during the 1940s, as possibilities for employment in agriculture diminished. The majority were poor, living in poor housing conditions exacerbated by social marginalization along racial grounds, which intensified as the Indian urban population grew.[74] Indians made up a quarter of Durban's urban population in 1942, but owned only 4 per cent of the city. Fears of 'swamping' were fuelled by racial stereotypes of unhygienic, avaricious Indians. 'Colonial-born' activists and Indian merchants were thus drawn into conflict with white authorities, especially in the wake of the 1943 Trading and Occupation of Land Restriction Act – more memorably known as the 'Ghetto Act'. In practice, the Act introduced a form of segregation for Natal's Indian population, prompting a campaign of resistance that would draw on transnational influences, and would itself shape broader movements of resistance to apartheid after 1948.

Indian residents in Durban and elsewhere faced similar pressures to those encountered by the burgeoning African urban population in South Africa, not least that of securing housing. Yet radicals such as Yusuf Dadoo distilled the social crisis into a political one, meaning that citizenship and trading rights remained the key platforms upon which radical leaders campaigned in the late 1940s. With the example of the movement for independence in India as an ideological backdrop, passive resistance was South African Indians underwent 'political and cultural translation' as the Gandhian quest for spiritual truth was transformed into a campaign for democratic rights.[75] This was a South African campaign, but one rooted in a transnational community that by definition drew powerfully upon ideas, values and repertoires transplanted from the Indian subcontinent. Dadoo, who had studied in both India and London in the interwar years, was the personification of this transnational radicalism: a long-serving member of the Communist Party, his politics was at the same time deeply inscribed with a sense of Indian national identity. Not only did he become a central figure in the development of the multiracial Congress movement in the 1950s, he was popularly described as 'Gandhi's favourite son' and an embodiment of Indian politics in its widest sense.[76]

Although a small minority – no more than 3 per cent – of the total population, Indian South Africans became a particular focus of political debate in the 1940s, as the Smuts administration acceded to demands for greater control over Indian residence, particularly in Durban. Efforts to 'peg' Indian property ownership culminated in the Asiatic Land Tenure and Indian Representation Act of 1946, which formalized residential segregation in Natal and elsewhere, and provided a precursor for the Group Areas legislation introduced by the apartheid state.[77] In response, Indian Congress leaders launched passive resistance protests, occupying spaces in Durban that had been defined as 'white' zones under new regulations. Harassed by European youth and the police, the protests were suppressed and ultimately unsuccessful, but sharpened the focus of international debates on the issue underway at the United Nations.

Popular support for passive resistance campaigns against the so-called Ghetto Act declined as segregation began to provide solutions for some of the long-term concerns of Indian workers, notably the provision of services and municipal housing. Furthermore, the establishment of settled – if segregated – urban communities provided a concrete sense of place and belonging in South Africa. Efforts to promote a unified communal identity within the South Asian diaspora, such as those undertaken by reformist Hindu missionaries in South Africa in the 1930s, had met with some enthusiasm, but religious diversity and communal identities did not develop into significant lines of fracture within the South African Indian community, as they did within South Asia.[78] By the mid-1940s, Indian identities began to coalesce around the social experience of existing as a transnational community within South Africa and 'being Indian in a South African way'.[79] Moreover, there was continued popular engagement with the notion of imperial citizenship, as testified by Indian participation in the formal welcome to the British Royal Family during their South African tour in 1947.[80] Despite the importance of radical leaders such as Dadoo in the political struggle against segregation and apartheid, South African Indian identities appeared to have become increasingly marked by the sense of an 'Indian-ness' forged in Africa, and individual experiences of both connection and disconnection across the Indian Ocean.[81]

International opinion and the United Nations

In October 1945, Jan Smuts stood overlooking San Francisco Bay, no doubt contemplating the shape of the new world order that would emerge in the aftermath of the war. While in South Africa his reputation was under threat from rising Afrikaner nationalism, on the international stage he was a kind of global elder statesman, an embodiment of the highest ideals of the British Empire. During the war, he had again been a member of the British War Cabinet, where his presence underlined the contribution of the Dominions to the imperial war effort. At the end of the war, he was invited to participate in the discussions around the formation of the United Nations Organization, and drafted the preamble to the UN Charter. It was an attempt to provide an inspirational text that would encapsulate the aspirations of the new organization, but its emphasis on the 'dignity and worth of the human person' and 'fundamental human rights' appears dissonant in light of Smuts's segregationist principles. But, in Smuts's mind, they conveyed a need to restore the moral and spiritual worth of the individual, and were not designed to be read as a principled statement of equality among all peoples.[82]

The notion of 'human rights' emerged in the 1940s as a useful rhetorical tool for international leaders, providing a vague but promising universal principle that would differentiate post-war international structures from the failed efforts to build legal frameworks for international relations in the mid-century. But human rights, coupled with the principle of self-determination, became a reference point for the claims of anti-colonial movements. Smuts's perception of human rights was an extension of the notions of trusteeship and organic national and racial unity that had underpinned his understanding of segregation in the interwar years. On this basis, human rights were determined along civilizational lines, a position that became increasingly at odds with the claims of anti-colonial nationalists, who contended that rights could only be delivered to equal citizens of a sovereign nation state.[83]

South African race politics thus became a particular focus of attention in the formative years of the United Nations, speaking as it did to both the moral principles that underpinned the definition of rights and liberties in the post-war order, but also – and often more forcefully – as a test of the scope of the new organization's powers. San Francisco saw wide-ranging debates around the scope of the new organization's competency, particularly its capacity to intervene in the internal politics of member states. African-American activists, including W. E. B. Du Bois, argued strongly that the treatment of minority groups should be a direct concern for the UN. While Du Bois ultimately failed to win support for the proposal, lobbyists continued to exploit the UN as a transnational arena within which grievances against national governments might find a hearing.[84]

The question of South African racial policies thus became one of the first tests of the competence of the UN, when in 1946 the Government of India, still nominally under British control, lodged a complaint about the treatment of Indians in South Africa. A response to the introduction of legislation limiting Indian property rights under the 'Ghetto Act', it created an opportunity for Congress leader Jawaharlal Nehru's newly formed transitional Government of India to adopt the role of anti-colonial champion at the UN.[85] The Indian delegation, led by Nehru's sister, Vijaya Lakshmi Pandit, lodged a complaint against the treatment of South African Indians by the Smuts government. In what would become the standard response of South African officials to criticisms of the country's race policies at the UN, Smuts dismissed the complaint as an unwarranted intervention in South African domestic affairs, but the UN General Assembly's Security and Legal Committees nonetheless adopted a joint resolution calling the two governments to agree on measures that ensured that the treatment of Indians in South Africa conformed to existing bilateral agreements.[86]

On one level, the debate in December 1946 suggested that the UN might offer an institutional challenge to the assumptions that underpinned colonialism.[87] But, at the same time, the discussions around the treatment of South African Indians also revealed the constraints of the emerging politics of the Cold War. The Indian delegation's charges against South Africa gained strong support from the Soviet Union, who saw the benefits of exploiting the issue to discomfort Western powers. For the Indian delegates, the South African issue enabled them to engage as an independent entity on the international stage, and the question would go on to become a focus for international criticism of apartheid throughout the 1950s. It was also a catalyst for international anti-apartheid activism, with Indian students in London involved in protests outside the South African Embassy in Trafalgar Square. In 1949, in protest against alleged government complicity in violent clashes between Indian and African rioters in Durban, campaigners burned an effigy of the National Party leader D. F. Malan.[88] While the 1949 riots revealed a local politics of identity that contradicted the discourse of anti-apartheid 'solidarity', the high-level debates at the UN had nonetheless established a key forum for scrutiny of South African race relations.

Subject to ongoing criticism at the UN, white South African politicians came to regard the institution with suspicion and a degree of contempt.[89] Alongside the bruising debate with India, Smuts announced that South Africa intended to incorporate the territory of South-West Africa (Namibia) into the Union. The plan was aligned with Smuts' concept of the post-war British Empire repackaged as a 'progressive Commonwealth' in a way that would appease US anti-colonial sentiments and enhance the influence of regional powers such as South Africa.[90] However, the Allied Powers had agreed at the Yalta conference that the League of Nations Mandates would be placed under a new United Nations Trusteeship system. From its inception, South Africa found itself at odds with the UN over the Mandated Territories and consistently refused to acknowledge the UN's legal right to determine future arrangements for the administration of South-West Africa. It was a forthright challenge to the UN, and a determined effort to push back against the organization's redefinition of Trusteeship.

Almost as soon as Smuts had made South African intentions clear, the BaNgwato regent Tshekedi Khama in Bechuanaland (Botswana) initiated a campaign against incorporation. As had been the case during his brushes with colonial authorities in the 1930s, Khama was instinctively opposed to any threat of South African expansionism, and interpreted the incorporation plans as a step towards South Africa putting into action its long-held ambitions to establish control over all of the southern African Protectorates.[91] Using his connections with the Anti-Slavery Society in London, as well as those within South African liberal networks, Khama was able to generate publicity both regionally and on the international stage, and his efforts played a significant role in ensuring that Smuts's application to formally incorporate the territory into the Union was rejected by the UN in late 1946.

It was a significant blow to Smuts' reputation and contributed to the waning of his political power. But it was by no means the end of the story, as Malan's nationalists showed little inclination to respect the authority of the UN on this issue. Following the National Party's election victory of 1948, South African diplomats took an increasingly hard line on attempts to exert international oversight over the territory, and disengaged from UN bodies when faced with criticism. Thus, the South African delegation was absent in 1949 when the anti-apartheid campaigner Michael Scott testified before the UN Trusteeship Committee on behalf of the Herero people of South-West Africa. The address undermined South African claims that the indigenous population had been consulted on the question of incorporation, and crystallized the contemporary critique of the legitimacy of colonialism.[92] Trusteeship, Scott argued, implied the coming of a moment when the 'ward' would inherit the sovereign rights of citizenship.[93] South Africa deliberately set out to define itself as being outside of this debate, refusing to acknowledge the competence of the new UNO.

The internationalization of South African political struggles was encapsulated in late 1946 when ANC President Alfred Xuma, Indian Congress representatives H. A. Naidoo and Sorabjee Rustomjee, and the white Senator Hyman Basner travelled to New York to lobby delegates at the UN. The months prior to their journey had seen Smuts introduce the 'Ghetto Acts' and the suppression of the African mineworkers' strike on the Rand. In New York, CAA leaders, Paul Robeson, Max Yergan and W. E. B. Du Bois, as well as the Indian delegation to the UN, provided assistance. Xuma noted grimly that it had taken an intercontinental journey to meet with his prime minister. For his part, Smuts – the great international statesman – could draw on the support of the British Attorney General, Hartley Shawcross, who flew into New York directly from the Nuremberg trials where he had been acting as a chief prosecutor. The issue of racial discrimination in South Africa might well have appeared to have been a perfect illustration of a transformative moment in post-war world politics. The great leaders of the first half of the twentieth century found themselves at odds with the democratic aspirations of an emerging world. Although the South African government remained unshaken in its refusal to countenance UN competence to intervene in its affairs – and as such provided one of the first major tests of the post-war international order – the United Nations nevertheless posed a significant challenge to the legitimacy of the white supremacist state in South Africa. Through to the 1960s, as its membership expanded with the process of decolonization, international action against South Africa coordinated by the United Nations seemed a real possibility.

Summary

The end of the 1940s did not appear auspicious for black leaders in South Africa. The Durban riots were a reminder of the interethnic tensions that made unified opposition difficult, while the development of apartheid seemed destined to compound racial fractures. The transformation of South Africa that had taken place during the war years, notably the rapid development of manufacturing industries and the headlong expansion of South African cities, seemed to have prompted the hardening of a determination to maintain white supremacy, given the added dimension through the ethnic nationalism of Malan's Afrikaner nationalists. Apartheid reflected a response to challenges of the 1940s – it was not the only response that had been available, and it built on some of the developments associated with the fleeting embrace of more welfarist policies in the early years of the war, not least in terms of the interventionist state that was necessary to manage the system of racial separation that began to be envisaged. The South African experience of the 1940s was shaped powerfully by local conditions, but nevertheless was not unique, but similar to a range of experiences elsewhere and marked by the impact of international developments, not least the organization of international politics itself, in the shape of the United Nations.

Further reading

Ballantine, Christopher John. *Marabi Nights: Jazz, 'Race' and Society in Early Apartheid South Africa.* [New edn]. Scottsville, South Africa: University of KwaZulu-Natal Press, 2012.

Dubow, Saul. 'Smuts, the United Nations and the Rhetoric of Race and Rights'. *Journal of Contemporary History,* 43 (1) (1 January 2008): 45–74.

Dubow, Saul and Alan Jeeves, eds. *South Africa's 1940s: Worlds of Possibilities.* Cape Town: Double Storey, 2005.

Duffy, Joanne L. *The Politics of Ethnic Nationalism: Afrikaner Unity, the National Party, and the Radical Right in Stellenbosch, 1934–1948.* London: Routledge, 2006.

Fredrickson, George M. *Black Liberation: A Comparative History of Black Ideologies in the United States and South Africa.* Oxford: Oxford University Press, 1995.

Furlong, Patrick. *Between Crown and Swastika: The Impact of the Radical Right on the Afrikaner Nationalist Movement in the Fascist Era.* Hanover, NH: University Press of New England, 1991.

Giliomee, Hermann. *The Afrikaners: Biography of a People.* London: Hurst, 2011.

Hyslop, Jonathan. '"Segregation Has Fallen on Evil Days": Smuts' South Africa, Global War, and Transnational Politics, 1939–46'. *Journal of Global History,* 7 (3) (2012): 438–60.

Landau, Paul Stuart. *Popular Politics in the History of South Africa, 1400–1948.* Cambridge: Cambridge University Press, 2010.

Mazower, Mark. *No Enchanted Palace: The End of Empire and the Ideological Origins of the United Nations.* Woodstock, UK: Princeton University Press, 2009.

Moodie, T. Dunbar. *The Rise of Afrikanerdom: Power, Apartheid, and the Afrikaner Civil Religion.* Berkeley, CA: University of California Press, 1975.

Shearar, Jeremy Brown. *Against the World: South Africa and Human Rights at the United Nations 1945–1961.* Pretoria: Unisa Press, 2011.

Von Eschen, Penny M. *Race against Empire : Black Americans and Anticolonialism, 1937–1957.* Ithaca, NY: Cornell University Press, 1997.

CHAPTER 6
APARTHEID AND COLD WAR

The changes to the international political order in the late 1940s had significant implications for South Africa. Whereas the systems of differentiated sovereignty, citizenship and civil rights that had developed since Union had been largely compatible with international norms before 1945, post-war principles of democracy, self-determination and the emergent discourse of human rights were a direct challenge to the principles of segregation. The election of an Afrikaner nationalist government under D. F. Malan in 1948 thus brought a more rigid and thoroughgoing model of segregation into being, just as colonial administration elsewhere was being reformulated, first in line with models of social and economic development and then, by the end of the 1950s, by decolonization. Apartheid, the race policy of Malan's nationalists, was elaborated during the 1950s in an array of new legislation that extended and entrenched segregation.

Exactly what apartheid meant in practice emerged slowly over the course of the 1950s, not in line with a specific ideological blueprint, but as a series of policies connected by a racialized world view and ethnic nationalist agenda.[1] To a great extent, it was a compromise between the desire to tightly regulate race relations and to enhance the conditions of life for Afrikaners. During the same period, popular African nationalism fashioned mass resistance to apartheid as a struggle for sovereign rights and democracy; anti-apartheid campaigns in the 1950s were thus defined as a struggle against a political system that was at odds with international norms. Shaped in the context of decolonization and the Cold War, apartheid was defined by post-war international political culture as much as it represented the particular context of South Africa. Thus, despite the burgeoning strength of the South African economy, boosted by the wartime boom, the actions of newly elected Nationalist government were subject to international contingencies. On the surface, the formation of a Nationalist government in 1948 suggested a step towards isolation and a break from Britain, but global economic entanglements would continue to influence on government policy throughout the apartheid era.[2]

The slow genesis of apartheid

The general election of 1948 is, rightly, seen as a transformative moment in South African history. The victory of the National Party under Malan was unexpected and narrow and, aside from the rhetorical power of apartheid as a campaign slogan, there was little clear sense of the detail of this new policy when Malan formed his first Cabinet. The essence of the National Party's proposed race policies were signalled prior to the election with the publication of the report of the Sauer Commission, a body of Afrikaner intellectuals who recommended a tightening of controls over African movement to and residence in urban areas. It contrasted with the findings of the Fagan Commission, appointed by the Smuts government in 1946, which had suggested the need for a policy to stabilize the urban population through a gradual relaxation of 'influx controls'. Apartheid signalled nationalists' determination to address black migration, but beyond this was ill-defined, a function of the coalition of Afrikaner intellectuals, powerful farmers and business leaders that came together within the National Party in the late 1940s.[3]

Popular representations of apartheid tend to emphasize its distinctiveness, but South African apartheid, like colonial administrations elsewhere, relied on an interventionist state and the construction of a complex state bureaucracy.[4] Across Africa, French and British officials reacted to post-war popular protest, trade union activism and anti-colonial nationalism by instigating reforms that would, they hoped, stabilize the industrialized workforce, ameliorate tensions between town and country, and promote the interests of 'moderate' and 'modernizing' Africans. The 'parting of the ways' in the 1950s between the South African apartheid state and the European powers on a path towards decolonization nevertheless reflected 'opposite fictions of rule'. One set of colonial authorities framed policy in terms of universalism and a faith in modernization, the other in a retrenched vision of essentialized racial difference.[5]

The National Party's first major race legislation strengthened controls over physical relations and 'mixed marriages' across the colour line. The Prohibition of Mixed Marriages Act (1949) and the Immorality Act (1950) thus policed the 'interior frontier' of the society, building upon pre-existing segregation legislation.[6] Further legislation established the form of apartheid: the Population Registration Act (1950), which set out a legal framework for the categorization of all South Africans; the Group Areas Act (1950) used those categories to map racially defined zones across South Africa in much more detail than had been undertaken hitherto; the subsequent reform of the Pass Laws amalgamated the collection of documents that Africans were required by law to carry into a single pass book – the loathed 'dompas'. Together, these policies structured a racial discourse that avoided explicit reference to discredited notions of biological difference, but at the same time embedded such distinctions into law, the institutions of state, and everyday practice.[7] Alongside this disguised racialism, apartheid was distinguished by coordinated use of the apparatus of the development state to establish more efficient systems of social surveillance and discipline. Apartheid policies reflected fundamental ideological principles, but were at the same time responses to external social and political conditions. The Bantu Education Act (1953) was defined by critics and supporters alike as a simple reaffirmation of racist assumptions regarding intelligence, and the need for education to do no more than prepare blacks for unskilled labour. The Act undoubtedly created a racially differentiated education system, but it also provided a mass education system that addressed a crisis in urban black youth unemployment.[8]

International responses to apartheid in the late 1940s and 1950s reflected the vague definitions of apartheid that were obscured by its surface certainties. Many commentators pondered the meaning of and prospects for 'apartheid' in the wake of

Malan's election victory, but few seemed entirely certain of its precise meaning beyond 'complete separation between the European and non-European'.[9] But, as critics of the 'doctrine of apartheid' noted, National Party policy seemed clearly at odds with the rights and freedoms itemized in the Universal Declaration of Human Rights signed in December 1948.[10] Apartheid evoked comparisons with fascism, Afrikaner nationalism with the rise of European fascism, and the 'tragic history of the Weimar Republic seems to be repeating itself in South Africa', as union leader Solly Sachs claimed in 1946.[11] Two decades later, the South African communist Brian Bunting claimed that 'the attitude of mind which produced … inhumanities in Nazi Germany' had been fermented by apartheid and Afrikaner nationalism.[12]

Often, however, accusations of fascism reflected the political sympathies of anti-apartheid activists; rather than pre-war fascism, apartheid more clearly resonated with post-war approaches to planning and development in so-called multiracial societies around the world. The language of pluralism was adopted by both liberal intellectuals and apartheid officials during the 1960s and 1970s as apartheid came increasingly to be defined in 'ethnic', as opposed to 'racial' terms.[13] Even before the end of the 1950s, apartheid social planning along explicitly racial terms lost legitimacy, as colonial rule itself was viewed in increasingly negative terms. Across the continent, anti-colonial nationalists argued that the organization of social and economic development was only viable within the contours of a sovereign nation state, and the justification of apartheid as 'separate development' needed also to adapt to the idea of forms of 'ethnic' independence.

'New African' culture and resistance

Apartheid focused in particular on the contest for control of urban space. State-led 'influx control' was systematically and aggressively enforced through a process of population removal and 'slum clearances', symbolized by the destruction of well-established mixed communities in Sophiatown in Johannesburg and District Six in Cape Town. Under apartheid, African urban culture became reconfigured, unconsciously, as a form of resistance. During the 1940s and 1950s, the forms of popular cultural style that had embodied interwar urban life became the representation of a 'New African' culture that paralleled the development of a more assertive, mass-oriented and Africanist political culture. Penny whistle players such as Willard Cele popularized what became known as *kwela*, presented as an authentic expression of South African urban culture. Artists such as the Zimbabwean Dorothy Masuka provided voices of resistance to apartheid with songs such as 'Chief Luthuli' and a tribute to the Congolese leader, 'Lumumba' on the mainstream Troubador record label; their commercial success outweighed political caution.[14]

Radio programming aimed at an urban African audience began to be broadcast by the South African Broadcasting Company in the post-war period, producing, by the 1950s, a variety of African-language programmes. The evolution of apartheid during the 1950s hindered, but by no means halted, the development of multiracial musical culture in South Africa. Although subject to the same unequal racial hierarchies that affected South African society more broadly, white promoters such as the organizer of Johannesburg's 'African Jazz and Variety' shows, Alfred Herbert, often exerted undue control over professional musicians. Efforts were made to organize multiracial support networks, such as Union Artists, led by the trade unionist Guy Routh, which allowed greater artistic freedom for black musicians. Union Artists also fostered international opposition to apartheid, lobbying the British theatrical union, Equity, to call on its members to boycott segregated performances in South Africa.[15] *King Kong*, a jazz opera centred on the life of the boxer Ezekiel 'King Kong' Dlamini, whose early success was followed by a fall into crime and alcoholism, presented township life in all its shades and complexities. First produced in 1959, *King Kong* transferred to London in 1961, and launched the careers of a number of black performers who would go on to have successful international careers, including Miriam Makeba, Hugh Masekela and Abdullah Ibrahim. Their work, along with *King Kong*, exemplified the syncretic nature of urban black culture, a hybrid mix of local and global influences that were fused together in the urban environment.

International perceptions of life in apartheid South Africa shaped the accounts of émigré writers such as Peter Abrahams, who in the early 1940s had established himself in pan-African circles in London. His book *Mine Boy* (1946) detailed the hardships of labour migrancy, achieving both international attention and success within South Africa.[16] Alan Paton's internationally successful *Cry, the Beloved Country*, published in the year of Malan's election victory, provided a deeply moralizing account of the anxieties of white liberals. Rooted in a paternalist Christian world view and highly ambivalent with regard to African urbanization, Paton's book described the degeneration of city life through the eyes of the rural African priest, Father Kumalo. But, despite its success, Paton's work represented the dilemmas and declining confidence of white liberal writers in the face of the challenge of nationalism – both Afrikaner and African.[17] During the 1950s, black writers became the dominant literary interlocutors of urban South Africa, as a new generation of younger writers came to prominence, particularly those associated with *Drum* magazine. The 'Sophiatown writers', Can Themba, Lewis Nkosi and Bloke Modisane, all worked as journalists on the magazine, before going on to become recognized authors themselves. The style of their writing, with its evocations of jazz and fast-living, provided a portrait of Sophiatown that was at once escapist and at the same time a bold expression of the realities of African urban existence in defiance of – and to an extent an act of resistance against – the bonds of apartheid.[18]

Ultimately, the urban culture that inspired this creative output would come into conflict with the apartheid state. The racially mixed Johannesburg suburb of Sophiatown had emerged as an important centre for African urban culture and politics, with institutions such as the Odin Cinema – one of the largest picture houses on the continent – which, in addition to films, provided a location for jazz performances and political meetings. But, in February 1955, police moved to remove the inhabitants of Sophiatown to the euphemistically named Meadowlands, a stark new municipal housing development on the edge of Soweto, despite attempts to organize mass resistance led by the ANC and other leading figures in the community, including the head of the Anglican Mission in the suburb, Trevor Huddleston.[19] Sophiatown symbolized the ambition of apartheid's engineers to reshape the physical landscape of South Africa in political vision of its ruling elite. By the early 1960s, most of its buildings had been demolished, replaced by a working-class white suburb named 'Triomf' (Triumph).

In South Africa, as in other African colonial cities, control over urban space became a metaphor for wider struggles around citizenship and as a result African city life was often marked by a culture of resistance.[20] The marginal and unlicensed nature of urban living, with its gangs of youths, crime, illicit drinking and *marabi* dance embodied a refusal of the precepts of segregation – it was a culture that refused to acknowledge the claims of the apartheid ideologues who saw Africans as 'tribal' beings. At the same time, the inhabitants of places like Sophiatown aspired to respectability and social acceptance just like their white neighbours.[21] It was within the cauldron of these urban centres that the new African politics of the 1940s had emerged, and South African cities, Johannesburg in particular, would be the centre of resistance to apartheid in the 1950s and beyond.

Congress and the mobilization of popular resistance to apartheid

The politics of resistance to apartheid in the 1940s rested upon the establishment of a national mass-oriented movement that, while centred on African leadership, drew together political leaders from across South Africa's ethnic communities. There had been attempts to forge links between the ANC and Indian political leaders in the 1940s, partly as a result of the dangers of interracial tension that had been starkly illustrated by the Durban riots of 1949. African leaders had also been impressed by the assertive tactics employed by the Indian passive resistance campaign against the Ghetto Act and civil disobedience was formally adopted by the ANC in its Programme of Action of 1949. The outline of the Programme was influenced by key members of a new generation of activists associated with the ANC Youth League, including Walter Sisulu, Oliver Tambo and Nelson Mandela. All three joined the national executive of the ANC in 1949 under its new President Dr James Moroka, who was more inclined to support more forceful action against the new Afrikaner nationalist government and its policy of apartheid.[22]

The political campaigns launched under the umbrella of Congress were formed from a blend of Africanism, international socialism, Christian liberalism and Gandhian non-violent civil disobedience. The tactics adopted in 1949 moreover represented an amalgam of the various strands of South African black politics, but also reflected transnational influences. At the 1945 Pan-African conference in Manchester, Peter Abrahams and Mark Hlubi addressed delegates on the conditions of black South Africans, while Congress leaders – unable to attend in person – sent messages of support. Transnational connections provided both a material link between Congress and the broader African anti-colonial movement, as well as sense of solidarity and unity.[23]

The tactic of non-violent civil disobedience had roots in the history of black South African political campaigns, but it was also a modular tactic of anti-colonial struggles throughout the world, from India to Ghana. The first nationally co-ordinated protest organized by Congress was the Defiance Campaign of non-violent civil disobedience, launched in June 1952, following a broadly successfully day of protest against national celebrations of the tercentenary of the arrival of the Dutch in the Cape.[24] The Defiance Campaign was officially a protest movement in support of Congress leaders' call for the abolition of five 'unjust laws' that constituted the backbone of apartheid, and called for volunteers to openly defy key apartheid laws, by entering racially segregated residential areas without permits, or by flaunting 'petty apartheid' restrictions on the use of public amenities. At the same time, the campaign was a moral expression that resonated with Christian leaders within the movement. Albert Lutuli, who had replaced Moroka as ANC President in 1952, called for the campaign against apartheid to be built upon a Christian 'spirit of defiance'.[25]

As an attempt to overwhelm the authorities with a wave of popular disobedience, the Defiance Campaign was by no means a success. Participation in the campaign was noticeably patchy, centred on large cities and the Eastern Cape, where in Port Elizabeth and East London the non-violent campaign disintegrated into rioting and the deaths of several protestors and bystanders. The riots signalled the end of the Defiance Campaign, and with the introduction of new laws extending the government's powers to suppress protest, the focus of ANC campaign tactics shifted to demonstrations and boycotts. The Defiance Campaign was nonetheless effective in extending the influence of the ANC through a significant expansion of the numbers of local branches across the country.[26] While the ANC would continue to struggle to make inroads in rural areas, it became, following the Defiance Campaign, an indisputably national movement.[27]

In an attempt to build on its new-found mass support, the President of the Cape ANC, Z. K. Matthews called for a 'Congress of the People … to draw up a Freedom Charter for the Democratic South Africa of the future'.[28] In 1954, leaders from the African and Indian Congress movements, the South African Coloured Peoples' Organisation and the Congress of Democrats (a small but influential group of left-wing white campaigners) set out ambitious plans for a nationwide consultation on the Charter. Preparations for Congress were disrupted by banning orders – harsh legal sanctions limiting the public activities of political activists – and criticism from potential supporters, such as the multiracial Liberal Party, who argued that communists from the Congress of Democrats had undue influence over the organization of the convention. Nevertheless, the Congress, which took place in June 1955, brought 3,000 multiracial delegates together to adopt the clauses of the Freedom Charter that had been drafted on the basis of an array of suggestions from across the country. A mixture of vague socialist nostrums and the declamatory language of liberal constitutions, the Charter was by no means a blueprint for working-class revolution, but its vision of multiracial democracy was radical in itself.[29]

The 1950s saw the emergence of significant new forms of black resistance, not least the coordinated campaigns against the imposition, for the first time, of controls over black women in urban areas. Militant anti-pass campaigns led by groups such as the Federal of South African Women bore testimony to the radicalizing effect that post-war social transformations and apartheid restrictions had upon African politics.[30] And yet, while the ANC had established itself as a popular movement with the ambitions for national mobilization made explicit in the Freedom Charter, the task of connecting national political agendas with those of local communities was never fully resolved during the 1950s. Efforts to campaign against the Bantu Education Act in 1954, for example, foundered on the unwillingness of many parents and children to boycott the new school system, and, despite attempts to establish underground schools and 'family centres', many opted to enrol in the new government schools. Churches, the mainstay of African education, did little to oppose the new system and, with the exception of the Catholic Church and Anglican schools in Johannesburg, largely complied with the order to hand over schools to government control.[31] And although of symbolic importance, local ANC leaders in Sophiatown were unable to weave together elite and grassroots opposition into a coherent campaign against the removal plans.[32] Other local protests, such as the Alexandra bus boycotts of 1958, were almost entirely disconnected from Congress control, although exhibiting a transnational dimension, with subtle and uncoordinated interactions with the burgeoning civil rights movement in the United States.[33]

Congress leaders recognized the value of international support, and looked, from the time of the Defiance Campaign, to develop contacts with activists around the world. In the United States, support for the civil disobedience campaign in South Africa came from civil rights activists, Christian groups and peace campaigners, which coalesced with the formation of the American Committee on Africa (ACOA) in 1953 under the leadership of Methodist Minister and co-founder of the Congress of Racial Equality, George Houser.[34] A branch of ACOA was established in California by Mary-Louise Hooper, who had worked as an assistant to Lutuli. In contrast, the Council on African Affairs had dwindled in support and influence, in part as a consequence of Max Yergan's political journey towards ardent anti-communism during the McCarthy era and the departure of W. E. B. Du Bois to Ghana in 1957 hastened the demise of the Council.[35]

In Britain, early anti-apartheid activism centred on the activities of church figures including Michael Scott, and Canon John Collins of St Paul's Cathedral, along with anti-imperial campaigners such as the Labour MP Fenner Brockway, whose Movement for Colonial Freedom provided an organizational focus for anti-apartheid in the late 1950s. Scott and Collins used public platforms to condemn apartheid and to raise funds to support participants in the Defiance Campaign. In 1954, public reaction to the implementation of Bantu education came in the shape of an appeal on behalf of British churches for funds to bolster the efforts of missionary societies in southern Africa. This was by no means radical opposition to apartheid, but instead marked a resurrection of humanitarian concerns for distant others that bore resemblance to – and drew explicitly upon – the language and ideologies of its nineteenth-century forebears.[36] In Britain, anti-apartheid emerged as a moral cause that drew echoes of an earlier benevolent imperialism. But campaigners consciously aligned themselves with African opinion and political agendas, none more so than Huddleston, whose account of life as a priest in Johannesburg, *Naught for Your Comfort*, was published on his return to Britain in 1956.[37]

The book provided a best-selling indictment of the impact of apartheid on the lives of black South Africans, well-received by critics.

Communism, Cold War and the international relations of apartheid in the 1950s

During the 1950s, South African government officials routinely described the country as a bulwark against the influence of communists in Africa, and set apartheid legislation within this Cold War framework. Broad legal restrictions against political opposition were introduced under the Suppression of Communism Act of 1950, which established measures to restrict the political, professional (and indeed social) activities of individuals and groups that had been 'named' as communist – or who were deemed to be acting in alliance with communism. Moreover, the Act defined communism in remarkably broad terms that included 'the promotion of disturbance and disorder' and the 'encouragement of feelings of hostility between the European and non-European races'.[38] But, while the Act exploited the threat of communism as a justification for authoritarian methods to suppress more general political opposition, it also represented ideological principles that were shared with key Western allies.

South Africa remained an important and strategic partner in the British Commonwealth, although the onset of decolonization made officials in London and Washington recognize the danger of unequivocal support for the apartheid state. From London's perspective, keeping South Africa within the Commonwealth was a priority, not least because of the consequences for the delicate plans for Central African Federation, which sought to balance settler and African nationalist interests in the colonial territories of Nyasaland, Northern Rhodesia and Southern Rhodesia. The election of Malan did, however, bring an end to the prospect of the incorporation of the British High Commission Territories, Basutoland, Bechuanaland and Swaziland. Nevertheless, although South African policy moved from formal expansion and towards informal influence, the High Commission Territories had, by the time of their independence in the late 1960 become 'virtual Bantustans' in the eyes of the South African government.[39]

After 1948, the National Party upheld the South African military and foreign policy alliances and South African officials were enthusiastic supporters of a multinational defence strategy for Africa, and maintained close links with their British counterparts.[40] Over the course of the 1950s, negotiations with the British government resulted in the handover of control over key military installations, including the Simonstown naval base at the Cape.[41] However, these agreements fell short of the more formal alliance and unequivocal commitment to the protection of white supremacy that South Africans had hoped to achieve.[42] By the late-1950s, as the Suez crisis of 1956 demonstrated, Britain no longer had the strength to operate the kind of independent imperial defence strategy envisaged by advocates of a 'white entente'.

South African communists did, in fact, play an important role in black politics during the 1950s. Although the Communist Party of South Africa had become marginalized in mainstream white trade unionism, its members had become a small but influential group close to the ANC. Similarly, communists held key positions in political movements during the 1940s, such as the Springbok Legion and the Campaign for Right and Justice.[43] Communist intellectuals and activists, and left-wing newspapers such as the *Guardian* and the *New Age* were a critical source of support for Congress and public critique of apartheid during the 1950s. Communists, such as Yusuf Dadoo, were also a key influence on the radicalization of Indian politics.[44] The formal banning of the Communist Party of South Africa in 1950 might also be seen as an attempt to stifle the threat of radicalism within African working-class movements. Just as communist-leaning unions were purged from the mainstream labour movement in the United States during the 1950s, trade union activity in South Africa – exemplified by the formation of the South African Congress of Trade Unions in 1955 – became more closely affiliated with nationalism than communism.[45]

Nevertheless, communists shaped key elements of Congress politics in the 1950s, including the Freedom Charter, which clearly bore the influence of CPSA member of its drafting committee, Lionel Bernstein. As such, government fears of communist influence had some justification, and were shared by leading figures within the Congress, regarding communist impact on African nationalism with some suspicion. Similar fears of communist influence meant that the multiracial Liberal Party were reluctant to enter into formal alliances with the Congress movement in the mid-1950s.[46] In sections of the ANC, concerns fed into wider dissatisfaction with the multiracial Congress Alliance, which culminated in November 1958 with the breaking away of Africanist members of the Transvaal ANC, and the formation of a new movement, the Pan-Africanist Congress (PAC).[47] With the editor of the *Africanist* newspaper, Robert Sobukwe, as president, the PAC saw themselves as representatives of a continental movement, often antagonistic towards Moscow, and the PAC manifesto looked instead to a wider African struggle rooted in 'African social conditions', inspired by the All-African Peoples' Congress held in Accra, Ghana in December 1958.[48]

Links with Moscow gave African leaders such as J. B. Marks, who attended international communist meetings in the 1930s, the opportunity to foster links between South African movements and anti-colonial counterparts overseas. But, during the 1950s, despite visits to the Soviet Union by Brian and Sonia Bunting and Ruth First, there was little formal contact between South African activists and the USSR before the 1960s. At the same time Soviet interest in what was becoming known as the Third World was evident from the late 1950s, with the establishment of the Soviet Afro-Asian Solidarity Committee and African Department of the Moscow Institute of Oriental Studies in 1956.[49] The South African Communist Party, as it was known after being secretly revived in 1953, remained therefore a significant partner in the Congress Movement, and one that would come to the fore in the crisis of the early 1960s.

Similarly, South Africa was a marginal foreign policy concern for the United States before 1960, although the State Department began to develop a more focused Africa policy over the course of the 1950s, which reflected in the formation its Bureau of African Affairs in 1958. South Africa stood a little apart from the rest of the continent, in the eyes of US officials, however. American investment in the country had been significant from the onset of industrialization, but from the 1950s, this was supplemented by interests in strategic resources, notably uranium. Washington's position on apartheid was shaped in part by a recognition of the need to balance the country's relations with Pretoria against its general support for post-war democratic ideals. In a sense, both the United States and Britain became 'reluctant referees' in the contest between Afrikaner and African nationalism.[50] South Africa remained a 'strongly anti-Communist and pro-West' ally, but the authoritarian nature of the apartheid state began to sound a warning to US officials anxious that Africans across the continent would begin to view the Soviet Union as a more trustworthy partner.[51]

By 1960, apartheid appeared increasingly at odds with the rising hopes of Third World leaders, whose vision of sovereign independence and a decisive break with Western colonialism was set out at the Bandung Afro-Asian summit in April 1955.[52] The end of the 1950s saw a surge of optimism with regard to decolonization, which seemed to offer new visions of sovereignty.[53] The end of empire reflected Cold War contingencies, but was also bound up with the emerging post-colonial desire to reject the rigid cage of East–West power relations and the chance to forge an autonomous unity grounded in a shared experience of colonialism.[54] In Britain, political leaders sought to frame decolonization around visions of a recalibration of empire into a free association of self-governing states within the British Commonwealth. The independence of Ghana in 1957 and federal experiment in Central Africa both signalled a desire for a carefully regulated process of change. Violent protests in Nyasaland and the killings of African detainees at the Hola Camp in Kenya seemed, in the minds of British officials, to signal that greater dangers lay in seeking to control anti-colonial nationalism than more rapid moves towards independence.[55] Macmillan's oft-quoted call for the South African government to recognize the 'winds of change' in Africa in February 1960 was a symbolic shift in the trajectory of Anglophone African politics. In February 1960, at the climax of his tour of Africa, the British prime minister addressed the South African Parliament in Cape Town, arguing in his speech that Britain – and by implication South Africa – could no longer ignore the 'wind of change' represented by African nationalism.[56]

The Sharpeville crisis and the turn to armed struggle

The US Ambassador to the UN, Ralph Bunche, predicted that 1960 would be the 'year of Africa', as the continent entered a 'renaissance in terms of heightened and unified aspirations for true self-determination, human rights, rapid economic transformation and the assertion of collective dignity and unity'.[57] In South Africa, meanwhile, the Pan African Congress (PAC) declared that 1960 would be a 'year of destiny', bringing 'independence and self-determination'.[58] Over the course of the year, seventeen African states had achieved independence; this initial optimism would however be offset by a sense of developing crisis on the continent, not least in South Africa.

In the late 1950s, pan-Africanist movements across Africa had begun to call for an international isolation of South Africa. At the Accra Congress in 1958, continental leaders urged on a coordinated response to apartheid, including economic sanctions and a boycott of South African goods.[59] In South Africa, both the ANC and the PAC began to develop plans for further campaigns of civil disobedience, and the latter announced at the end of 1959 that a renewed anti-pass protest would be launched the following spring. Drawing on the language of Nkrumah in Ghana, the PAC called on its members to prepare a campaign of 'positive action' that would be the first step towards what they confidently asserted would be freedom within three years. When the protest began, on 21 March 1960, support for the PAC was at its strongest in the Western Cape and townships around Vereeniging in the Transvaal. In Sharpeville, south of Johannesburg, a crowd of thousands gathered at the police station in Sharpeville; after a standoff lasting several hours, the police opened fire without warning, killing over sixty protestors.[60]

Within hours, news of the massacre had reverberated around the world, imprinting an image of the apartheid state as one committed to the suppression of opposition. In Cape Town, after riots on the night of the massacre were followed by mass arrests of PAC supporters, thousands marched to the city's police headquarters on 25 March. Philip Kgosana and other PAC leaders, with the Liberal editor of *Contact* magazine Patrick Duncan acting as a not-entirely-welcome intermediary, agreed for a compromise with the police and the crowds dispersed. But within days, the government had declared a state of emergency, and banned both the ANC and PAC. A second march in Cape Town attracted tens of thousands of protestors onto the streets, who dispersed only after Kgosana was promised a meeting with the Minister of Justice. Instead of the meeting, Kgosana was arrested, and the leading centres of PAC support in Langa and Nyanga townships were besieged by police.[61]

Even before the Sharpeville crisis, apartheid was coming to be seen around the world as an epitome of racial oppression. In Britain, a campaign to boycott South African consumer products, inspired in part by pan-Africanist debates at Accra, had been launched in June 1959 by the Committee of African Organisations.[62] The Sharpeville massacre came at the end of the 'Boycott Month', and spurred the formation of a permanent British Anti-Apartheid Movement. Similarly, opposition to the ban on Maori players during the New Zealand rugby tour of South Africa in 1960 had led to major public demonstrations, laying the groundwork for the development of a popular anti-apartheid movement in the country.[63] Around the world, public antipathy to the apartheid state peaked in response to the shootings, which seemed to underline the isolation of settler colonialism in southern Africa.

The crisis in South Africa affected sharpened international opinion, with 80 per cent of respondents to a Gallup poll in Britain declaring their opposition to apartheid in the aftermath of Sharpeville. The economic impact was particularly dramatic, as South Africa's foreign reserves halved by the end of 1961, and capital of around 12 million rand a month left the country in the wake of the crisis.[64] Verwoerd himself was resolute, in public at least, in his adherence to unremitting pursuit of apartheid policy. An attempt on his life at the Rand Show in early April, however, took the main architect out of the scene for some weeks and the confidence of the white population seemed to ebb. Some business leaders called for a re-examination of race policies and the opening of consultations between the government and moderate black political leaders.[65] Both the PAC and ANC were banned, and the effective suppression of civil protest arguably created the conditions for a shift in policy towards armed resistance. Despite evidence of support for compromise, the hard-line response of Verwoerd – mirrored by some within the ANC and PAC – meant that South African political struggle would be structured around an authoritarian state and militant resistance.[66]

Events in South Africa were also a constituent part of a wider 'African crisis' that included both the endgame of the anti-colonial struggle in Algeria and the descent of the newly independent Congo into political chaos and violence. As the new United Nations session was convened in September – with former colonial states in Africa and Asia forming a majority in the General Assembly for the first time – South Africa was being bracketed alongside the Congo as it fragmented into civil war. Despite the efforts of UN Secretary-General, Dag Hammarskjöld, who visited South Africa in early 1961, many saw little scope for any agreement between an uncompromising Verwoerd and international leaders – despite South African fears of isolation.[67] Some, like Nkrumah, who described the deportation of the Anglican Bishop of Johannesburg, Ambrose Reeves, as evidence of the 'corrupt and corrupting monster' of apartheid, had hardened their own position – at least rhetorically.[68] At the level of international relations, the legacies of the Sharpeville crisis were superficially dramatic, but did not in themselves provoke a crisis in white supremacy.

In the year following the shootings, South Africa's relationship with the Commonwealth was dramatically transformed, first as the country was declared a republic following a referendum in October 1960. The adoption of a republican constitution required a formal request for continued membership of the Commonwealth, which, despite the opposition of newly independent African states, appeared possible at the 1961 Commonwealth Conference in London, until discussions broke down and Verwoerd withdrew the application, breaking the link with Commonwealth.[69] A new South Africa Act in 1962 re-established many of the trade agreements associated with Commonwealth membership, but Britain's relationship with South Africa was set on an ambiguous path between formal support for the apartheid state and informal support for its opponents.[70] In a sense, South African withdrawal from Commonwealth was as much as anything else a reflection of the re-stabilization of the apartheid state after the crisis, rather than an indication of its isolation. Other Commonwealth heads of state, including Kwame Nkrumah, were willing to enter into a degree of compromise in 1961; Verwoerd's ultimate refusal to follow suit was an expression of confidence, not weakness.

Prior to his covert departure from South Africa in January 1962, Mandela had taken a central role in the formation of an armed wing of the ANC, Umkhonto we Sizwe (commonly known as MK). Prior to Sharpeville, the Congress movement had maintained its commitment to non-violent civil disobedience, but the suppression of mass resistance movements during the state of emergency proved to be a catalyst for a change of tactic. In the aftermath of its banning, Mandela and other more militant Congress leaders became disillusioned with attempts to mobilize mass protest through strikes and 'stay away' campaigns, despite evidence that strikes in mid-1960 had a real impact on economic activities in major ports and industrial centres.[71] The turn to armed struggle was a decisive moment in the development of South African liberation movements, but it was by no means a uniquely 'top down' process. There had been outbursts of insurrectionary violence in rural areas of South Africa since the 1940s, notably in Zeerust in the western Transvaal in 1957–58, in Sekhukhuneland in 1958, and in Pondoland in the Transkei in 1960.[72]

The decision to instigate guerrilla-style action within Congress came after long and fraught discussions with ANC moderates including Lutuli. On 16 December 1961, less than a week after he had been presented with the Nobel Peace Prize in Oslo, MK launched a series of sabotage attacks that marked an initial stage of what they hoped would become a wider popular struggle. The MK campaign was, however, to be short-lived. Soon after his return from overseas in July 1962, Mandela was arrested after US CIA operatives informed South African authorities of his whereabouts. And then, in June 1963, many of the leading members of the MK 'High Command', including Govan Mbeki, Ahmed Kathrada and Walter Sisulu, were arrested at Liliesleaf Farm in the northern Johannesburg suburb of Rivonia. At the subsequent trial, during which Mandela set out a careful and eloquent defence of the decision to resort to violence, the leadership of MK were sentenced to life imprisonment on Robben Island.

MK was not the only anti-apartheid organization to turn to armed struggle in the early 1960s. In July 1964, just weeks after the conclusion of the Rivonia trial, white liberals connected to the African Resistance Movement bombed the main Johannesburg railway station, resulting in the death of an elderly white commuter. The activist responsible, John Harris, was subsequently captured and sentenced to death in the following year.[73] PAC supporters launched armed campaigns under the name Poqo ('pure' or 'alone'). The origins of Poqo lay in PAC activities in the Western Cape in the aftermath of Sharpeville, and the increasingly violent rhetoric of campaigns that called for general insurrection by blacks against white rule. It was a genuinely grassroots organization, with cells across the Western Cape. Elsewhere in South Africa, especially in areas where support had been strongest in the run-up to Sharpeville, armed resistance by Africanists was more closely aligned with formal PAC structures, while the movement's leader Potlake Leballo established headquarters in Maseru, Lesotho. From there, Leballo sought to coordinate a nationwide uprising that would achieve 'independence by 1963', but aside from an uprising in Paarl in November 1962, no coherent national struggle emerged. The arrest of hundreds of PAC activists across the country in 1962 and the following year saw the effective suppression of the movement. Nevertheless, the Poqo/PAC insurrectionary movement constituted the largest grassroots armed campaign of the 1960s.[74]

Black politics in exile

With internal opposition supressed by the mid-1960s, representatives of the ANC, PAC and SACP began to work to rebuild their movements overseas. But the constraints of apartheid had narrowed opportunities for black South Africans across a range of activities beyond political activism and the emerging diaspora of South African exiles, as we have seen, included performers such as the jazz trumpeter Hugh Masekela and the singer Miriam Makeba. In fact, many in the circles of writers and poets that developed in South African cities in the post-war years began to depart the country, including *Drum* writers Lewis Nkosi, Can Themba and Bloke Modisane.[75] The array of creative talent that left South Africa during the 1960s would ultimately come to construct a transnational version of South African culture that, although not always explicitly political in form, nevertheless provided narratives that cut across and challenged the strictures of apartheid.

The post-Sharpeville clampdown on South African opposition movements nonetheless prompted significant efforts by anti-apartheid activists to establish operations overseas. The deputy president of the ANC, Oliver Tambo, left South Africa shortly after Sharpeville, accompanied by the white editor of *Africa South* Ronald Segal. In London, together with Yusuf Dadoo and Tennyson Makiwane, Tambo began to establish a headquarters for the ANC and develop links with anti-apartheid supporters.[76] The PAC also established external bases of operations in the aftermath of the Sharpeville crisis, beginning with the PAC office in Accra, Ghana, set up by Peter Molotsi and Nelson Mahomo who had been despatched overseas by Sobukwe in March 1960.[77] In mid-1960, South African political activists overseas agreed to form a South African United Front, with offices in London, Accra and Dar es Salaam. It was a short-lived effort at unity, however, and was dissolved by 1962.[78] Both the ANC and PAC saw newly independent African states as key to their success and long-term survival in the face of the effective suppression of mass internal resistance by the end of 1960. Initially, the PAC, with its pan-Africanist credentials, received a warmer welcome than the ANC in certain quarters, notably Ghana. The ANC began to more carefully develop support following the 1962 conference of the Pan-African Freedom Movement for East and Central Africa in Addis Ababa, marked by a speech by Mandela that presented the ANC as a genuinely African – and Africanist – political movement.[79]

The early 1960s saw significant numbers of South African activists depart the country, many travelling as students, often under the covert sponsorship of the ANC. One of the first to leave was Thabo Mbeki, son of the leading MK and SACP activist, Govan Mbeki. At the University of Sussex, Mbeki led a delegation of students to Downing Street in 1964, presenting a petition calling the British government to lobby the South African authorities not to impose the death penalty on the Rivonia accused. After his studies in the UK, Mbeki travelled to the Soviet Union, where he joined several South African students connected with the ANC Youth and Students Section (YSS), including Joe Nhlanhla, Walter Sisulu's son, Max, and the future ANC health minister Manto Tshabalala.[80] The students were evidence of increasing Soviet support for the SACP, which had become more firmly established from 1960, when Yusuf Dadoo and Vella Pillay met formally with their counterparts in Moscow. Although initially cautious on the question of armed struggle, the Soviet Union established a training centre for MK fighters in Odessa in 1963, while ANC leaders including Tambo worked increasingly closely with Soviet authorities to develop the military and political education of ANC activists.[81] Meanwhile, the only substantive material support for Congress from Western states had been provided by Scandinavia – largely channelled through the non-governmental organization set up by Canon Collins, International Defence and Aid – and expressly earmarked for non-military use.[82]

Building on the Soviet support and training, Tambo, along with the SACP general secretary Moses Kotane, worked from 1962 to establish bases of operation in Africa and secure material support from communist states, taking control of the military dimension of the movement from the imprisoned leadership of MK.[83] While the Soviet Union came to provide the bulk of the military funding for MK, links were maintained with China during, despite the worsening relations between the two communist powers, as ANC leaders consciously refrained from aligning themselves exclusively with either Moscow or Beijing.[84] By the mid-1960s, MK fighters were receiving training in the Soviet Union, Czechoslovakia and China, along with Egypt and Algeria. Camps at Kongwa and Morogoro in Tanzania served as holding centres for hundreds of increasingly frustrated MK fighters. Meanwhile the ANC began to forge links with anti-colonial movements across southern Africa, including those in Portuguese territories – FRELIMO in Mozambique and the Angolan MPLA – that had initiated a 'bush war' on home soil.[85]

In 1967, groups of ANC fighters joined compatriots from the Zimbabwe African Peoples' Union (ZAPU) to infiltrate Zimbabwe with the intention of reaching South Africa. After series of skirmishes with Rhodesian security forces in the Wankie district, the majority of the fighters were killed or captured. A second incursion in 1968 met with a similar fate.[86] Taken together, the Wankie and Sipolilo campaigns were of ambiguous value – while they demonstrated a level of organization and commitment among MK and ZAPU fighters, they failed in achieving their strategic aims; while they ultimately did little to alleviate frustration within the MK camps, they provided a focus for discussions that aimed to refocus the general aims and tactics of the ANC.

Just weeks before the launch of the Wankie campaign, Albert Lutuli died following an accident on train lines close to his home in Stanger. Remembered in the international press as a 'middle man of good will', his death marked the passing of an older generation of Congress activists.[87] Two years later, in the wake of the Wankie and Sipolilo campaigns, the ANC convened a consultative conference at its base in Morogoro, Tanzania. An attempt to bring strategic coherence to the movement in exile, the conference resulted in the extension of ANC membership to non-Africans, and Yusuf Dadoo, Joe Slovo and Reg September were appointed as members of the movement's Revolutionary Council. A new programme retained the fundamentals of the Freedom Charter, but signalled the intention of the movement to focus on the urban working classes as the primary focus of the struggle, eschewing the peasant-based insurrectionary programme adopted by other Third World liberation movements.[88] By the end of the 1960s, then, ANC and

SACP leaders had begun to draw the varied strands of the movement in exile into a coherent organization; at the same time, MK activist Ronnie Kasrils secretly recruited a number of young British sympathizers to smuggle cash and propaganda materials into South Africa. Using leaflet 'bombs' developed by the engineer Ron Press and tested in London and Bristol, these recruits operated in South Africa in isolated groups between 1968 and the early 1970s, and gave the liberation struggle a renewed degree of public prominence.[89]

Similarly, leaders of the PAC sought to build an exile movement in the wake of the suppression of their ill-fated attempt to launch a mass insurgency in 1962–63. Nelson Mahomo worked with Patrick Duncan, who had joined the PAC in 1963, to appeal for support and funds in Europe and the United States. By 1964, however, the PAC was beset by tensions and quarrels among its exiled leadership. Disputes over finances resulted in the suspension of Mahomo and other key figure, while Leballo faced a revolt among activists in Maseru. From 1964, Leballo joined other PAC representatives in Dar es Salaam, Tanzania, and sought to establish a new headquarters in Lusaka in 1967, but further factional tensions resulted in the entire movement being expelled from Zambia the following year.[90]

Despite its internal strife, the United Nations in 1969 recognized both the ANC and PAC equally as representative of the South African people, and at least until the mid-1970s, both groups were weighted equally in international perceptions of the liberation struggle. The tensions between the PAC and ANC continued to influence the international relations of South African liberation movements, however. In Tanzania in 1969, Leballo informed Julius Nyerere of a coup plot against him, cementing the support of the Tanzanian authorities for the PAC – and his leadership. In contrast, the ANC leader Oliver Tambo refused to testify against the coup plotters and in response Nyerere expelled the organization. Shortly after, the ANC established what would become its long-term African headquarters in the Zambian capital, Lusaka, and relations with Nyerere would not be re-established until the late 1970s.[91]

Both the PAC and ANC had struggled during the late 1960s to establish an organized structure in exile. The ANC had survived, and during the 1970s would seek to establish itself both in Western capitals and independent African states as the primary representatives of the South African struggle against apartheid. The pan-Africanist strand of South African liberation movements also remained as a counterpart and counter discourse to the ANC/SACP. While its power would eventually diminish, and was already showing signs of weakness by the end of the 1960s, the affinities between the PAC and post-independence African leaders would continue to underscore support for the South African pan-Africanists into the late 1970s. In the 1960s, foreign intervention in debates around apartheid was constrained by inertia at the level of intergovernmental action, but gained momentum through the increased involvement of supranational bodies associated with sport and other cultural and social links between South Africa and the wider world. The principle of international pressure was established as a fundamental dimension of global opposition to apartheid during the 1960s. It was a category that encompassed anti-apartheid movements, NGOs and official foreign policy.

Sanctions, boycotts and international solidarity

South African withdrawal from the Commonwealth in 1961 might be regarded as a major step towards international isolation, but the country in fact maintained significant links with the Commonwealth in trade, politics and culture. But the first half of the 1960s saw concerted efforts to intensify international pressure on the apartheid regime, through official international organizations such as the UN but also through the auspices of an emergent international anti-apartheid lobby, as activists turned to the imposition of formal sanctions against South Africa. Calls for sanctions were not new: they had been initiated briefly by the Government of India in the 1940s, were raised as a possibility by campaigners in the mid-1950s, and had been proposed by various African and Caribbean states at the end of the same decade. In the early 1960s, however, sanctions became a central focus of global anti-apartheid debate, encapsulated in the major conference on sanctions in 1964 sponsored by the British Anti-Apartheid Movement. It aimed to engage with debates underway at the UN around international action against apartheid, under the auspices of the organization's Special Committee against Apartheid, which had been formed in 1962 following a General Assembly resolution that called members to impose diplomatic and trade sanctions against South Africa.[92] This, taken together with the voluntary arms embargo initiated by the UN Security Council in August 1963, formed a diplomatic environment in which activists could conceive of the possibility of formal international action against South Africa.[93] The 1964 sanctions conference was thus a crystallization of early 1960s anti-apartheid sentiment, anti-colonialism and non-alignment. It represented Third World repugnance of apartheid and the desire to push beyond the UN arms embargo; for leading Western powers, though, the embargo had been a tactical manoeuvre designed to appease Third World nations. US support for the arms embargo was, it seemed, designed to diminish the possibility of economic sanctions, not open the door to further action.[94]

Major Western powers, with significant trade and investment interests in South Africa, were unconvinced by the arguments in support of sanctions, and worked actively to build a case against them. In 1963, the British government set up a Cabinet Working Party to investigate sanctions, concluding that they would have little impact on the South African economy without the imposition of a major military blockade. Moreover, the danger that sanctions posed to British trade with South Africa were tied to the fear that the deliberate isolation of the apartheid state would result in the degeneration of relations between the UK and the settler-dominated territories north of the Limpopo as the centrepiece of British policy in the region – the Central African Federation – had begun to unravel. Sanctions would, it was thought, push the hard-line political leaders in Southern Rhodesia into closer alliance with Pretoria, thereby further undermining British influence in the region.[95] For the United States, moreover, southern Africa

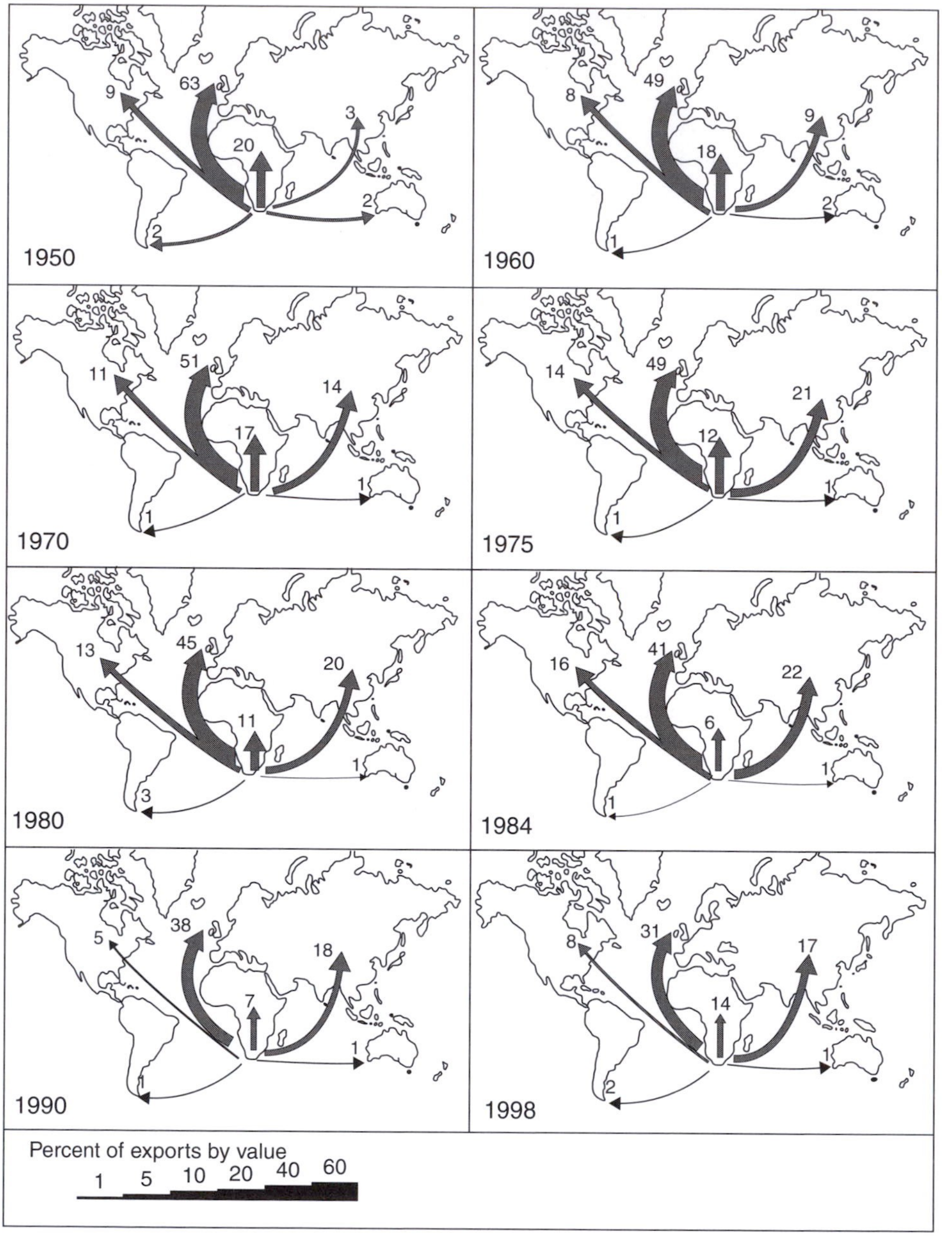

Map 4 South African exports, 1950–98.

Source: 'Exports from South Africa, 1950–98, by continent': A. J. Christopher. *The Atlas of Changing South Africa*. London: Routledge, 2001, pp. 194, 228.

remained a key source of strategic minerals such as chromium and vanadium that were vital for military and arms production. Despite a slight decline in the period between 1958 and 1962, returns on US investments in South Africa were particularly strong, especially in the mining sector.[96]

Calls for international sanctions were ultimately sidelined by the manoeuvres of the Western powers, and it would not be until the 1980s that sanctions would again become a major element of foreign intervention against apartheid. The failure to implement a large-scale international response to apartheid, coordinated by the UN, was not, however, a simple matter of self-interest. The United States and the UK recognized that the issue of apartheid was powerful for its new members and the African Group in particular. The liberal internationalist principles that had given birth to the UN were under increasing pressure, first in the face of ideological struggles linked to the Cold War, but more urgently through the increasingly loud calls for social and economic justice being made by representatives of Third World states. During the first half of the 1960s, the United States found itself a 'reluctant referee' in diplomatic battles between the apartheid state and emerging independent states in Africa.[97]

South Africa was a significant ally of the United States in the Cold War, founded in no small part on the strategic importance of its agreement in 1950 to supply uranium ore to the United States and the UK. By 1960, concerns over South African race policies gained ground over strategic imperatives, resulting in an increasingly hesitant policy towards the apartheid state.[98] The ambivalence of US policy continued under the Kennedy administration, despite the new president's reputation as an opponent of colonialism with sympathies for the Third World, derived largely from his time as chair of the African Subcommittee of the Senate Foreign Relations Committee in the late 1950s. Kennedy nevertheless viewed the ANC and PAC with suspicion and preferred to foster links with the white liberal opposition. Although some US officials (notably the Assistant Secretary of State for African Affairs, G. Mennen Williams) sought to establish closer links with the ANC, US policy towards South Africa continued to be based upon a belief that the ANC and PAC were fronts for communist activity and that US interests required cordial relations with Pretoria.[99] Instead, Senator Robert Kennedy visited South Africa in 1966 at the invitation of the National Union of South African Students (NUSAS). Kennedy had, while he was the Attorney General under his brother's administration, met with Patrick Duncan – much to the disapproval of South African officials. During his tour of the country, Kennedy met with key individuals, including the (albeit marginalized) ANC leader Albert Lutuli, spoke at a number of public events and called for South Africans to work towards racial reconciliation.

At the same time, pressure groups and activist movements in the United States urged a more vocal and active official response to apartheid. Civil Rights leaders, in particular, voiced opposition to apartheid consistent with their struggle against racial injustice within the United States. In 1962, US Civil Rights leader Martin Luther King Jr issued a joint statement with Lutuli on racial injustice, made explicit reference to apartheid in a number of major speeches, and in 1964 called for a 'massive movement for economic sanctions' against South Africa.[100] King subsequently sought permission to visit South

Africa in 1965, but was denied a visa. Similarly, the radical black leader Malcom X had been influenced by pan-Africanist ideologies since the 1950s, and increased contacts with African leaders after leaving the Nation of Islam in 1964. Over the course of that year, he made three separate visits to the continent, attending the Organisation of African Unity (OAU) meeting in Cairo as well as meetings with officials across North and West Africa. Like King, he spoke publicly about the connections between the United States and South Africa, and talked at a press conference in Ghana of the way in which apartheid and Portuguese colonialism in southern Africa were sustained by US support; 'until you expose the man in Washington', he told African reporters, 'you haven't accomplished anything'.[101]

Malcolm X's indictment of US official support for South Africa illustrated the struggle to define the image of American geopolitical power in the mid-1960s. Irwin has detailed the shift in US and British policy towards the latter part of the decade, as criticism of US involvement in south-east Asia made Washington less amenable to the views of Third World representatives and more determined to bolster its allies in southern Africa. As the process of decolonization played out, the United States had sought to create a 'legitimate hegemony' at the UN; as optimism faded at the UN, America began to be regarded as a new form of imperial power.[102] By the 1970s, then, material interests were the primary driver of US policy towards Pretoria. The Cape sea route continued to be of major significance in the world economy, as a vital connection between the West and the oil states of the Middle East. From 1967 until the mid-1970s the Suez Canal was closed to shipping, meaning that much of the crude oil supplies to the United States were shipped in a new generation of super tankers using routes that passed close to Cape Town. At the same time, the Soviet navy increased its operations in the Indian Ocean just as Britain, following the defence review initiated by the Wilson government, withdrew much of its military strength in the Gulf and South-East Asia.[103]

In the nexus of decolonization and civil rights, anti-racism became a predominant value in international relations from the late 1960s, but it was cultural contacts that would provide the main platform for the development of international anti-apartheid in the 1970s. Sport came to be a particular focus of anti-apartheid activism, in part as a reflection of its perceived importance for white South Africans.[104] Although formally disconnected from government, the politics of international sport paralleled that of the nation state itself, while sporting power did not necessarily overlap with political power, and in the aftermath of decolonization, representatives of smaller and newly independent states were able to lobby the Olympic Committee, FIFA and other sports bodies for the exclusion of South African teams.

From the late 1950s, South African ministers had shown an increasing willingness to take an interventionist approach to ensure that sporting bodies complied with apartheid principles, prompting activists to organize rival bodies designed to promote multiracial sport. Then, as African states achieved independence in the 1960s, pressure grew on international bodies to exclude South Africa from competition. Despite support from its president, Avery Brundage, the Olympic movement excluded South Africa from the

1964 Olympics in Tokyo, withdrew its invitation to participate in the Mexico Olympics in 1968, and then banished the country altogether in 1970. South African officials did little to aid their cause by heavy-handed attempts to force the Olympic committee to reverse its decision, which Prime Minister B. J. Vorster described as a return to 'the jungle'.[105]

Like their counterparts in the banned liberation movements, anti-apartheid activists in sport were subject to banning and imprisonment as the South African authorities sought to limit the impact of their campaigns. The president of the South African Non-Racial Olympic Committee (SAN-ROC), Dennis Brutus, had travelled to the 1963 meeting of the IOC despite a banning order and was arrested and imprisoned on Robben Island on his return to South Africa. After leaving South Africa in 1966, Brutus established a base in London and continued to coordinate efforts to exclude South Africa from international sport.[106] Exile was also an option for black South African sportspeople unable to compete at international level, most notably the Coloured cricketer, Basil D'Oliveira, who had travelled to Britain in 1960 and made his international debut for the England cricket team in 1966. When selected for the tour to South Africa in 1968, D'Oliveira became the centre of a major political controversy, as officials, including Vorster, called for his removal, forcing the tour to be abandoned.[107]

Protests against South African sports teams intensified in the late 1960s, culminating with the launch in Britain of the Stop the Seventy Tour (STST) campaign, organized by South African Young Liberal Peter Hain.[108] In late 1969, STST campaigners tested direct action tactics against the Springbok rugby tour of Britain, while the Irish Anti-Apartheid Movement declared that competition against South African teams constituted 'agreement with segregation'.[109] Following the chaotic scenes during the rugby tour, the Labour Prime Minister Harold Wilson was eventually persuaded to call on cricket authorities to reconsider plans for the South African tour, citing the threats to both sporting relations with Commonwealth countries and increased social tensions within Britain.[110] In the wake of the successful campaign, protests were launched against South African rugby tours of Australia in 1971, and New Zealand in the following year.[111]

The apogee of apartheid

On 10 March 1970 in Port Elizabeth, the South African cricket team completed an overwhelming victory against Australia, sealing a dominant performance by the home side over the four-match series. Widely regarded as the strongest international team of its day, it was the last time a South African team would play an official international cricket match until 1991. Like South African cricket, the national economic performance also appeared worthy of celebration at the start of the 1970s. Since 1945, it seemed that the South African economy had grown rapidly and consistently, and white South Africans experienced living standards that were remarkably high by international standards. Many lived in expanding suburban developments, facilitated by levels of car ownership that were second only to those of the United States.[112] Apartheid, it seemed (and its opponents began to argue) was synonymous with a flourishing capitalist economy.[113]

Economic growth had been particularly impressive in manufacturing, resulting in the main from import substitution stimulated by official controls over the inward shipment of foreign commodities. The development of the car manufacturing industry was given particular encouragement, and over the course of the 1960s multinational companies significantly expanded production of vehicles in South Africa. Contemporaries viewed the rising value of secondary industry as an indication that manufacturing had become the prime driver of the economy, an ambition that underpinned official attempts to promote the automobile industry. However, most of the component parts of the vehicles built in South Africa continued to be imported, leaving the factories as little more than assembly plants. Despite the interest in manufacturing, primary industries remained of critical importance to the South African economy. Rather than inexorable decline, as was predicted in the 1940s, gold output grew in the post-war period, in large part due to the extension of mining into new fields in the Orange Free State.[114]

The major force in the development of the new goldfields was the Anglo-American Corporation, which became the largest gold-producing company by the late 1950s. Moreover, Anglo-American expanded its interests across a wide range of industries and services, to the extent that by the end of the 1970s it was claimed that Anglo-American companies accounted for 50 per cent of the shares traded in the Johannesburg stock market.[115] Overall, South Africa had growing international investment in the 1950s, interrupted only by the withdrawal of foreign capital in the immediate aftermath of the Sharpeville crisis. While this was a shock that presaged the conditions that would pertain in the 1980s, confidence returned as the state reasserted its authority and suppressed resistance by the middle of the decade. At the same time, local investors had stepped in to the gap, including the significant body of Afrikaner capital that had been bolstered under the National Party over the course of the 1950s and 1960s. By the early 1970s, Afrikaner capitalist interests, such as the Sanlam Corporation, had become the primary backers of the National Party. But, as well as fostering the growth of private capital, the state also promoted economic growth through significant public investment. The creation of parastatal bodies such as the South African Coal, Oil and Gas Corporation (SASOL), formed in the early 1950s, represented a policy of 'economic nationalism' directed through the Industrial Development Corporation formed by Smuts's United Party administration in the 1940s.[116] Fearing the potential of international sanctions, public investment was directed into schemes such as the coal to oil conversion process developed by SASOL, while the defence company Armscor was formed as a response to the UN arms embargo imposed in 1963.[117]

In 1970, the Minister of Bantu Administration, M. C. Botha, guided legislation through parliament that, in many ways, represented the high-water mark of 'grand' apartheid. The Bantu Homelands Citizenship Act transferred the citizenship of black South Africans to the ethnic 'Homelands', or 'Bantustans', that had been established over the course of the previous decade. It represented – in principle if not in reality – the moment at which total separation between black and white had been achieved. The chief architect of apartheid, Hendrik Verwoerd, had not lived to see his achievement, however, killed by a parliamentary messenger, Demetrios Tsafendas, in 1966.[118]

Verwoerd's successor, B. J. Vorster, promised to continue the transformation of the former reserves into autonomous self-governing 'Homelands'. During the 1950s, apartheid visionaries had promoted the complete separation of the rural reserves, building on the provisions of the 1951 Bantu Authorities Act. Verwoerd, however, notwithstanding his reputation as the leading ideological force behind apartheid, had taken a pragmatic approach to the development of the Bantustans, casting aside the full recommendations of the Tomlinson Report of 1955, which had determined that state aid of over £100 million would be required to stabilize the economies of the reserves. The Promotion of Bantu Self-Government Act of 1959 was thus an attempt to provide a political solution to African ambition, based on 'ethnic' rather than racial division, and cast as a form of internal 'decolonization'. The policy was neither entirely coherent – embodied in the disjointed geography of scattered territories such as Bophuthatswana – nor financially viable. In effect, most became labour pools for industrial centres, maintained at significant cost to the government in Pretoria.[119]

By the late 1970s, ten Homelands had been established, all purportedly mapping onto the historical origin of South Africa's ethnic groups. Three – the Transkei, Bophuthatswana and the Venda – had gained nominal 'independence' by 1979. Alongside the development of the Bantustans, the apartheid state refined and extended its technocratic powers over African urbanization, although the inadequacy of housing provision and administrators' inability to regulate labour meant that control over the black urban population took an increasingly authoritarian guise. Pass law offences proliferated, and an estimated 3.5 million people (or over 10 per cent of the country's population) were removed from urban areas in the two decades after 1960.[120] Under Verwoerd and Vorster, the Bantustans became the centrepiece of a huge effort of social engineering designed to maintain white privilege and based upon a highly bureaucratic form of racial domination. During the 1960s, racial segregation became, in the eyes of officials, a question of technocratic management, as policy shifted from a more pragmatic first phase into the grander ambition of the 'apartheid project'.[121] But the apartheid state was, arguably, never entirely secure and in the 1970s and 1980s, it would face new challenges from within and without.

Summary

During the 1950s, the average annual increase in the black population of South Africa was over 2.5 per cent, which increased to 3 per cent in the following decade.[122] As elsewhere in the developing world, rural poverty fostered population growth as well as migration from countryside to town. Migration away from rural areas was exacerbated by apartheid policies that sought to remove African tenants from white-owned farms. But unlike Latin American countries, which saw rural populations move into rapidly expanding urban sprawls such as Brasilia, the strictures of apartheid required the 'surplus' populations of the countryside to be relocated in the appropriate ethnic Homeland. As a consequence, the population of the Bantustans had increased by 70 per cent in the period 1960–70.[123] The result was the development of a series of 'rural slums', with the population density of cities. This process of 'displaced urbanization' became one of the key social characteristics of apartheid through to the 1980s, resulting in social dislocation and economic hardship as residents of locations such as Botshabelo near Bloemfontein in the Orange Free State engaged in the lengthy commute to work in the nearest city.[124]

While the rest of Africa underwent a process of rapid decolonization, apartheid entrenched colonial relationships that had led to increasing isolation – a trend that would continue with the breakdown of Portuguese colonial rule and white supremacy in Zimbabwe. But South Africa was never as insulated from the rest of the world as the apartheid regime or its critics contended. Trade and investment links between South Africa and its Western allies were, anti-apartheid critics argued, 'deeply grafted into the politics and economics of apartheid', and that attempts to impose economic isolation on the country were doomed to fail.[125] Ultimately, the question was not so much one of actual isolation, but rather that, during the 1960s and 1970s, an 'isolationary' discourse began to shape both attitudes towards South Africa and thinking within the country's white elites. Government policy, business strategies and popular consciousness began to be shaped around the idea that South Africa stood apart from the wider world. Consumer boycotts were always designed to arouse public conscience in South Africa's major Western markets as much as they were motivated by a confidence in their actual economic impact.

Further reading

Berridge, Geoff R. *South Africa, the Colonial Powers and 'African Defence': The Rise and Fall of the White Entente, 1948–60*. London: Macmillan, 1992.

Bonner, Philip, Peter Delius and Deborah Posel, eds. *Apartheid's Genesis, 1935–1962*. Johannesburg: Witwatersrand University Press, 1993.

Bonner, Philip and Lauren Segal. *Soweto: A History*. Cape Town: Maskew Miller Longman, 1998.

Borstelmann, Thomas. *Apartheid's Reluctant Uncle: The United States and Southern Africa in the Early Cold War*. Oxford: Oxford University Press, 1993.

Borstelmann, Thomas. *The Cold War and the Color Line: American Race Relations in the Global Arena*. Cambridge, MA: Harvard University Press, 2001.

Ellis, Stephen and Tsepo Sechaba. *Comrades against Apartheid: The ANC & the South African Communist Party in Exile*. London: James Currey, 1992.

Fredrickson, George M. *Black Liberation: A Comparative History of Black Ideologies in the United States and South Africa*. Oxford: Oxford University Press, 1995.

Guelke, Adrian. *Rethinking the Rise and Fall of Apartheid: South Africa and World Politics*. Rethinking World Politics. Basingstoke: Palgrave Macmillan, 2005.

Irwin, Ryan M. *Gordian Knot: Apartheid and the Unmaking of the Liberal World Order*. Oxford: Oxford University Press, 2012.

Lodge, Tom. *Black Politics in South Africa since 1945*. London: Longman, 1983.

Lodge, Tom. *Sharpeville: An Apartheid Massacre and Its Consequences*. Oxford: Oxford University Press, 2011.

Minter, William, Gail Hovey and Charles E. Cobb, eds. *No Easy Victories: African Liberation and American Activists over a Half Century, 1950–2000*. Trenton, NJ: Africa World Press, 2008.

Onslow, Sue, ed. *Cold War in Southern Africa: White Power, Black Liberation*. London: Routledge, 2009.

Posel, Deborah. *The Making of Apartheid, 1948–1961: Conflict and Compromise*. Oxford: Clarendon Press, 1991.

CHAPTER 7
LIBERATION STRUGGLES

Like the apartheid 'project', the development of a culture of resistance to white supremacy in South Africa can also be usefully set within a global context. Opposition to apartheid reflected – and influenced – transnational struggles for democracy and 'liberation', the latter becoming a central point of reference for southern African anti-colonial movements and their international supporters during the 1970s and 1980s. The language of liberation struggle envisaged a future free from forms of colonialism, but the ideological and philosophical foundations of the idea of 'liberation' had a post-colonial dimension, inspired by both a long tradition of black politics, and the world that emerged from the process of decolonization. Popular support for anti-apartheid had moral and ideological roots that reflected global shifts in norms, values and political culture, built on post-war notions of self-determination and the pre-eminence of the sovereign nation state, but shaped also by an emerging discourse of human rights that added a new dimension to claims regarding citizenship and political entitlements. The concept of universal human rights, as laid down in the Universal Declaration of 1948 had, by the 1980s, become a framework that allowed civil society to exert power over the institutions of the nation state, and opened a channel for transnational influence over the politics of the South African state.

Black Consciousness and the Soweto Uprising

In July 1969, a small group of black students broke away from the liberal and multiracial National Union of South African Students (NUSAS), and launched a new movement, the South African Students Organisation (SASO). The first president of SASO, Steve Biko, used his column in the *SASO Newsletter* to articulate a political ideology that would become known as Black Consciousness (BC). Biko's philosophy centred on the belief that freedom from apartheid required black South Africans to liberate themselves from the psychological servitude of white domination; black South Africans, he suggested in 1976, had 'developed a certain state of alienation, he rejects himself, precisely because he attaches the meaning white to all that is good'.[1] SASO members represented a new generation of black youth, born into the system of apartheid and with few formal connections to the banned ANC and PAC. Although they drew on Africanist strands of the Congress movements and were influenced by African Christianity, they built their critique of South Africa's racially determined socio-economic and cultural world from the ground up. They also drew upon ideas that had influenced the worldwide upsurge of student protest in the latter part of the 1960s, alongside ideologies of Black Power and Third World revolution inspired by the anti-colonial writings of Frantz Fanon.[2] Theirs was, to some extent, a South African interpretation of the ideologies of the New Left, inspired, like their compatriots in Paris, New York and London, by the works of thinkers such as Herbert Marcuse.[3] But Black Consciousness was at its heart a reflection of the South African context, and its advocates articulated the particular concerns of black South Africans, called for black solidarity, self-help and a collective effort by blacks to free themselves from the cognitive restraints on their freedom.

The concept of 'blackness' defined by Biko and others around SASO was not exclusive, nor indeed did it conform to the apartheid vision, as some state officials had assumed. It centred on an attitude of mind that could be shared by all individuals that were classified in segregationist discourse as 'non-white'. It could therefore appeal to Coloured and Indian groups, whose lives had equally been shaped by apartheid doctrines of 'parallelism'. During the 1960s, both groups had seen the establishment of 'parallel development', with the creation of separate political and administrative structures, such as the South African Indian Council, and advisory body established in 1969.[4] Faced with similar constraints and grievances, apartheid began to unify the experience of black South Africans, and Black Consciousness offered an ideological foundation for a shared political agenda. Moreover, the influence of Black Consciousness could be discerned in African performance culture in the 1970s. As the state sought to shape culture along apartheid lines, through the establishment of Radio Bantu by the South African Broadcasting Corporation, and broadcasting services associated with Bantustans, performers such as Julian Bahula aligned themselves explicitly with SASO. Even where musicians sought to steer a path between popular politics and state control, groups such as Harari provided a focal point for new forms of cultural identity that challenged apartheid norms.[5] The Black Consciousness movement recognized the value performance culture in promoting new forms of black identity, and SASO established a Cultural Committee that promoted radical black theatre in townships during the 1970s.

In 1972 a Black People's Convention was created as a national coordinating body that oversaw the formation of BC-oriented trade unions and Black Community Programmes engaged in social health and welfare projects, notably in the Eastern Cape. These activities had attracted the attention of the security services, and in 1973 Biko and other BC leaders were issued with banning orders. In the same year, student dissident Abram Ongopotse Tiro, who played a role in both SASO and the South African Students Movement (SASM), which had emerged in the late 1960s to represent black high school students, left for Botswana, where he was killed by a parcel bomb in early 1974.[6] At the same time, white radicals from NUSAS, together with religious organizations such as the Christian Institute, began to forge links between Black Consciousness and white liberals, although their search for 'multiracial' alternatives prompted a critical response from black intellectuals such as Biko. In particular, divisions between white radicals and Black Consciousness activists emerged over the relative significance of race and class in South Africa, but while dialogue between black and white groups prompted the former to pay increasing attention to black living conditions and develop new forms of political mobilization, no common ideological framework emerged to transcend issues of race and class.[7]

Concurrent with the expansion of activities associated with the Black Consciousness movement, the early-to-mid-1970s saw a new phase of militancy among black workers. A series of strikes in factories around Durban in 1973 brought public attention to the resurgence of labour unrest, but perhaps more significant was the development of new unions, such as the African Metal and Allied Workers' Union, which brought new forms of organization to black factory workers, particularly in the manufacturing industries. Unlike their forebears in the South African Congress of Trades Unions (SACTU) in the 1950s, the new unions tended to prioritize local workplace grievances rather than national political issues.[8] Nevertheless, by the end of the 1970s, independent labour organizations had become an established presence that, on the one hand, presented a channel for negotiation between black workers and their employers, but on the other also had the potential to provide a platform for the organization of community protest.

The reappearance of worker militancy coincided with dramatic change in economic fortunes, not only in South Africa, but across the world. The proximate cause of the crisis was the embargo of oil production announced by the Organization of Petroleum Exporting Countries (OPEC) in October 1973, in protest at US support for Israel during the Arab-Israeli War. By the early months of the following year, the price of crude oil had quadrupled. But the crisis came as the structures established in the 1940s to maintain stability in the world economy were beginning to break down and the short-term spike in oil prices resulted in the longer-term suppression of growth across the developed world. The oil shock of 1973 had a significant impact on the South African economy (as would the subsequent increase in oil prices following the Iranian revolution at the end of the decade). The impact on manufacturing was particularly marked, as the global rise in commodity prices that followed the 1973 crisis increased the costs for manufacturing industry, even as the value of the rand increased in real terms.[9] The hoped-for reorientation of the South African economy towards the export of manufactures did not transpire, and instead, the inherent weaknesses that had been obscured during the boom years began to be revealed – with important social and political consequences. While the post-war economic performance of South Africa was strong in comparison to the developed world, it has been shown that it stood less well when set alongside the growth experienced by emerging economies in the same period.[10]

By the second half of the 1970s, then, social and economic conditions were already beginning to place strains on the system of apartheid. Economic pressures had gradually cut into the living conditions for black South Africans, placing pressure in particular upon state provision of key services, including education. These were brought into sharp focus with the dramatic resurgence in popular unrest in 1976, sparked by the brutal suppression of a protest by high school students in Soweto. On 16 June, some 15,000 students marched to a school in Orlando, in a protest organized by the Soweto Students' Representative Council (SSRC), an offshoot of SASM. The protestors were met by a significant body of police who opened fire, killing two demonstrators including the thirteen-year-old Hector Pieterson, whose image (captured by the photographer

Sam Nzima) would come to define the events in public consciousness.[11] After the initial demonstration had been dispersed, riots broke out across Soweto, and within days the unrest had spread across the Rand. During early August, the protests extended into a fully fledged nationwide revolt, which, according to official estimates, left over 500 dead.[12]

In the aftermath of the uprising, the government-appointed commission offered little by way of explanation, save that the revolt pointed to a lack of official awareness of the levels of dissatisfaction within the black population. While largely uncoordinated, the revolt represented a generational shift in popular opposition to apartheid that drew inspiration from language and symbols of Black Consciousness.[13] Vorster nonetheless blamed the events of a series of 'agitators', with the heaviest burden of guilt being placed on the BC movement. A number of organizations and individuals associated with BC were banned, along with a range of others including the leading critic of apartheid in the Dutch Reformed Churches, Beyers Naudé. Biko, the figurehead of the BC movement, was arrested and killed by police in September 1977, his death becoming a focal point for local and international denunciation of the apartheid regime. In November, the UN Security Council adopted a mandatory arms embargo against South Africa, extending the provisions of the voluntary ban imposed in 1963, while the General Assembly declared 1978–79 as International Anti-Apartheid Year. Although SASM activists had begun to make links with the ANC prior to the uprising, it was in the aftermath that established black movements began to fully acknowledge the significance of protest.[14] Thousands of black youths left South Africa in the aftermath of the uprising, many of whom found their way into exiled liberation movements, swelling the ranks of ANC activists and MK cadres in particular. The Soweto uprising had engendered a fundamental transformation of the political landscape in South Africa, and reinvigorated the transnational dimension of the resistance movements. At the same time, external pressures on the apartheid state were intensified as a consequence of major transformations in regional politics.

Internal and external pressures – from 'dialogue' to 'total onslaught'

In the late 1960s, South African regional dominance seemed increasingly secure. Despite being granted independence, Botswana, Lesotho and Swaziland were economically dependent members of a customs and monetary union with South Africa, while Namibia remained an incorporated appendage to the Republic despite continued debates at the United Nations. Importantly, the Portuguese colonies of Angola and Mozambique, along with the self-declared independent settler state of Rhodesia, provided a buffer zone of colonial territories between South Africa and the rest of the continent. Vorster sought to further bolster South African standing in the continent by promoting an 'outward-looking' policy of engagement with independent states, including Malawi and Zambia – the former established diplomatic relations with the apartheid state in 1968 and its President, Hastings Banda, made an official state visit to South Africa in 1971. Vorster also sought to engage key African states in dialogue, notably Gabon and the Ivory Coast, breaking down – at least for a brief moment – unified African opposition to apartheid.[15] The zenith of Vorster's policy of detente came in 1975, when he met Zambian President Kenneth Kaunda at the Victoria Falls, aiming to seek a collective solution to the developing crisis in Rhodesia.[16]

But events in Europe in 1974 were a catalyst for the reassessment of Pretoria's policy in the region. A military coup in Lisbon in April, led by veterans of Portuguese colonial conflicts, overthrew the authoritarian Estado Novo regime of Marcello Caetano. The following year saw democratic elections and the end to the colonial wars that had consumed a major part of the country's budget. Thereafter followed a rapid withdrawal of Portuguese forces and officials and the formal granting of independence to Mozambique and Angola in 1975.[17] In the former, the Frente de Libertação de Moçambique (FRELIMO), formed in exile in Tanzania in 1962, took power with its leader, Samora Machel, as the independent country's first president.[18] The situation in Angola was more complex, because the anti-colonial war had been fought by three rival nationalist movements, rooted in geographical and ethnic divisions. Founded in the 1950s and based in the capital Luanda was the Soviet-backed Movimento Popular de Libertação de Angola (MPLA), which formed the official government in 1975. To the north, the Frente Nacional de Libertação de Angola (FNLA) represented the ethnic-nationalist interests of the Bakongo and was supported by the Mobutu regime in neighbouring Zaire. To the south, Jonas Savimbi led the União Nacional para a Independência Total de Angola (UNITA), and its support was rooted in the Ovimbundu. In the lead-up to independence, UNITA broke away from the MPLA government and set up a rival administration in the southern city of Huambo.

Ostensibly to protect South African interests and investment, Vorster despatched a military force to southern Angola in October 1975, which in turn prompted Cuba to commit troops in support of the MPLA. As independence drew closer, many thousands of Portuguese settlers fled the country, destined for Portugal, Brazil and South Africa. The threat to white settler regimes increased as the liberation war in Rhodesia intensified. Fighters from the Zimbabwe Peoples' Revolutionary Army (ZIPRA), led by Joshua Nkomo, operated in the east of the country with bases in Zambia, while the Zimbabwe African National Liberation Army (ZANLA) led by Robert Mugabe was closely aligned with FRELIMO in Mozambique. As the war on its borders escalated, Pretoria cooperated closely with security services in Rhodesia, who were themselves engaged in cross-border efforts to destabilize black nationalist movements. Rhodesian security forces sponsored the formation of Resistência Nacional Moçambicana (RENAMO) as a counter-revolutionary force in Mozambique and launched a series of cross-border raids on ZIPRA and ZANLA camps.[19] By the late 1970s, the cordon of colonial states that surrounded South Africa had begun to dissolve, replaced by a zone of instability.

Conversely, independence in Angola and Mozambique helped to strengthen South African liberation movements, and the ANC in particular. As a counter to the influence of Pretoria, the formation of the Frontline States provided an umbrella for political and military initiatives against southern Africa's minority regimes, while the Southern African Development Coordination Conference (SADCC), which sought to promote economic development as a counter to South African dominance of the region, was launched in 1979. With support from the Frontline States, MK fighters were able to operate from bases in Angola and Mozambique, increasing their capacity to operate within South Africa itself. Moreover, both FRELIMO and the MPLA strongly supported the ANC's claim to be the primary representative of the South African majority, enhancing the movement's influence both within the region but also within international organizations such as the UN and the OAU.[20]

The regional instability of the late 1970s, together with the recrudescence of popular protest within South Africa, was accompanied by renewed international debate on apartheid, with Britain and the United States, while remaining key strategic partners, began to cool their relations with Pretoria. In 1977, Britain backed a Commonwealth agreement against sporting contact with South Africa, while US officials became increasingly intemperate in their public pronouncements on apartheid. In late 1977, the formerly voluntary UN arms embargo was superseded by a mandatory ban.[21] The combined effect of these new challenges prompted efforts to revise apartheid policy, with security concerns taking an increasingly prominent position in the minds of apartheid officials led by a new Prime Minister, P. W. Botha. The former Defence Minister came to power in 1978 after Vorster resigned following a series of revelations regarding the covert appropriation of state funds to finance a programme of propaganda. The scandal, inevitably nicknamed 'Muldergate' after the Minister of Information, Connie Mulder, involved attempts to purchase of foreign newspapers such as the *Washington Star* and the *Guardian* in the UK.[22] Thus Botha, the conservative pragmatist, came to power rather than Mulder, who prior to the scandal had been regarded as a likely successor to Vorster. Even before his appointment, the new Prime Minister had been a leading advocate of 'total strategy' – a composite set of policies, centred on defence, but comprising military, diplomatic and economic efforts to engage what Botha described as a 'total onslaught' against the country.[23] On becoming Prime Minister, Botha made 'total strategy' official government policy and sought to revive attempts to create a 'constellation of states' amenable to the apartheid state. With the formation of SADCC and the failure of attempts to create a moderate power-sharing administration in Zimbabwe-Rhodesia, the military strand of 'total strategy' would come to dominate the regional policy of Pretoria under Botha.[24]

Botha's succession represented an unmistakable shift in power towards military and defence interests in South Africa. While 'total strategy' was responsive to external stimuli, it was also a reflection of the ideological and material concerns of the security services, whose vision of 'total onslaught' was shaped by the thinking of the French military strategist André Beaufre, with its emphasis on the interconnections between security, social and economic policies.[25] Although the collapse of the colonial regimes in Angola and Mozambique, and the loosening grip of settler colonialism in Rhodesia, might be seen as catalysts for the greater emphasis on security, repressive responses to internal resistance and political instability in South Africa during the 1980s, the interplay of elements within Afrikaner nationalist politics were also critical factor. The creation of 'frontline states' on the borders of South Africa, similarly, are often seen as

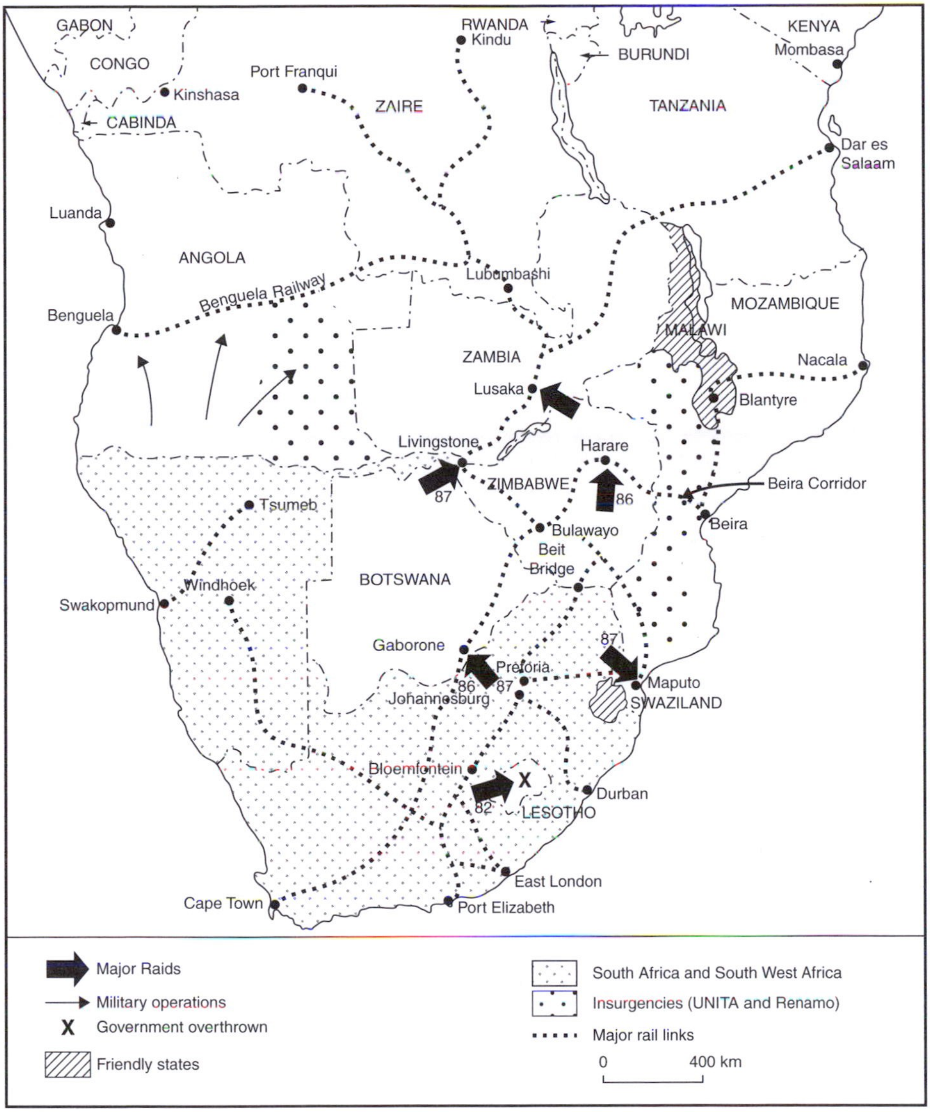

Map 5 Regional destabilization in the 1980s.

Source: 'Destabilization in Southern Africa in the 1980s': A. J. Christopher. *The Atlas of Changing South Africa*. London: Routledge, 2001, p. 185.

factors in the gradual undermining of the isolation of the apartheid state. But, perhaps a different set of questions need to be asked, centred on the assumption that instability within South Africa and the retreat of settler regimes in the wider region were symptoms of the same process of transformation. While the catalyst for decolonization in Angola and Mozambique was the coup in Lisbon, the process of political change in Portugal was bound up with the escalating costs of colonialism. Similarly, the expense of military conflict against ZANLA and ZIPRA forces in Rhodesia had played a significant role in bringing about the 'internal settlement' in 1978. When power-sharing arrangements were rejected by nationalist forces, further negotiations in Lancaster House, London were sponsored by the newly elected Conservative government under Margaret Thatcher, which resulted in new elections that brought the ZANU wing of the Patriotic Front to power under the leadership of Robert Mugabe. Apartheid South Africa, the dominant power in the region, was able to withstand the challenge to white supremacy for longer, but ultimately its leaders had to face the prospect that colonial forms of power were no longer sustainable in their crudest forms.

The 'reform' of apartheid under P. W. Botha

In a speech to parliament in 1979, P. W. Botha informed his party and supporters of his belief that they must 'adapt or die': reform was necessary in order to ensure the survival of white South Africa. As such, the policy changes he introduced in the early 1980s were designed to recognize and account for rising black power while maintaining white dominance.[26] The initial plans for reform were prompted by the desire to address the perceived roots of the unrest of the mid-1970s, and two commissions of enquiry were established to examine the possibilities for reform of trades unions and so-called 'influx controls' that had been at the heart of apartheid since the 1940s. The Wiehahn and Riekert Commissions reported in mid-1979, with the former recommending that black trades unions be given official recognition, while the latter concluded that blacks with residential rights in towns should effectively be treated as a stable urban middle class, while at the same time increasing controls over the 'influx' of new workers to cities. At the same time, the apartheid state sought to extend its links with business, setting up major conferences between state officials and business leaders at the Carlton Hotel in Johannesburg in 1979 and then again in Cape Town in 1981.

The reforms would have important effects over the following decade, not least by allowing trades unions to become a legally sanctioned organizations for the expression of black interests – albeit under government control. In legislative terms, the reform programme was initiated in 1982 under the auspices of the development minister, Piet Koornhof, who introduced bills designed to implement the Riekert proposals on the stabilization of the urban African population, while the Black Local Authorities Act of the same year extended the power of township councils. These were followed by fundamental changes to the structure of the South African state itself. In 1981, the Senate was abolished and replaced by a President's Council whose members included representatives from white, Coloured and Asian groups. The following year, more wide-ranging constitutional changes were proposed for the creation two new houses of parliament: the House of Representatives, elected by Coloured voters, and the House of Delegates, representing South African Indians. There were no changes for the majority of South Africans, however, whose citizenship was formally linked to the Homelands, but attempts were made to inject a form of democracy to local government and introduce greater representation within the governance of townships. The new constitution introducing the tricameral parliament, and also abolishing the office of prime minister and replacing it with a president holding enhanced executive powers was approved in a whites-only referendum in 1982.

Many within South Africa viewed Botha's reforms as focused on building support for the political system, rather than systematic reform of apartheid. It was an attempt to build a black middle class with a degree of investment in the status quo, rather than a genuine attempt to overturn the structural inequalities built into the system. It reflected attempts to deal with internal political tensions within South Africa, but also within the Afrikaner constituency, where an emerging divide between more liberal 'verligte' and hard-line 'verkrampte' viewpoints on apartheid were threatening the unity of the National Party. Following the proposals for the new tricameral system, a group of National Party MPs, led by the member for Waterberg in the northern Transvaal, Andries Treurnicht, broke away to form the Conservative Party (CP). Despite these signs of deeper fractures in the National Party, Botha was able to steer the constitutional changes through parliament, becoming elected to the new office of State President in 1984.

Botha's reforms were a response to changing circumstances within South Africa and the wider region, but the ideological underpinnings of the reform agenda also reflected global trends. Botha and his allies sought, some have argued, to legitimate apartheid rather than change it.[27] As such, the language of reform was suffused with the vocabulary of contemporary political thinking associated with the neo-liberal social and economic discourse of South Africa's primary allies in the United States and Britain.[28] As such, the Botha reform agenda drew on the key tenets of neo-liberal political discourse, with its focus on superficially 'pragmatic' policy, on the shrinking of the state, and of the predominance of individual liberties. Moreover, Botha's reform strategies were clearly influenced the work of American political scientists such as Robert Rotberg and Samuel Huntington, both of whom suggested that the political system in South Africa could be modernized under the guidance of an authoritarian state.[29] Thus, while its major Western supporters were primary advocates of privatization and the slimming-down of the state, officials in Pretoria constructed an increasingly elaborate set of institutions designed to simultaneously maintain authoritarian control, with military and security services in key positions. From 1979, the National Security Management System operating under the control of Botha's State Security Council established a network of institutions designed to provide intelligence and maintain partnerships between civilians and security forces at local levels. Security concerns shaped the foreign relations of the apartheid state, as Pretoria sought to build partnerships with states willing to assist it to circumvent the arms embargo. During the 1970s, under Vorster and the Botha, South African officials forged links with Israel in particular, securing access to arms and training – as well as allegedly sharing expertise and resources in the development of South Africa's nuclear weapons programme.[30] By the mid-1980s, the style of 'neo-liberalism' performed by the apartheid state more closely resembled the practices of autocratic regimes in Latin America and Asia, that combined counter-insurgency activities with wholesale attempts to restructure civil society.[31]

The change of focus was a consequence of the response of South African civil society to the reform programme set out by Botha in the early 1980s. Unified opposition to the programme coalesced in 1983 with the formation of the United Democratic Front (UDF), which joined existing strands of civil society together into a focal point for resistance. For South African Indians, the tricameral constitution represented the form of parallel institutions that had been promised since the 1960s, but 'parallelism' had ultimately been an empty political chalice until at least the late 1970s. Elections had been introduced for the South African Indian Council in 1974, and in 1981 it became a fully elected body; its purely advisory role was extended in 1976 to cover oversight of education and social welfare policies. Indian parties contested the first elections under the tricameral constitution in 1984, with the main parties being the National People's Party (NPP), which had controlled the SAIC since 1981, and Solidarity, whose leader J. N. Reddy focused on economic growth and the need for foreign investment.[32]

Alongside Indian politics, the UDF brought together a coalition of groups associated with black politics in the post-Soweto period. Coloured activists in the suburbs of Cape Town had been particularly dynamic in the organization of civic groups in the early 1980s, their efforts focused on community-led campaigns to improve facilities. By the formation of the UDF in 1983, civic groups had been set up across the country, with an emphasis on concerns including transportation, rents and local services. Alongside the civics, a series of community-based unions had emerged, in part as a response to the new regulations brought into being under the Industrial Conciliation Act in the wake of the Wiehahn Commission. But, unlike those unions affiliated with FOSATU, the community unions took a highly politicized approach, and sought to connect trades union activity with grassroots protests. In addition, the UDF drew on the support of youth and student groups, who had continued to provide a focus for black resistance in the years following the Soweto Uprising. While SASO and the Black People's Convention had been banned, new groups such as the Congress of South African Students and the Azanian Students' Organisation had emerged as a focus for black youth. Both black student activists and their white counterparts in NUSAS provided a 'cutting edge of political radicalism', drawing on international influences that included the revisionist analyses of the history of South African racial inequalities as well as theories of Third World dependency developed by Latin American scholars.[33]

Church leaders played a significant role in the protest movements of the 1980s, signalling a decisive shift from the cautious liberalism that had dominated the churches' response to apartheid in the 1950s. Starting with the Cottesloe Consultation in 1960, which had been sponsored by the World Council of Churches (WCC) in response to the Sharpeville shootings, Christian leaders had begun to take an increasingly assertive stance against institutionalized racial discrimination in South Africa. The WCC took an increasingly assertive stance towards apartheid, condemning the policy through the auspices of its Programme to Combat Racism launched in 1969. In the following year, the WCC announced that it would provide financial assistance to the South African liberation movements, notwithstanding their advocacy of armed struggle. The decision prompted the members of the WCC affiliate, the South African Council of Churches

(SACC) to examine their association with the world body. All decided to remain, and while many Christians were uncomfortable with the WCC's support for the ANC and PAC, South African churches sought increasingly to assert their independence from the apartheid state.[34] In the 1970s, groups such as the SACC and Christian Institute would seek to work alongside leaders of the new generation of black activists associated with Black Consciousness, which itself drew on the influence of Black Theology, developed in the United States in the 1960s. Alongside Black Theology, more radical South African Christians were also inspired by Latin American liberation theology that sought to connect the work of the church to the needs of the poor and dispossessed. The language and methods of liberation theologians such as Gustavo Gutiérrez, including the focus on 'praxis' or practice over theological doctrine, were taken up by Black Consciousness activists in South Africa.[35]

By the 1980s, a new generation of black church leaders were coming to embrace the call for Christians to work against the racial injustice embedded in the apartheid system. This meant that even those leaders who were not advocates of liberation theology found themselves at the forefront of campaigns against apartheid. One particularly prominent example was Desmond Tutu, who was general secretary of the SACC between 1976 and 1978 and became a vocal critic of apartheid both within South Africa and on visits overseas. Notwithstanding the authorities' efforts to dissuade him from his activities, which saw his passport withdrawn and a brief period of imprisonment, Tutu became a focal point for anti-apartheid protest in the early 1980s, a figure of international prominence whose advocacy of non-violence was recognized with the award of the Nobel Peace prize in 1984. While the Dutch Reformed Churches had effectively broken with the 'English-speaking' churches after Cottesloe, Calvinists continued to influence opposition to apartheid. The DRC minister Beyers Naudé, as we have seen, played an important role in the Christian Institute, while the keynote speech at the launch of the UDF in 1983 was given by the Reverend Allan Boesak, who at the time was president of the World Alliance of Reformed Churches, who had expelled the Dutch Reformed Church in 1982 because of its ongoing support for apartheid.

Figures such as Boesak, as well as former Robben Island prisoners and an older generation of nationalist figures such as Albertina Sisulu, gave the UDF a symbolic connection with traditional forces of opposition in South Africa. While the UDF drew together a coalition of groups with a wide range of influences, it also provided a clear link back to the Congress movement of the 1950s, expressing support for the principles of the Freedom Charter. Although it emerged as a direct response to Botha's reforms, and began with a public campaign calling for a boycott of elections to township councils in 1983 and the Indian and Coloured chambers of the new tricameral parliament in 1984, the UDF embodied a resurgence of nationalist consciousness that had been evident since the late 1970s. Thus, while movements on the left such as the Azanian People's Organisation (AZAPO, formed in 1978 by former BC activists) played an important part in the mobilization of protest during the 1980s through organizations such as the National Forum, the principles and symbols of the ANC would come to the fore as a prominent aspect of popular resistance from the mid-1980s.

The campaign against the elections in 1983 and 1984 were a marked success. In Soweto, participation was no higher than 10 per cent, while the rates of participation in the Coloured and Indian elections in the following year reached no higher than 18 per cent across the nation as a whole. Elections to the House of Delegates did prompt a contest between the NPP and Solidarity, with the South African Indian Congress, the historic centre of anti-segregationist politics, taking the lead in promoting the election boycott amongst South African Indians. Perhaps as importantly, support for the elections was further undermined by opposition from the Zulu political leader, Mangosuthu Buthelezi. As a result, the NPP established a narrow majority over Solidarity, but underwhelming levels of participation meant that the legitimacy of the elected body was severely shaken. In urban areas, participation was particularly low with only 10 per cent of the electorate of the township of Lenasia near Soweto taking part.[36] The boycott campaign demonstrated that Botha's attempt to reform apartheid from within had not quelled the burgeoning discontent, and instead protest against apartheid returned with a new intensity.

Resistance and repression

The decade between 1984 and the first elections under a universal franchise in 1994 was marked by violent struggle between the state authorities and resistance movements which bordered on civil war. This low-intensity conflict combined with ongoing military involvement in Angola and Mozambique to create a culture of crisis that undermined the long-term sustainability of apartheid and would have long-lasting consequences for the post-apartheid state. The burden of the crisis weighed most heavily on black urban residents, particularly in the major cities and industrial centres, but rural areas were also affected by the crisis, not least because of the impact of the removal policies of the 1960s and 1970s.

The upsurge in violence began with a series of protests across the Vaal Triangle, the industrialized belt south of Johannesburg that incorporated Vereeniging, Vanderbijlpark and Sasolburg in September 1984. The protests were rooted in ongoing campaigns by students (a national schools boycott had been in operation since April that year) and civic groups (in response to rent increases). Rioting followed a stay-away on 3 September, and by the end of the month – in an unprecedented move – the authorities deployed SADF troops in the Vaal townships. By October, the protest had spread to other parts of the region, and by the end of the year civic groups, students and trades unions affiliated with the UDF had staged protests in the Eastern Cape. In addition to the urban centres of Port Elizabeth and East London, UDF organizers built up significant networks of support in rural townships. The protests continued until July 1985 when the government declared a state of emergency in the centres affected by the protest.[37]

Even before the state of emergency, the brutality of the clampdown on protest had been underlined by the killing of the Eastern Cape UDF organizer Matthew Goniwe, as the authorities began to target UDF leaders, cutting off the national leadership from the movement by arrests, imprisonment and the imposition of banning orders, as well as extrajudicial killings. Over half the national and regional leadership of the UDF were removed from political activities during the emergency, but unlike the 1950s, these tactics did not result in the suppression of grassroots protests. Instead, UDF-affiliated campaigns shifted focus, moving to a repertoire of localized consumer boycotts organized by street-level committees. The key characteristic of the protests of the 1980s was that local grievances were effectively linked to national questions in ways that had not been achieved in the past, often led from the ground up, with the national leadership 'trailing behind the masses'.[38] In the second half of the 1980s a culture of resistance had been established in South African townships that effectively isolated many pockets of the country from government control.

The first state of emergency had failed to extinguish popular protest against and it was lifted in March 1986. Just two months later, however, a new, nationwide state of emergency was declared in advance of protests to mark the tenth anniversary of the Soweto Uprising. The second state of emergency would last until the end of the decade, and saw an intensification of authoritarian controls under what was, in practice, military rule across large parts of the country. Townships and urban areas had been a focus of political protest in the 1950s and 1960s, but the tenor of the struggle in the 1980s was different, more intense, drawing whole communities into a mode of living shaped by resistance, on the one hand, and levels of state intervention without parallel in earlier phases of mass protest against apartheid.

During the 1980s, the liberation movements in exile were able to re-establish closer connections with internal resistance than had been possible prior to the Soweto Uprising. This was partly a consequence of a consolidation of ANC dominance over anti-apartheid resistance, both internally and externally. In the early 1980s, despite its increasing prominence within the Frontline States, the ANC continued to share a stage with the PAC in international organizations. The transformation of regional power that resulted from Angolan and Mozambican independence strengthened the regional standing of the ANC, as in both countries the post-independence ruling parties had been allied with the ANC since the early 1970s.[39] Together with the continued support of Kenneth Kaunda, the ANC came by 1985 to be recognized within the subcontinent as the principal representative of the people of South Africa. Together with its alliance with the black trades union movement in South Africa, its connections with the Eastern Bloc through the SACP, and the increasing density of its networks of supporters in Europe and the United States, the ANC had established itself as the predominant political force in the struggle against apartheid, signalled most effectively in 1987 with the adoption of the Freedom Charter by the United Democratic Front and the Congress of South African Trades Unions.[40]

The ANC had sought to build on the resurgence of its support and influence after the Soweto Uprising by engaging more directly in internal politics. In the early 1980s, even before the resurgence of domestic resistance under the UDF, MK activists broadened their efforts to attack strategic targets including the Sasolburg fuel refinery in 1980 and the Koeberg nuclear reactor in 1982. ANC propaganda efforts included Radio

Freedom, the broadcast service supported by Western donors and produced in studios in Lusaka.[41] This phase of 'armed propaganda', which continued through to 1984, had the intention of creating a following within South Africa that could, when necessary, be moulded into more formalized support. In January 1985, the ANC in exile called upon its supporters to 'render South Africa ungovernable', but despite the increasing crisis in the townships, it is unclear to what extent the ANC directly influenced popular resistance in the 1980s. The large majority of MK fighters remained outside South Africa, and while some were engaged in active service against UNITA in Angola, most remained in limbo at various camps across southern Africa. Maintaining morale amongst MK fighters was not easy, particularly within the atmosphere of suspicion engendered by the movement's internal security organization, Mbokodo, which operated a notorious detention centre in Angola, known as 'Quatro'.[42] While MK fighters continued to infiltrate South African townships, more intangible influence was perhaps more significant. The symbols and slogans of the ANC and MK became rallying points for resistance, regularly encountered at public events such as the funerals of 'comrades'.

Over the course of the 1980s, the breakdown of state authority in the townships was in some areas almost total – community actions such as rent and school boycotts and the targeting of township officials as 'collaborators' meant that the official grip in some urban areas was loosened, leaving a void into which various groups could establish local power. UDF supporters across the country shared broad visions of 'national democracy', as well as (often vaguely defined) socialist definitions of working-class solidarity, but notions of 'people's power' embraced a spectrum of activities that ranged from formalized community-led structures of civic authority through to the brutal and arbitrary imposition of popular justice through beatings and killings, often by means of the infamous 'necklace', when a petrol-filled tyre was hung around the necks of alleged collaborators and set alight.[43]

Perhaps the only institutions that maintained legitimacy both within the state and the townships were churches, who have been defined as becoming a 'site of struggle' in themselves in the 1980s.[44] The leadership of the UDF was closely associated with official churches, while organizations such as the South African Council of Churches gave overt and explicit support for the liberation movements. In 1985, the Institute for Contextual Theology issued the Kairos statement, arguing that South Africa had reached a crisis point in which the apartheid state should not be regarded as a legitimate authority, effectively calling on Christians to engage in civil disobedience. While many found it difficult to embrace the Kairos message, it arguably 'gave theological direction and impetus' to a significant body of Christians opposed to the apartheid state.[45] But churches were by no means united in their views on apartheid, with deep-seated racial divisions continuing to exert a powerful influence over their members through to the 1990s. Pentecostal churches, although initiated through international links in the early twentieth century, had developed distinctive South African forms by the 1950s. African Pentecostal churches such as the Zionist Christian Church (ZCC) expanded rapidly in the second half of the century. The ZCC, together with other African Initiated Churches, claimed nearly half the African population as members by the early 1990s. In many cases these churches were largely apolitical or, as was the case with the Apostolic Faith Mission (AFM), marked by strict racial divisions.[46] The Pentecostal movement was largely acquiescent in the face of apartheid, although prominent exceptions could be found, perhaps the most important being Frank Chikane, who was ordained as an AFM pastor in 1980, but continued to engage in political activities, became a leading figure in the discussions leading to the publication of the Kairos document, and became general secretary of the SACC in 1987.

While black South Africans, particularly the increasing numbers living in urban areas and rural slums, found their lives dominated by the cycles of resistance and repression by the late 1980s, many white South Africans remained insulated from the violence and faced few profound changes to their privileged living conditions. But the sense of crisis was nevertheless pervasive, and many young South Africans had direct experience of the struggles inside and outside of South Africa through military service, often as conscripts. In many ways, the experiences of these soldiers paralleled those of other conflicts in the late twentieth century, including the war in Vietnam. Anxieties resulting from the brutality of conflict, the relentless presence of death in everyday life, and the dehumanization of an 'enemy' were common factors; in the South African context, however, the diffuse notion of an enemy was also shaped by deep-seated casual racism and a belief that the military were engaged in a struggle to maintain 'law and order' against 'agitators and terrorists'.[47] In around 1986 the tactics employed by the security forces began to shift, with black police and informal 'vigilantes' engaged in direct confrontation with black resistance movements, while the military, under the directorship of the National Security Management System (NSMS), began to focus on welfare and development programmes designed to 'win the hearts and minds' of township residents. By the late-1980s, state policies had transformed, with 'reform' seen as an adjunct to 'security', focused on efforts designed to effect the 'reconstitution of the very fabric of civil society'.[48] As such, the apartheid state drew again on lessons learned by other colonial powers, and networks of shared intelligence.[49]

The world against apartheid?

The Soweto Uprising spurred a resurgence in global anti-apartheid activity, similar to its impact on resistance within South Africa. And just as domestic protest movements coalesced in the early 1980s, transnational anti-apartheid movements also reacted to the reform policies of the Botha administration, just as leading Western powers moved to promote forms of 'constructive engagement' with Pretoria. In the decade following the International Year Against Apartheid, worldwide movements made concerted efforts to persuade governments and businesses to isolate South Africa through sanctions and disinvestment. These campaigns called again on ordinary people to support the struggle in South Africa in their everyday lives, by refusing to purchase South African products, and by raising funds to support South African protestors. Across the world, a consistent set of messages and tactics were elaborated in support of the liberation movements, although each movement reflected the national political cultures within which they operated. Finally, international organizations such as the UN and the Commonwealth continued to provide a forum for the international politics of anti-apartheid.

At the same time, the cultural boycott remained an important pillar of international opposition to apartheid. The break in sporting contacts with South Africa that had been contested in the late 1960s and early 1970s continued, given formal recognition by the Gleneagles Agreement by Commonwealth states in 1977. During the 1980s, South African sports authorities sought to undermine the boycott by promoting a series of 'rebel' cricket tours with teams from England and Australia. Although national authorities responded with bans on participating players, the ambiguity of their position was revealed by their willingness to facilitate the inclusion of South African-born players in their own teams. More politically contentious was the decision taken by the British government in 1984 to fast-track the UK citizenship of athlete Zola Budd in order to enable her to compete for Britain in the 1984 Olympics, which became a focus of criticism in the year in which Britain welcomed an official visit by P. W. Botha.[50]

In addition to the main centres of activity in Britain and the United States, anti-apartheid became a genuinely global social movement during the 1980s. Not only were movements around the world connected through shared ideologies and protest repertoires, but their activities constituted a transnational force that operated across and beyond national borders, often dissolving the boundaries between nations in the process. The anti-apartheid movement acted as advocates for the South African liberation movements, ensuring that governments and businesses around the world were accountable for their links with the apartheid regime.[51] For some commentators, the anti-apartheid movement formed part of a nascent 'global civil society' that had begun to take shape, reflecting the potential structural economic and political connectivity that emerged in the wake of decolonization.[52] Increasing calls for sanctions and disinvestment might also be regarded as a reflection of new norms in international relations, in which systemic racial discrimination was framed as an antithesis of the accepted values of liberal democracy.[53]

These global threads nevertheless operated within specific national settings. In some parts of Europe, anti-apartheid became an object of governmental policy rather than a concern restricted to the sphere of non-governmental organizations. In Sweden, sanctions were introduced in 1979 and 1987, with substantial cross-party support. Until his assassination in 1986, the official anti-apartheid policies in Sweden were most prominently associated with the Social Democratic Party leader, Olof Palme. In 1971, shortly after visiting southern Africa, Palme increased official humanitarian aid to South African liberation movements, with the ANC developing a particularly close and beneficial relationship with Swedish social democrats.[54] The Norwegian government also provided funds for the ANC from the late 1970s, while the Norwegian Council for Southern Africa coordinated public support from its formation in the late 1960s[55]. The Irish Anti-Apartheid Movement, meanwhile, had been an important influence on official attitudes towards southern Africa in the early 1970s, although the effects of public activism were tempered after the country joined the European Community in 1973.[56]

One of the most well-established anti-apartheid movements was that of the Netherlands, where the Comité Zuid-Afrika had been launched in the aftermath of Sharpeville, followed by the more radical Anti-Apartheid Beweging Nederland in 1971. Like their compatriots elsewhere Dutch anti-apartheid activists organized consumer and sporting boycotts, lobbied for sanctions and disinvestment, with a particular focus on the Anglo-Dutch Shell Oil company and imports of Outspan oranges; historic links with Afrikaner nationalism were, however a source of tension, characterized by the ransacking of the Amsterdam headquarters of the Dutch South Africa Association in 1984.[57] In France, anti-apartheid activism was organized by the Mouvement Anti-Apartheid, formed in 1975, while movements were also formed in West Germany, Belgium, and Switzerland, among other European states.[58]

In Britain, the movement was rekindled in the aftermath of the Soweto Uprising, although its popular support expanded most rapidly after the South African security clampdown in 1984. The national membership and numbers of local groups rose dramatically in the wake of media coverage of events in South Africa, and as a result of high-profile interventions in the public debate, including popular cultural endeavours such as the Birmingham pop group the Specials' song 'Free Nelson Mandela'. Songwriter Jerry Dammers's song followed in the footsteps of a number of anti-apartheid protest songs, dating back to Vanessa Redgrave's 'Hanging from a Tree' (1963), but perhaps its most well-known predecessor was Peter Gabriel's 'Biko', a paean to the Black Consciousness leader recorded after his death in 1978. What distinguished Dammers's song, however, was that it interlocked with the ANC's campaign to promote Mandela as the global symbol of the anti-apartheid struggle, initially conceived to mark his sixtieth birthday in 1978. Dammers had organized a charity concert to mark Mandela's birthday in 1983, and went on to work with the producer Tony Hollinsgworth to organize the birthday tribute to Nelson Mandela at Wembley Stadium in June 1988. The concert was broadcast by the BBC and transmitted to nearly seventy countries worldwide, attracting an estimated audience of 600 million people.[59]

Prime Minister Thatcher sought to counter claims that she supported the apartheid system, and in fact what motivated her antipathy to the anti-apartheid movement was her ideological opposition to sanctions which were regarded as an example of state intervention in economic activity at odds with the neo-liberal ideals upon which her policies of privatization and deregulation were based. For British officials, South Africa remained 'half-ally, half-untouchable' throughout the apartheid era.[60] In this, Thatcher shared the belief of US President Ronald Reagan that change in South Africa was best served by 'constructive engagement', a form of critical friendship that relied on maintaining – or indeed extending – business and trade links with South Africa. The US Secretary of State, Chester Crocker, was perhaps the key architect of Reagan's policy of 'constructive engagement', which he saw as an antidote to the ineffective and confrontation policies of the Carter administration in the late 1970s. Crocker's approach was to maintain investment and business connections with South Africa, with the belief that economic growth would be 'the principal engine of constructive change in all fields'.[61] From the late 1970s, many US businesses operating in South Africa had pledged to abide by a set of principles drafted by the Reverend Leon Sullivan, a director of General Motors. The Sullivan principles called on companies to operate a desegregated workplace, to ensure equal play and working conditions, to provide training for and advancement opportunities for their black employees. In practice, however, this was a loose and voluntary code, which was highly difficult to put into practice in the context of apartheid legislation.[62]

As in Britain, cultural contacts with South Africa became points of political tension. In 1985, artists and producers Steve van Zandt and Arthur Baker formed 'Artists Against Apartheid', a one-off collective that drew together an array of major stars to produce the anti-apartheid song 'Sun City', a critique of performers who had willingly accepted invitations to play in the casino complex of that name located in Bophuthatswana. More complex questions of cultural politics and ethics were raised in the following year, when US songwriter Paul Simon released his *Graceland* album, which featured performances by a number of South African artists including the band Ladysmith Black Mambazo and Ray Phiri, recorded in Johannesburg. The album, released as Botha extended the state of emergency across South Africa, was critiqued as a naive form of cultural 'constructive engagement' at odds with the UNESCO boycott on performances within South Africa. While political ambiguous, the record undoubtedly helped to launch the South African artists' international career and represented a reciprocal moment in the transnational cultural influences that crossed the Atlantic.[63]

Anti-apartheid in the mid-1980s had the capacity to become, in part at least, a front for a critique of 'Reaganomics' and its British counterpart, 'Thatcherism'. It was certainly the case that left-wing groups implacably opposed to the policies of the New Right were particularly enthusiastic in their support for anti-apartheid. At times, the result was that anti-apartheid became a proxy for wider political tensions, as was the case with the City of London Anti-Apartheid Group, whose high-profile non-stop picket outside South Africa House in Trafalgar Square obscured deep tensions that led to the group's eventual disaffiliation from the national Anti-Apartheid Movement (AAM).[64] Apartheid was also a particularly salient issue for black community activists in Britain, and groups such as Black Action for the Liberation of South Africa articulated a powerful pan-Africanist message of racial solidarity influenced by wider discourses of resistance to white supremacy. Not all black activists took an uncompromisingly exclusivist position on apartheid, but the lack of focus on broader questions of racism from within the AAM tended to give the movement the appearance of a white middle-class campaign, disconnected from the political agendas of black Britons. The AAM maintained a diligent focus on the issue of sanctions and solidarity with the liberation movements rather than extend its campaign into a broader critique of race politics and racism in Britain as well as in South Africa; as such, the formation of the AAM Black and Ethnic Minority committee in May 1989 represented a belated recognition of the importance of black support.[65]

The upsurge in British public interest in apartheid in the mid-1980s was shaped by greater prominence of apartheid in political debate, stimulated by the controversial state visit of P. W. Botha to Britain in 1984 (the first official visit since Verwoerd had attended the

Commonwealth conference in 1961). The controversy over Botha's visit and the support provided by the UK government for the South African athlete Zola Budd contributed to a sense that the Thatcher administration were, at the very least, comfortable with the Botha programme for reform, although the visit, part of an unprecedented tour of Western Europe, was chiefly motivated by the desire to maintain South African support in the proxy-Cold War conflict in Angola.[66] Despite the widespread condemnation of the invitation to Botha, sympathetic accounts of the Thatcher administration's position on apartheid suggest that its flexibility gave confidence to reformers within the National Party.[67] Set in the context of the year long strike by mineworkers and protests against the siting of US nuclear missiles in the UK, anti-apartheid might be viewed as a key element of foreign policy for the 'enemy within', the composite amalgam of trades unionists, militant socialist activists, and counter-cultural groups that aligned themselves against the norms of 'Thatcherism' in the mid-1980s.[68] But the picture was more complex, and efforts to mobilize popular support for anti-apartheid were by no means simply anti-Thatcherism by proxy.

Anti-apartheid campaigns were having an impact on individual businesses with interests in South Africa. During the 1970s, campaigners had persuaded churches in the UK, including the Church of England, to divest their financial interests in South Africa. With the support of the British Council of Churches, and groups such as Christian Concern for South Africa, efforts continued in the 1980s to promote support for anti-apartheid in Christian churches.[69] Perhaps the most significant victory for anti-apartheid campaigners came with the decision, announced in 1985, that Barclays Bank would cut its connections with its South African arm. The campaign against Barclays in the 1980s had originated in the short-lived campaign launched by the Haslemere movement in the late 1960s, and built on the campaign against Midland Bank launched in the mid-1970s by the group End Loans to South Africa (ELTSA). Led by a Methodist minister, David Haslam, ELTSA tactics included attempts to mobilize shareholders at annual meetings and strenuous efforts to persuade individual and corporate customers to withdraw their business. While the extent of its influence has been difficult to judge, ELTSA clearly contributed to the loss of confidence in international investors in the second half of the 1980s.[70]

In the Commonwealth, anti-apartheid groups had been established in Canada, New Zealand and Australia, where campaigns often focussed on sporting boycotts. In Australia, anti-apartheid activism played a role in a process of redefining Australian identities as multicultural and cosmopolitan, in contrast to the racially monochrome identity that had prevailed throughout most of the century.[71] Official support for sanctions against South Africa had increased during the 1970s and early 1980s, particularly from former colonial territories, but it was not until the second half of the decade that these efforts began to bear fruit. In the face of the ongoing violence and state repression in South Africa in 1985, opponents of sanctions against South Africa began to find it harder to sustain their case. At its Heads of Government meeting in 1985, Commonwealth leaders persuaded a reluctant Margaret Thatcher to agree to a plan to despatch an Eminent Person's Group to South Africa, co-headed by the Australian Prime Minister Malcolm

Fraser, and the Nigerian government head, General Olusegun Obasanjo, with the aim of establishing a process of negotiation between the South African government and the liberation movements. Members of the group visited South Africa between February1986 and May 1986, meeting with South African leaders, including the imprisoned Nelson Mandela. During the group's final visit to South Africa, the SADF launched cross-border attacks on camps in Botswana, Zambia and Zimbabwe – a demonstration of hard-line determination that was not lost on its members. At the Commonwealth summit in August 1986, British reluctance was finally overcome and leaders announced a package of sanctions against Pretoria.[72]

Just days after the Commonwealth summit, the US Senate passed the Comprehensive Anti-Apartheid Act, a package of sanctions that included a ban on new investment, on the import of a range of South African goods, and on the export of oil and computers from the United States. Reagan moved immediately to veto the Act, but this was overturned by an unprecedented bipartisan vote in Congress. Significantly, the Act did not simply prescribe measures against Pretoria, but also set out the preconditions under which sanctions might be lifted, which were the effective dismantling of apartheid. Significantly, it also placed pressure on the ANC to suspend the armed struggle and enter into negotiations with the government.[73] US sanctions followed in the wake of a popular anti-apartheid movement that reached the height of its influence in the mid-1980s. Focused on disinvestment, sanctions and consciousness-raising efforts, anti-apartheid activism was coordinated both by established groups such as TransAfrica and the American Committee on Africa, but also the newer Free South Africa Movement. The new organization extended the repertoire of anti-apartheid, bringing forms of 'political theatre' to the movement and effectively extending public awareness of events in South Africa. The success of the US anti-apartheid movement reflected a genuine divide between popular sentiment and the administration's realpolitik with regard to apartheid, and built on the premise that it 'more thoroughly understood public sentiment than Reagan's foreign policy experts'.[74]

The apartheid state in crisis

Despite implacable opposition from British and US political leaders, sanctions and disinvestment were critical elements of global anti-apartheid campaigns, and arguably its most significant tool of persuasion. But the economic pressures that the apartheid state faced in the late 1980s were rooted in structural weaknesses and broader pressures beyond those imposed by Western governments. Moreover, the escalating crisis in the townships did little to encourage the confidence of business and trading partners. In August 1985, shortly after the first state of emergency had been declared, Botha opened the National Party congress in Durban with a speech that many had expected would signal a decisive break from apartheid, accelerate the pace of reform and open up negotiations with the ANC. Instead, Botha delivered a rebuke to his critics and announced his determination to continue with the reform programme as it stood, insisting that any other direction would result in a 'drift into faction strife, chaos and poverty'.[75] Unsurprisingly, the speech was not welcomed by the ANC, who argued that Botha had effectively confirmed their assertion that 'apartheid cannot be reformed'.[76] Of more immediate impact was the response of international investors, who had already begun to lose faith in the stability of the South African economy. In the aftermath of Botha's 'Rubicon speech', the US Chase Manhattan Bank declared that it would no longer make loans to the South African government, and that outstanding debt would need to be repaid. Unable to service its debts, South Africa saw levels of international investment fall rapidly, while a range of major businesses, including General Motors and IBM (in addition to Barclays, described earlier) withdrew from South Africa.[77]

These developments exacerbated the crisis in the South African economy, which had been in recession since the early 1980s. South African debt to foreign lenders had grown significantly in the early 1980s, as the government sought to balance the costs of maintaining apartheid in the face of structural weaknesses, particularly with regard to trade and labour. Despite the increasing importance of manufacturing, the mining sector, and gold in particular, continued to be a critical element of the national economy. The combination of falling gold prices and rising wages, spurred by the reforms to trades union legislation, meant that the revenue from gold exports was no longer a reliable cushion against economic pressures.[78] Added to this were the increasing costs of the system of apartheid itself. By 1984, the ministry responsible for the oversight of the black population (once 'Native Affairs', but by then 'Co-Operation and Development') claimed 10 per cent of the total budget for the state. Almost the same again was spent on the administrative costs of the ten Bantustans, while the state was also obliged to fund fifteen separate education departments. Furthermore the level of expenditure on security, including both South African military engagements in the region and the maintenance of emergency powers within the country, had spiralled in the years of 'reform'.[79]

While the 'Nkomati Accord' of 1984 had reduced South African involvement in the civil war between the Mozambican government and RENAMO rebels, the apartheid state continued to engage in extensive military operations in the region. As the Commonwealth Eminent Persons Group discovered in 1985, South African forces regularly launched incursions into neighbouring territories throughout the 1980s. To the northwest, fighters from the South-West Africa People's Organization (SWAPO) began from the early 1980s to launch attacks into Namibia, prompting the deployment of SADF forces in southern Angola. By the mid-1980s, South African forces were deeply committed to the conflict, which had become a proxy for Cold War antagonism. The MPLA government, in addition to Soviet financial support, was backed by a Cuban military force of over 30,000, while the United States maintained covert support for Jonas Savimbi's UNITA. As fighting intensified in the second half of the 1980s, South Africa committed increasing numbers of its forces, many of them conscripts, to the conflict.

In August 1987, the SADF and UNITA launched a major attack against the Angolan military in the southern town of Cuito Cuanavale. While the mission was initially a success, South African forces were unable to overcome Cuban reinforcements and by March 1988 had begun to suffer setbacks that revealed the underlying vulnerability of the hitherto powerful South African military. Significantly, the South African air force, hampered by the effects of the arms embargo, was unable to provide adequate support for the attack on the town. At the same time, the costs of the war, coming on top of the economic crisis exacerbated by the withdrawal of international loans, meant that long-term military efforts were no longer viable.[80] In the context of an emerging rapprochement between the Soviet Union and the United States, South Africa agreed to allow elections in Namibia in 1989 as part of a deal that saw Soviet and Cuban military withdrawal from Angola. Cuito Cuanavale therefore marked a turning point in the political dynamics of the region.

The crisis inside South Africa had also reached a level that seemed intractable. The security forces, drawing on methods employed by paramilitary groups such as Koevoet in the border war, engaged in covert and brutal activities against UDF 'comrades' and others involved in resistance movements. But, by the late 1980s, the apartheid state had increasingly begun to deputize its struggle against internal resistance to black allies, including Bantustan authorities, but also more diffuse and irregular groups of vigilantes and migrant labourers. Vigilante-style activities had been evident since the 1970s, but coordinated vigilantism expanded dramatically in the period 1985–86. Groups would impose control over neighbourhoods, seemingly with the approval of the police and state authorities. Often, groups would enforce 'order', allowing township authorities and the military to begin activities designed to 'win the hearts and minds' of local residents. As contemporary observers noted, South African vigilantes appeared to resemble similar phenomena across the Third World, notably in the Philippines and Central America. Effectively, it seemed as if state repression had been privatized, with unofficial groups taking the place of the formal security services. In early 1986, a group known as Witdoeke attacked informal settlements in Cape Town, displacing around 70,000 people over the course of a few weeks, and thereby effecting 'removals' that state officials had been unable to complete.[81]

Vigilantism was often associated with attempts to establish or maintain political power within Homelands. In 1985, the Chief Minister of KwaNdebele, Simon Skosana, established Mbokotho, what was in effect a private army deployed in support of his ambitions to secure 'independence' from Pretoria. After a series of violent episodes, including the abduction and beatings of hundreds of residents, Skosana was forced to abandon his plans.[82] The most intense violence associated with Homeland politics was experienced in the region of Natal between Durban and Pietermaritzburg. Here, UDF-supporting activists became engaged in what has been described as a 'low intensity civil war' with supporters of Inkatha, an ethnic nationalist movement that had its roots in a Zulu cultural organization established by King Dinuzulu in the 1920s. The movement had been revived in the mid-1970s by the leader of the Kwazulu Homeland, Mangosuthu Buthelezi. By the early 1980s, Buthelezi, a former ANC supporter, had moved closer to Pretoria and had come to be regarded by some (notably the British Prime Minister Margaret Thatcher) as a potential alternative national leader for black South Africans. From 1984–85, however, violence between Inkatha supporters and organizations affiliated with the UDF escalated into a vicious spiral of violent attacks and reprisals.

The authorities did little to address the violence and intimidation undertaken by Inkatha supporters, while many hundreds of UDF activists were arrested and detained.[83]

The deepening crisis in South Africa in the second half of the 1980s prompted tentative moves towards negotiation between the government and the ANC, by that time established within the international community as the primary voice of the majority. Hardliners in government remained convinced that 'counter-insurgency' measures would eventually bring stability, but already more fundamental reforms of the apartheid system were beginning to emerge. Pass Laws were abolished in 1986, along with other key elements of apartheid, including the legal ban on mixed marriages. While these changes, together with increased recognition of the need to improve the training and conditions of black workers, continued to focus on urban 'insiders', it was clear that some of the fundamental principles of the apartheid system were being undermined. This was particularly clear within the realm of the economy where, as Feinstein suggests, 'the retreat from the economic dogmas of previous decades was largely complete' by 1986.[84] In the 1960s and 1970s, South African corporations, such as Anglo-American, had been able to expand their domestic interests in order to offset restrictions on their ability to engage in investment overseas; by the mid-1980s, however, the limits of domestic expansion – without dramatic redistribution – were clear, and a negotiated settlement seemed the only path to globalization.[85]

From 1985, the ANC began to host meetings with South African business leaders whose concerns over the economic impact of the crisis were beginning to outweigh their antipathy towards majority rule. In 1985, Gavin Relly, chair of Anglo-American, led a delegation to meet Oliver Tambo and other ANC leaders in Zambia.[86] Botha denounced the meeting as a 'betrayal', and it seemed clear that business leaders were moving decisively towards active engagement in the political process. In 1986, the leader of the Progressive Party, Frederick van Zyl Slabbert, stepped down from parliament and took a leading role in the formation of the Institute for a Democratic Alternative for South Africa. Under its auspices, he organized a meeting between Afrikaner intellectuals and an ANC delegation in Dakar, Senegal in 1987. These meetings went some way to dispel fears that the ANC was instinctively anti-business and driven by a visceral hatred of Afrikaners. At the very least, the meetings signalled to the South African government that the ANC was a serious contender for power that could not simply be treated with disdain.[87] At the same time, the public discourse of business began to take on board the language of resistance; even as campaigners in Europe were picketing their petrol stations in protest against their support for apartheid, Shell placed an advert in the South African press declaring that 'You can't silence the people'.[88] Through the second half of the 1980s, reformist whites and ANC representatives used transnational spaces as neutral territory upon which to slowly build a dialogue that would eventually lead to formal negotiations.

In 1986, a conference on South African education in New York provided an opportunity for a meeting between Pieter de Lange, chair of the Afrikaner Broederbond, to meet figures from the ANC, including its International Director, Thabo Mbeki. Over the next four years, Mbeki carefully developed lines of communication between the ANC in exile and influential Afrikaners, including the academic Willie Esterhuyse, who attended a series of meetings at Mells Park, the English country house owned by Consolidated Gold Fields.[89] Mbeki, a skilled and intelligent diplomat, was able to build working relations with Afrikaner interlocutors, making it possible to imagine negotiations between the ANC and the government itself. Key to the process was the imprisoned leader, Nelson Mandela, who had publicly rebuffed Botha's offer in 1985 to release him from jail if he abandoned the armed struggle. The following year, Mandela made initial attempts to engage officials in discussion, which resulted in a meeting with the Justice Minister, Kobie Coetsee, in 1987. Soon, Mandela was in regular contact with a small group of officials, including Niël Barnard, the intelligence officer to whom Esterhuyse had reported details of the ongoing meetings with Mbeki.[90] Thus, by around 1988, both the ANC and key figures closely connected with the South African government had concluded that stalemate was all that could be achieved through the cycle of resistance and repression that had developed in the years following the Vaal Uprising. In a clear signal that state repression was no longer able to completely stifle resistance, the virtual banning of UDF activities in February 1988 prompted the formation of a coalition of opposition groups, notably the UDF and Congress of South African Trade Unions (COSATU), under the banner of the Mass Democratic Movement (MDM).

For the state authorities, a critical shift came in January 1989 when Botha suffered a stroke, inhibiting his ability to engage in negotiations on Namibia's future and prompting him to resign his leadership of the National Party. The new party leader, F. W. de Klerk, took over as acting State President in August and began to put in place a strategy for political change. The elections in September gave further evidence that the National Party was losing ground to its rivals at either end of the political spectrum, suggesting that there was a popular appetite for a change in political direction. In the week after the election, tens of thousands of anti-apartheid protestors marched in Cape Town, led by church leaders and the city's mayor. De Klerk grasped the moment of opportunity that came with the rapid collapse of Soviet hegemony in Eastern Europe. Many in the ANC had already begun to realize that a shift in superpower relations, resulting from the foreign policy of the new Soviet leader Mikhail Gorbachev, had profound implications for their ability to sustain an armed struggle. Tambo met with Gorbachev in Moscow in 1986, and an official ANC mission was established in the following year. Initial confidence in the new regime's support for the ANC were tempered, however, by the growing emphasis on detente within the Soviet political elite, particularly the Minister for Foreign Affairs, Eduard Shevardnadze, whose ambiivalent position on violent resistance raised questions regarding future directions of the country's engagement with South Africa.[91]

A further signal that the South African movements could no longer rely on the single most important source of funds for MK came when the Soviet military transported MK fighters from Angola to Uganda following the diplomatic agreement to remove multinational forces from Angola and allow Namibian independence. For de Klerk, the fall of the Berlin Wall in November 1989 was a moment of opportunity to seize the initiative; for the ANC it was the moment at which many of their fundamental assumptions were shaken. De Klerk moved quickly. After visiting key European political leaders, including Margaret Thatcher and Helmut Kohl, de Klerk announced in parliament, in February

1990, that key apartheid legislation would be repealed, that all liberation movements would be unbanned and that all political prisoners would be released.

In its August 1989 Harare Declaration, the OAU Committee on South Africa gave its endorsement to the conditions that the ANC had laid down before it would enter into formal negotiations with the South African government. Despite receiving the backing of both the OAU and the United Nations, the ANC were initially outmanoeuvred in efforts to secure international support during the negotiation process. Both Mandela and de Klerk recognized the importance of international support in the period after 1990. Although the South African government was particularly keen to persuade Western powers to end the series of sanctions that had been imposed during the late 1980s, it was clear to both sides that the support of African states was critical to their success. From 1990 to 1992, Mandela made multiple visits to Kenya and Nigeria, while de Klerk combined visits to both countries with unprecedented official state visits across the continent. South African economic power was brought to bear as a diplomatic tactic, with a large business delegation accompanying de Klerk to Nigeria in 1992. The success of de Klerk's 'soft power' initiatives went some way to dilute the reality of support for the ANC that had been implied in the Harare Declaration. By 1992, he had, it seemed, had succeeded in 'reforming apartheid just enough to allow South Africa's return to the international community, but without entirely surrendering to the ANC'.[92]

The global dimensions of the 'negotiated revolution'

Mandela's walk to freedom on 11 February 1990 was an event for which the description 'globally significant' was no exaggeration. In part, of course, this was because the presence of television news reporters from across the world made it so. But Mandela's release was more than an exercise in media communication. It was, as his biographer Anthony Sampson eloquently described, a mythical moment, embodying the 'triumph of the human spirit, the return of the lost leader'.[93] Alongside the image of Berliners dancing on the wall that had divided their city, photographs of Mandela walking from Victor Verster prison captured a genuine spirit of the times, a moment of optimism. Mandela was, in short, presented as a saviour of liberal democracy. The process by which South Africa came to hold fully democratic elections some four years later was, however, to prove complex, difficult, chaotic and marred by violence.

The scope of de Klerk's speech in parliament that prefigured Mandela's release surprised most onlookers. In unbanning all the liberation movements, including the Communist Party, de Klerk signalled both the seriousness of his intentions and the degree of confidence he felt in securing a settlement that might entrench minority interests and limit the power of the ANC. Many of the leaders of the ANC remained in exile, while Tambo himself was seriously ill after suffering a major stroke in late 1989. The year 1990, however, saw the rebuilding of an ANC organization within South Africa as its leaders returned, and the forging of an alliance between Congress, the SACP and COSATU – known as the 'Tripartite Alliance' – which would go on to dominate post-apartheid parliamentary politics into the twenty-first century. By 1991, when formal negotiations got underway at the Convention for a Democratic South Africa (CODESA), the positions of the ANC and other major political groups were clear. The ANC, confident in the support of the majority of the population, stood firm for a strong unitary state; the National Party sought the protection of minority rights and leaned towards federalist arrangements. Inkatha, which Buthelezi had transformed into the Inkatha Freedom Party, held out firmly for a federalist structure, as did other former Bantustan leaders. But, while clear divisions dogged the process, points of compromise began to emerge, notably around the protection of property rights and measures to safeguard the interests of private capital. The National Party were willing to give ground on formal power-sharing on racial lines, while the ANC began to dampen its socialist rhetoric around the nationalization of mines, embedded in its commitment to the principles of the Freedom Charter, and publicly restated by Mandela on his release.[94] The breakthrough came in 1992, when SACP leader Joe Slovo wrote of the need to offer 'sunset clauses' as concessions to the white establishment, especially civil servants and other officials whose support was critical to a peaceful transition.[95]

Outside the negotiation process, South Africa witnessed increasing violence, mainly between supporters of the ANC and Inkatha. As in the late 1980s, the most intense violence was associated with the continuing struggle between the ANC and Inkatha in Kwazulu-Natal. In March 1990, in what came to be known as the 'Seven Day War', the 'comrades' in and around Pietermaritzburg faced a renewed onslaught from Inkatha supporters, resulting in over 100 deaths and the destruction of 3,000 homes.[96] At the same time, the conflict between ANC and Inkatha supporters spread to the Rand townships through migrant workers. Fearing that the violence represented a deliberate attempt to stall the progress of negotiations, the ANC began to speak publicly of the existence of a 'Third Force' of elements within the security forces and others who were set against any form of democratic transition. As subsequent reports suggested, the intransigent elements within the state had indeed sought to manipulate the progress of negotiations by fermenting violence. Despite denials of state involvement, and despite the ANC formally ending the armed struggle in 1991, the period of negotiations was the most violent phase of the apartheid era, with around 14,000 deaths in the years between the release of Mandela and his inauguration as president in 1994. Even where the violence was not obviously coordinated, the culture of killings and counter-killings reflected the degree to which weapons had been almost indiscriminately distributed by both sides in the late 1980s and early 1990s. In their attempt to secure the support of 'the people' the security services and MK had facilitated the creation of local factions whose political agendas often blurred into criminal activities.[97]

A moment of crisis in 1992 came close to bringing the collapse of the negotiations. That June, residents of the Boipatong township south of Johannesburg were attacked by hundreds of Inkatha supporters, mostly residents of a nearby hostel for migrant workers. More than forty township residents were killed in what was one of the bloodiest examples of a phenomenon that had come to mark political tensions on the Rand since the start of negotiations – between 1990 and 1992, nearly fifty massacres had taken place in the

Vaal region, resulting in over 1,200 deaths.[98] Boipatong, however, was transformed into a political crisis when the ANC accused the South African authorities of complicity in the massacre, and withdrew from the formal negotiations process. ANC leaders including Mandela, Mbeki and Joe Modise successfully lobbied the OAU ministers' conference in Senegal for a strong declaration of support, while the UN Security Council adopted a resolution condemning the violence (although, thanks to Britain and Nigeria, the final resolution watered down its direct criticism of the South African government).[99] Nevertheless, it took several months of behind-the-scenes discussions between the ANC's chief negotiator, Cyril Ramaphosa, and his opposite number in the National Party, Roelf Meyer before a formal Record of Understanding was agreed between the two parties in September 1992. Shortly before Mandela and de Klerk resumed formal discussions in September 1989, troops in the Ciskei capital of Bisho had opened fire on a crowd of ANC supporters led by Ramaphosa and Ronnie Kasrils.

The violence continued through to 1994, but negotiations continued, even after the murder of the MK leader, Chris Hani, by white right-wingers in early 1993. Although events in Kwazulu-Natal and on the Rand were perhaps the most damaging examples of the impact of Homeland politics on the negotiation process, events elsewhere underlined the difficulties that the fractured structures of apartheid created for the construction of an integrated democracy. For some Bantustan leaders, the process of negotiation was an existential threat to their personal power that they opposed to the last. In March 1994, the Bophuthatswana leader, Lucas Mangope, turned his back on the elections planned for the following month, prompting the Homeland's officials and police to strike. Mangope called for support from the right-wing Afrikaner leaders, but when armed militia from the extremist Afrikaner Weerstandsbeweging (AWB) arrived, the Bophuthatswana army mutinied and the white militia were forced into retreat. The defeat of the white right was brutally underlined when black police shot and killed two AWB fighters in full view of international news media. Finally, almost on the very eve of the vote in April, Buthelezi agreed to participate in the elections. And so, on 26 April 1994, South Africa's first wholly democratic elections began. The process was by no means flawless, but it was obvious that the poll was a genuine reflection of the popular will.

As with his release some four years earlier, the inauguration of Nelson Mandela as South Africa's first black president was a 'media event' of global significance. It was, in broadcasting terms, scripted as a form of democratic 'coronation', bound by tradition and enacting a ritualized social rite of passage.[100] If the narrative of South Africa's 'miracle' was shaped by contemporary media discourse, it was also in itself a significant moment in the historical development of a round-the-clock, globalized media network in the final decade of the twentieth century. Just as events such as the US-led military intervention in Iraq in 1991 were shaped by the development of twenty-four hour rolling news delivered by networks such as CNN, South African elections helped to cement the formation of a global telecommunications media. The tragedy of 1994, however, was that the agendas of global media in Africa were exposed by the contrasting treatment of contemporaneous events in South Africa and Rwanda. On 28 April, the final day of voting in South Africa, large numbers of refugees began crossing from Rwanda into

Tanzania, bringing stories of mass killings. International news corporations began to reassign reporters from South Africa – where the electoral process had been relatively undisturbed – to the Rwandan-Tanzanian border. At the time of the elections in South Africa, over 2,000 accredited journalists were present in the country. When the genocide took place in Rwanda, the number was less than twenty.[101]

The South African elections became a global broadcasting event for a number of reasons. In media terms, this was a culmination of events that had first swept through the international press and television in 1960 after the Sharpeville shootings (again, in contrast to the history of communal conflict in Rwanda, which began with the violence associated with the country's independence in 1959). In addition to time scale, the end of apartheid represented a triumph of liberal democracy and human rights. A constitutive part of the process of political negotiation between South African political parties aimed at establishing agreement on the conditions for new elections was the creation of a framework for a new constitution for South Africa. At its heart, constitutional change was a necessary precondition of a non-racial, universal franchise, but the set of rights and principles that was eventually adopted by the South African government went much further. It has become a truism of modern South African political and historical commentary to note that the post-1994 constitution was one of the most liberal and progressive constitutions anywhere in the world: it established equal rights on the basis of race, gender and sexual orientation.

Summary

The new South African constitution was in many ways a reflection of the global political and ideological influences present at the birth of the 'new South Africa'. The end of the Cold War and the collapse of the Soviet Union played a part in the political calculations that led to the opening up of a space for negotiations; the consequent shifts in global power also shaped the transition to democracy and the form that the new democratic state took. In a sense, the South African constitution embodied best practice in legal frameworks for human rights as conceived in the early 1990s, but it also represented the product of a 'top down' process directed by Afrikaner and African nationalist leaders, rather than the popular will. In the years following the Soweto Uprising, apartheid had been undermined by a combination of political, social and economic forces. The efforts and sacrifices of the South African people had been sustained in a popular struggle against a state whose legitimacy to rule was continuously challenged, which at the same time fostered social divisions that would test the post-apartheid governments. The new ANC-led government faced the challenge of reconciling the varied elements of South African society and politics in the construction of a stable democracy. Moreover, the final years of apartheid had seen the increasing influence of global political and economic factors, which both provided opportunities for South African political leaders and constrained their agency. Moreover, the politics of transition had been shaped by the shift to a 'unipolar' political order, in which liberal democracy and free-market capitalism became the norm. The emerging 'Washington Consensus' was a critical element of international relations during the period in which South Africa moved towards democracy; it would play a determining role in the direction of post-apartheid politics.

Further reading

Barber, James, John Barratt and South African Institute of International Affairs. *South Africa's Foreign Policy: The Search for Status and Security 1945–1988*. Cambridge: Cambridge University Press, 1990.

Dubow, Saul. *South Africa's Struggle for Human Rights*. Athens, OH: Ohio University Press, 2012.

Friedman, Steven and Doreen Atkinson, eds. *The Small Miracle: South Africa's Negotiated Settlement*. Randburg, South Africa: Ravan Press, 1994.

Klotz, Audie. *Norms in International Relations: The Struggle against Apartheid*. Ithaca, NY: Cornell University Press, 1995.

Lodge, Tom and Bill Nasson. *All, Here, and Now: Black Politics in South Africa in the 1980s*. London: Hurst, 1992.

Nesbitt, Francis Njubi. *Race for Sanctions: African Americans against Apartheid, 1946–1994*. Bloomington, IN: Indiana University Press, 2004.

Norval, Aletta J. *Deconstructing Apartheid Discourse*. New York: Verso, 1996.

Pityana, Barney, ed. *Bounds of Possibility: Legacy of Steve Biko and Black Consciousness*. London: Zed Books, 1992.

Price, Robert M. *The Apartheid State in Crisis: Political Transformation in South Africa, 1975–1990*. New York: Oxford University Press, 1991.

Seekings, Jeremy. *The UDF: A History of the United Democratic Front in South Africa, 1983–1991*. Oxford: James Currey, 2000.

South African Democracy Education Trust, ed. *The Road to Democracy in South Africa*. Vol. 2: *1970–80*. Pretoria: Unisa Press, 2006.

Thomas, Scott. *The Diplomacy of Liberation: The Foreign Relations of the African National Congress since 1960*. London ; New York: Tauris Academic Studies, 1996.

Thörn, Håkan. *Anti-Apartheid and the Emergence of a Global Civil Society*. Basingstoke: Palgrave Macmillan, 2006.

CHAPTER 8
GLOBALIZATION AND THE NEW SOUTH AFRICA

The first democratic elections in South Africa in 1994 were an event of global significance. In a standard popular narrative, the largely orderly election process seemed to represent a climactic moment in South African history that was in itself symbolic of a transformed global political situation. What better illustration could there be of the triumph of liberal democracy and the 'end of history' than the images of thousands of black South Africans queuing to vote across the country? The dominant narrative was one of negotiations and peaceful transition, at the centre of which was the guiding hand of extraordinary political leaders. In the years that followed, the process of constructing a new South Africa placed primary emphasis on the building of consensus, reconciliation, and a political order based upon liberal freedoms and equality. The establishment of majority rule marked an end point to an era of European colonialism and appeared to underline the construction of a new world order in the aftermath of the Cold War.

Such seductive narratives conceal, however, the contingencies, complexities and contradictions of the political and social transformations that took place at the end of the twentieth century in South Africa. Post-apartheid South Africa was nevertheless subject to significant global influences that differed, in both degree and form, from those that had pertained through to the end of apartheid. The coming of liberal democracy to South Africa resulted in a state that finally conformed to the post-war norms of sovereignty and popular democracy, just as the system of nation states was itself becoming corroded by global influences. The post-apartheid nation emerged at a moment when the various political, economic, social and cultural developments that have been conceptualized as a process of 'globalization' began to exert strengthening pressure on the system of nation states that had structured world politics since the middle of the twentieth century.

South African political and social experience since 1994 has been shaped by a number of interlinked but distinctive, dimensions of its relationship with the wider world. Post-apartheid South Africa has been powerfully influenced by the global discourse of human rights and the ideologies of liberal democracy, which emerged in part from the construction of the politics of the transition to democracy itself. Similarly, its political economy has been shaped by the processes of globalization that accelerated even as the country emerged from the apartheid era, and have – arguably – set limits on the capacity to effectively rectify the inequalities entrenched by colonialism, segregation and apartheid. By the end of the twentieth century, the 'New South Africa' had also been shaped by its connections with the region and continent, as the country positioned itself as an African power.

Rights and reconciliation

In early 1993, following the agreement between the National Party and the ANC, formalized in the Record of Understanding, a Multiparty Negotiating Forum was created to oversee the process of transition and prepare the way for the elections that were held in the following year. A particularly significant focus of the negotiations was the debate around the particular constitutional structures that would legitimate the transition. These discussions began a process of constitutional rebuilding that resulted in the third new constitutional arrangement in two decades, but the first to be centred on a formal Bill of Rights. The 1996 Constitution provided a model for a post-apartheid state that replaced parliamentary with constitutional sovereignty, overseen by a Constitutional Court. As with all constitutions, South Africa's was built not simply on the foundations of a process of national reconstruction and reconciliation, but reflected the wider body of ideas and knowledge that informed lawmakers at the historical juncture in which it was drafted. In the early 1990s, this meant a moment, in the immediate aftermath of the Cold War, in which 'liberal constitutional principles were hegemonic'.[1] The principles of human rights, upon which the post-apartheid state were founded, were not self-evident truths, but the reflection of contemporary ideological frameworks.

The language of individual rights had been widely employed as a counter to the discourse of apartheid, particularly by international observers. In 1958, the American Committee on Africa organized its Declaration of Conscience against apartheid, which self-consciously drew upon (and was timed to coincide with the tenth anniversary of) the Universal Declaration of Human Rights. Apartheid was a distinctive reference point in the developing discourse of human rights throughout the 1960s and 1970s. It had been a focus of discussion at the Tehran UN Conference on Human Rights in 1968, which, although a disappointment to many Western human rights activists, had provided an opportunity for Third World states to promote a reading of rights as a means of elevating collectivist definitions of rights over those that emphasized individual freedoms.[2]

In the aftermath of the Soweto Uprising and the death of Black Consciousness leader Steve Biko, international responses to apartheid were again framed with reference to human rights, and the thirtieth anniversary of the Universal Declaration in 1978 was marked by the proclamation of the International Anti-Apartheid Year.[3] In the case of Biko's death, questions of the legal rights of detainees and medical ethics were of particular concern.[4] At the same time, human rights took an increasingly important role in shaping US foreign policy towards South Africa. Material interests and economic realities continued to play a predominant role – even under President Carter, the most vociferous critic of the apartheid regime from the White House, human rights principles did not lead to economic sanctions. Nevertheless, some have argued that human rights concerns, as an embodiment of liberal values, came to override a realist approach in the face of the violence and apparent intransigence of the apartheid state in the mid-1980s.[5] There were apparent contradictions in Washington's position, of course, particularly when Reagan condemned apartheid during a speech on Human Rights Day in 1984 despite his firm opposition to practical measures against Pretoria – and the US government's own record in its sphere of influence, particularly in Latin America.

Despite the frequent references to human rights in the language of opposition to apartheid, until the late 1970s, these had invariably been tied to citizenship within the nation state, rather than rights in their broadest sense. During the latter part of the 1970s however, as legal historian Samuel Moyn has recently argued, a new interpretation of human rights as a transnational regime able to override sovereignty and discipline the behaviour of nation states, began to emerge.[6] While nationalist movements in southern Africa were primarily concerned with questions of political and civil rights, of citizenship and democracy, the transnational solidarity movement that developed to support these struggles began to take on board, and reshape, notions of rights – both because of their instrumental value, and because a transnational definition of rights was in closer accord with the organizational and ideological principles of an international solidarity movement. But even at the level of transnational activism, talk of human rights was more of 'an incipient protest language' than a fundamental principle of anti-apartheid, which was framed as anti-racist protest as often as it was pro-rights.[7]

The use of human rights by South African anti-apartheid and nationalist movement was similarly diffuse until at least the mid-1980s. In fact, some groups saw the language of rights at certain times as an anathema to black nationalism. One of the most severe complaints of Africanists in response to the Freedom Charter in the 1950s was its basis in an abstract rights rather than an anti-colonial struggle for independence.[8] By the 1980s, though, human rights were an increasingly important focus of opposition to apartheid, led by an emerging body of rights-oriented NGOs, including Lawyers for Human Rights and the Legal Resources Centre, which mounted legal challenges to the Pass Laws and other elements of apartheid legislation.[9] Similarly, internal resistance movements in the 1980s began to use the language of human rights both in the 'traditional' sense to refer to claims to political rights, but also as a way of addressing the actions of the state – and apartheid itself – as an abuse of fundamental human rights. Human rights entered South African political discourse in the second half of the 1980s and early 1990s, when the National Party and ANC almost simultaneously discovered the benefits of rights talk in legitimating their own political agendas. For both sides, the promotion of individual rights appeared to offer protections to their core interests – for the ANC, in order to promote democracy and for the National Party, to protect minority groups within a democratic system.

The language of rights came to play a dominant role in the process by which the new political dispensation after 1994 was legitimated, both inwardly in the minds of South Africans, and also in an outward facing sense, with regard to international observers. The new South African constitution is rightly regarded as a remarkably progressive and liberal document, with wide ranging provisions for the protection of citizenship rights as well as social and economic rights. Human rights were also embedded in the process of reconciliation in the years immediately following the 1994 election, most importantly through the operation of the Truth and Reconciliation Commission (TRC). At the heart of the public narrative associated with the new South Africa was the notion of reconciliation, that South Africans would come together to forge a new national identity based on the mutual respect of differences, and of collective ownership of the task of building a post-apartheid society. Such were the ideals promoted by national leaders in the early years of the post-apartheid state, designed with both a domestic and international agenda in mind. The idea of national reconciliation was seen as critical to ensuring the stability of the post-apartheid state, and that a formal reconciliation process was required in order to build a future on 'forgiveness'.[10]

The TRC first sat in 1996 to investigate abuses of human rights in the years between 1960 and 1994. The process was peculiar to South Africa's transition to democracy, but drew on a series of attempts to establish public processes of healing following periods of authoritarian rule. It built upon models of truth hearings established in Latin America, but diverged from them in significant ways. Notably, it included a series of amnesty hearings, in which perpetrators of human rights abuses might apply to have their crimes absolved in return for public acknowledgement of their actions. The decision to set aside retributive justice in the name of national reconciliation was an innovation that was by no means uncontroversial, and some prominent figures, such as the family of Steve Biko, refused to engage with the Commission as a consequence. Alongside the amnesty hearings, the TRC gave individuals an opportunity to present public testimony of their experiences. Testimonies, such as that of the family of the UDF activist Matthew Goniwe, revealed the extent of the brutal repression of political opposition by the apartheid state. But, for some critics, its structures individualized the nature of human rights abuses, and in so doing obscured the more generalized and systematic denial of rights under apartheid.[11] Others suggested that the narrow, Christian-redemptive narrative of the Commission, embodied in its Chair, the former Archbishop of Cape Town, Desmond Tutu, served as a platform for the legitimation of the liberal-democratic post-apartheid state.[12]

The TRC has been cast as both triumph and failure, as responsible for the broad acceptance of the post-apartheid political dispensation and as denial of justice. The ambivalence of political leaders from all sides meant that no real light was shed on the complicity of major figures in the brutalities associated with the struggle. Furthermore, the TRC tended to create a framework whereby responsibility for human rights abuses fell upon individuals, most notoriously Eugene de Kock, head of the counter-insurgency unit based in Vlakplaas near Pretoria, which operated as a death squad for the apartheid regime in the late 1980s. Although it is clear that the security forces operated under the oversight of officials, no political figures were or have been subject to investigation, while P. W. Botha himself refused to testify to the TRC. Similarly, the ANC refused to allow the Commission to examine its operation of MK camps in Angola or the activities of Mbokodo.

At the heart of the criticisms of the TRC has been its very particular definition of justice, or rather, of the way in which classic standards of retributive justice were sidelined in favour of reconciliation. In this view, 'reconciliation' excluded the possibility of justice for the families of high-profile victims of the apartheid state, including that of Steve Biko. Others have highlighted the ways in which the TRC represented a form of 'victor's justice', while others still have argued that the whole TRC process represented an attempt to legitimate the principles of liberal democracy and embed them at the heart of the political culture of the new South Africa. Perhaps most compelling, though, was the argument that the TRC sacrificed accountability in the name of building a 'culture' of reconciliation and human rights.[13] Rather than recognizing human rights as functional tools to protect individuals from abuse at the hands of the state and other institutions, the embrace of constitutionalism and human rights in the 1990s has often appeared more of an exercise in the legitimation of the post-apartheid state. Moreover, while the Constitutional Court has had some success in holding the powerful ANC government to account, not least with regard to the right of access to antiretroviral drugs, the politics of human rights in the post-apartheid period have been more fraught than the architects of the constitutional process may have hoped. As such, human rights and the constitutional protection of liberal democracy may have offered more of an indication of the global historical context in which the post-apartheid settlement was achieved, than a reflection of the principles underlying the political development of South Africa since 1994.

The new South Africa and the constraints of globalization

The processes associated with late-twentieth-century globalization have affected South Africa in varied ways, in some cases underlining the country's post-apartheid status as a middle-income country in the global South, but in other ways re-emphasizing the legacies of apartheid and the international connections that stemmed from its position within the economy of empire in the twentieth century. When assessing the impact of globalization, stark inequalities and underdevelopment have to be set alongside its regional dominance and relatively sophisticated infrastructure. Like many other countries, South Africa has undergone the processes of structural adjustment that characterize the latest phase of globalization, including deregulation of capital and financial markets, the liberalization of trade and the constraint of state interventions aimed at stimulating economic development. In the South African case, however, adjustment was initiated not by the diktat of international organizations such as the International Monetary Fund, but by the ANC government itself, as its leaders proactively instigated liberal reforms that certain policies, such as the tariff reductions of the late 1990s, went further than bodies such as the World Trade Organization deemed necessary.[14]

The apparent conversion of the ANC-led Tripartite Alliance to neo-liberal orthodoxies was identified by some critics as an indication of the superficial nature of the political transformation that had taken place in 1994 – nothing more, it was argued, than an 'elite transition', a handover of power from a white to a black oligarchy.[15] Others have highlighted the contrast between the skilful way in which the ANC conducted political negotiations in the lead-up to the 1994 elections with the lack of preparedness and expertise with which it entered into discussions over the economy. Having focused its attention and resources on developing its military capacity and political allies during its years in exile, the ANC found itself at a disadvantage. Mandela maintained his faith in an economic policy centred around nationalization, until persuaded by international leaders and centrists within the ANC that the realities of globalization would limit the capacity for an ANC government to pursue economic policies at odds with its major investment and trading partners.[16] The ANC policy began to shift as Thabo Mbeki emerged as the leading moderate figure determined to align the ANC and its partners in COSATU and the SACP with the global neo-liberal consensus.

As deputy president under Mandela, Mbeki coordinated the continuing recalibration of ANC economic policies after 1994. When it came to power, the ANC government had adopted the Reconstruction and Development Programme (RDP) as its framework for social and economic policy. The RDP focused on providing 'basic needs' in terms of services and housing, training and skills development. As such, the programme bore strong similarities both to the state-centred policies both of European countries in the aftermath of the Second World War and post-independence African governments. But, even here, despite the broadly social democratic nature of the programme, the impact of the 'Washington consensus' was apparent, and the RDP acknowledged the need to build economic growth in a world economy characterized by trade liberalization and 'reducing protection'.[17] By 1995, however, it was clear that the new government's economic policies were neither inspiring business confidence, nor providing the basic needs that its supporters had called for. Under the guidance of Mbeki, the government launched its Growth, Employment and Redistribution (GEAR) strategy in June 1996, which comprised a series of measures almost wholly in line with the kinds of structural adjustment programme that the World Bank and IMF had imposed upon debt-laden Third World states in the preceding decade. With an emphasis on debt reduction, liberalization of regulations, privatization and wage restraint, GEAR aimed to promote foreign investment and growth.[18]

This initial state-led structural adjustment programme was followed by an expansion of the overseas interests of the major South African conglomerates. South African businesses rapidly increased their interests in the region and African continent more widely – in the first four years after the election of the ANC government, Africa received over 40 per cent of South African foreign investment.[19] By the end of the twentieth century, major South African groups including Anglo-American and Old Mutual had moved their headquarters to London in order to facilitate access to capital and more effectively globalize their own business. These moves, encouraged by the government in the hope of stimulating foreign investment into South Africa, the major South African conglomerates and members of the black state elite – such as the former mineworkers leader Cyril Ramaphosa, who had opted to leave politics and join the private sector after Mbeki was chosen as deputy president of the ANC in late 1994 – were integrated within a transnational class of actors associated with global financial capital. South African globalization, initiated by the state as a response to crisis and the perceived necessity of alignment with global norms embodied in the Washington Consensus, was increasingly beholden to external forces. As it was, global forces would again intervene, in the shape of the 1997 Asian financial crisis, which began to affect the South African economy in the following year, leading to a significant fall in the value of the rand.[20]

The Asian crisis highlighted the extent to which the economic fortunes of post-apartheid South Africa remained tied to the vagaries of the global economy. On the one hand, it provided justification for Mbeki's position, namely that South African economic freedoms required the government to maintain an ongoing commitment to self-imposed structural adjustment, in preference to reliance on the support of global institutions with the result that similar policies would be imposed on the country anyway. In contrast, the Asian crisis prompted some countries to reconsider the principles of the Washington Consensus, turning instead to partnerships and agreements between individual states, rather than a reliance upon global institutions.

Relations between South Africa and India were a particularly prominent aspect of the globalized culture of post-apartheid South Africa at the turn of the twenty-first century. In the first decade of the century, trade between South Africa and India grew at over 20 per cent a year, alongside a comparable growth in investments and bilateral trade agreements. Strong historical connections between the two countries, the size of the South African diasporic Indian population, as well as South Africa's geographical location within the Indian Ocean 'world' provide some explanation for this.[21] South Africa's emergence from relative (although, as we have seen, far from complete) isolation under apartheid coincided with realignments in global trade and financial exchange that made connections between countries of the global South an increasingly important feature of globalization, reinvigorating in turn the importance of the Indian Ocean world itself. From 1994, South Africa also built up increasingly important links with other Asian states, notably Malaysia, which appeared to offer a model for the economic empowerment of an indigenous population in the aftermath of colonialism. Despite the Asian crisis, ANC leaders imported the Malaysian model for affirmative action almost wholesale, in some cases with South African businesses becoming intertwined with Malaysian counterparts.[22]

The 'Asian Renaissance' thus inspired Mbeki's vision of an 'African Renaissance'. But more directly, it helped provide a framework for the empowerment of black business, drawing on the *bumiputra* programme that had been instrumental in transferring economic power from Chinese into Malay hands under the New Economic Policy from the 1970s. By the start of the negotiation process in South Africa, black business leaders were beginning to point to the Malaysian example as they put pressure on the ANC to incorporate Black Economic Empowerment (BEE) policies into their agenda for a new South Africa. Mbeki, despite opposition within the ANC, worked to develop possible BEE initiatives as an aspect of post-apartheid policy – in the process bringing key black professionals into the centre of his circle of power within the ANC.[23] In 1998, a Black Economic Empowerment Commission was established, and published its recommendations in 2001. The aim of BEE, according to the commission, was to 'substantially and equitably transfer and confer the ownership, management and control of South Africa's financial and economic resources to the majority of its citizens'.[24] In practice, BEE initially comprised the large-scale transfer of equity into the hands of a small black elite, many of whom had close connections with the ANC government itself, and attempts were made to broaden the scope of its influence with the broad-based Black Economic Empowerment Act of 2003. In the same year, Mbeki began to reassess the GEAR strategy, and began to talk instead about a dual economy in South Africa, marked by dichotomies of success and failure of boom and dependence, of conspicuous consumption and abject poverty. In his 2006 Nelson Mandela Memorial Lecture, Mbeki decried the culture of acquisition that had been unleashed by liberation, an observation that many found difficult to square with his advocacy of the very policies that seemed to have enabled such a culture to take hold.

Mbeki, African Renaissance and HIV/AIDS

'I am an African'. With these words, Thabo Mbeki opened his speech to mark the passage of the South African Constitution Act in parliament in May 1996.[25] It was a dramatic and multilayered oration, which embraced the transnational communities that made up South Africa, and reflected on the multiple historical pathways that led to the construction of a new South Africa in the aftermath of apartheid. Mbeki spoke of the oppression and violence that had scarred the lives of South Africans, and reasserted the principles of equality, freedom and the rule of law that were embedded in the Constitution. Above all, it rooted the foundations of the new South Africa in Africa itself, and framed Mbeki's political vision in Africanist terms. Africanism and the concept of an African Renaissance lay at the core of Mbeki's political philosophy, and laid the foundations for the relations between South Africa and the wider continent under his leadership.

Under Mbeki, South Africa took a leading role in the promotion of key transnational political institutions. These efforts were underpinned by his conception of an 'African Renaissance', a project that would foster a dynamic political, economic and cultural transformation of the continent, with South Africa at its centre. Elaborating his vision of the African Renaissance in 1998, Mbeki lingered on the realities of corruption, inequality and violence that had blighted the post-colonial history of the continent. The path towards 'renewal' in Africa, Mbeki argued, was to be found in a 'rediscovery of our soul' and 'the restoration of our self-esteem', the simultaneous denial of colonial visions of African inferiority and the post-colonial 'corruption of political power' in the service of the enrichment of a few.[26] Mbeki took a leading role in the creation of the New Partnership for Economic Development, launched in 2001 with the aim of fostering economic regeneration, and South Africa hosted the launch of the African Union in 2002. Both developments marked an attempt to redefine international political institutions in Africa, and beyond the structures that had been established in the immediate aftermath of independence.

Alongside its involvement with multinational organizations, post-apartheid South African leaders have sought to play a more interventionist role in continental diplomacy. This has resulted in varying degrees of success, reflecting the complex intercontinental rivalries that were often obscured by the general opposition to apartheid and support for the South African liberation movements. During Mandela's presidency, tensions developed between his desire to take a principled public stand and the policy of 'quiet diplomacy' advocated by Mbeki. In 1995, Mbeki had persuaded Mandela to refrain from publicly engaging in the campaign against Nigerian President Abacha's imprisonment and trial of the writer Ken Saro-Wiwa. Despite Mbeki's efforts to broker a resolution, Saro-Wiwa was executed on the eve of the Commonwealth Heads of Government meeting in Auckland. Upon hearing the news, Mandela launched into angry condemnation of the Nigerian government's actions, and began to urge the country's expulsion from the Commonwealth and other international organizations, significantly undermining relations between the two governments.

Mbeki's approach to Nigeria in 1995 would prefigure his policy towards Zimbabwe in the early years of the twenty-first century, as the country descended into economic crisis and political chaos following the acceleration of the process of land reform under the veteran leader Robert Mugabe in 2000. As a symbol of resistance to colonialism, Mugabe retained strong support from Africanists in the ANC, while the racialization of the political struggle in the form of violent attacks on white farmers resulted in public condemnation of Mugabe from Britain and other Western powers. Although (like Mandela) Mbeki had little personal regard for Mugabe, and the lack of affinity between the ANC and ZANU-PF had deep roots in liberation struggle hostilities (the exiled ANC had always maintained a closer relationship with Joshua Nkomo's ZAPU), the South African president was determined to take a 'softly-softly' approach towards its neighbour. Recognizing the regional support for Mugabe in the Southern African Development Community (the successor to the apartheid-era SADCC), Mbeki refrained from providing public support to the Zimbabwean opposition Movement for Democratic Change (MDC), but instead sponsored behind-the-scenes talks between MDC and ZANU-PF officials.

Contemporary observers concluded that Mbeki had been outmanoeuvred by Mugabe, but the South African leader's lack of decisive action in support of the people of Zimbabwe was a choice, of deference to an elder statesman and rejection of international pressure to take a stand.[27] It was a moment when Mbeki's instinctive support for African leaders against what might be construed as racist criticism overrode his desire to promote human rights and democracy at the heart of an African Renaissance. At the same time, millions of Zimbabweans had crossed the border into South Africa, joining the burgeoning population of African migrants in major cities. By the end of the first decade of the twenty-first century, South African cities had become home to a number of transnational African communities; Zimbabweans, migrants from Nigeria and Somalia, as well as the wider southern African region, had begun to establish themselves alongside. At points, migrant groups became the focus of resentment, particularly in areas where levels of poverty and inequality had barely altered since 1994, such as

Alexandra in northern Johannesburg, which saw serious unrest in 2008. At the political level, Mbeki's approach to the crisis in Zimbabwe might be seen as an indication that his emphasis on Africanism was designed in part to ward off accusations that his exile experiences had distanced him from his African identity, that he had become a 'Black Englishman' during his studies.[28] But his failure over Zimbabwe coincided with, and was perhaps rooted in his motivations for, his most controversial intervention in global debate, namely his championing of 'dissident' views on HIV/AIDS.

The African HIV/AIDS pandemic was recognized as a major global crisis from the late 1980s, as infection spread from Central and East Africa down trade routes running south. Signs of the coming crisis were beginning to be recognized in the final years of apartheid (and by ANC leaders such as Chris Hani, who began to witness the impact of the disease on South African fighters in MK camps).[29] The arrival of the epidemic in South Africa thus coincided with the transition to democracy, confronting the post-apartheid state with a health crisis on an unprecedented scale, posing material challenges for state institutions, and threatening social and cultural cohesion. The treatment of people suffering from the subsidiary illnesses associated with HIV/AIDS was often hampered by social and cultural stigma, and many refused to acknowledge their own condition, or that of close relatives; death was often explained with reference to euphemistic descriptions of an un-named illness.[30]

Monitoring the spread of infection alone was a difficult task. The number of infections were difficult to estimate and have tended to be extrapolated from its prevalence in pregnant women, which rose from 25 per cent in 1999 to just under 30 per cent five years later. In 2005, the prevalence of HIV in the population aged over 25 had risen to 15.5 per cent and by 2013 it had increased to over 19 per cent.[31] A national strategy to tackle HIV/AIDS was launched in 1992, but during Mandela's presidency the issue became sidelined. Official policy was beset by scandals over funding of questionable schemes to tackle the crisis, most notoriously in the case of the cabinet decision to support clinical trials of Virodene, allegedly an alternative treatment for AIDS, but in reality a combination of industrial solvents. More significantly, the Virodene scandal was an early indication of the degree to which the HIV/AIDS crisis would result in the politicization of claims around scientific truth and authority.

The critical figure in these developments was Mbeki, who began to take up the question of HIV/AIDS as a kind of personal crusade against what he perceived to be a global pharmaceutical establishment. Questioning the link between HIV and the conditions associated with AIDS, Mbeki argued that poverty was the major cause of mortality, not the presence of HIV in an individual's bloodstream. When he made the claims at the opening of the World AIDS Conference in Durban in 2000, Mbeki provoked trenchant criticism, both within South Africa and internationally. In a particularly powerful critique, the Archbishop of Cape Town, Njongonkulu Ndungane, described the government's position as comparable with apartheid. On one level, Mbeki's stance reflected the dilemmas faced by all African political leaders when confronting HIV/AIDS, and was rooted in the undeniable impact that poverty has upon health. However, these dilemmas were compounded by the influence of AIDS dissidents, such as David

Rasnick, who had disputed the link between the human immunodeficiency virus and the syndrome that affects those infected with the virus, leaving them susceptible to secondary infections.

Mbeki therefore moved from the problematic, but less controversial, claim that poverty was a major cause of fatalities from AIDS to the outright denial of the medical consensus on the aetiology of the disease. Both he and his Health Minister, Manto Tshabalala-Msimang, began to call for African solutions to what was defined as an African crisis, and promoted claims that, rather than an expensive and complex regime of medication, those who were HIV-positive could maintain health through careful regulation of diet and nutrition. While Mbeki withdrew from public engagement with the issue in 2002, official sponsorship of alternative therapies for HIV/AIDS continued, which included the granting of permission to the German doctor Matthias Rath to market vitamin supplements as a treatment for HIV.

In opposition to Mbeki stood the Treatment Action Campaign (TAC), launched in 1998. Under the leadership of former ANC activist Zachie Achmat, the TAC pressed the government to establish a programme to prevent transmission of the virus to newborn children of HIV-positive mothers, successfully bringing a case against the government based on the claim that the government's refusal to deliver antiretroviral drugs to HIV-positive mothers was contrary to the Bill of Rights.[32] The TAC also – somewhat ironically – supported the government in its own legal battle with major pharmaceutical companies to allow South Africa the right to import cheap, generic versions of antiretrovirals. However, the South African government under Mbeki remained reluctant to establish a national programme of treatment. In the absence of official support, programmes such as the US President's Emergency Plan for AIDS Relief, which began under the Bush administration in 2003, began to provide access to drugs through private clinics. In 2012, HIV infection rates in South Africa remained the highest in the world.[33]

Explanations for Mbeki's AIDS-denialism have focused on the connections between his stance on HIV and his Africanist political philosophies. The African Renaissance, as we have seen, was centred on a process of self-renewal, which the HIV/AIDS crisis threatened almost at the moment of birth. The conjuncture of South African freedom and the genesis of a major health crisis centred on a sexually transmitted disease appeared to touch upon some of the crudest colonial stereotypes of a 'degenerate' Africa. When Mbeki shifted the focus from a virus to poverty, he was thus moving the issue from the field of African 'values' to the issue of 'development'.[34] And, of course, that moved the HIV/AIDS issue onto the same ground as that covered by Nepad and Black Economic Empowerment. As his biographer, Mark Gevisser, has noted, Mbeki took up the issue of HIV/AIDS at the same time that he began work on Nepad, in the aftermath of the Asian financial crisis.[35] As such, AIDS-denialism might be regarded as a form of anti-globalization, closely connected with his deep frustration at the continuing scepticism and Afropessimism exhibited by the West.

Mbeki's dealings with continental politics and the South African response to the African HIV/AIDS crisis cannot be judged in simple terms of success versus failure. As the successor to Mandela, the feted world statesman often characterized by international observers as an exceptional African, Thabo Mbeki was always likely to find his options for political manoeuvre limited; at the same time, they provided a powerful motivation to set out a new agenda, distinct from Mandela's nation-building through reconciliation. Mbeki set out to forge a new path for his country, based on regional and continental leadership, centred on the concept of African Renaissance, a complicated amalgamation of a celebration of the African spirit and an acknowledgement of the lamentable record of corruption, poverty and violence that had marred the post-colonial history of Africa. On top of all this, he came to power at a point when the very consensus upon which he had built his reputation – alignment with the 'Third Way' of global leaders such as Bill Clinton in the United States and the New Labour project of Tony Blair in Britain – was becoming tarnished. His first term as president saw the beginnings of a recalibration of world politics as the triumph of liberal democracy in the 1990s began to be undermined by ultimately misguided interventionism on the part of the Bush administration. Mbeki was left with the task of guiding the normalization of a country in a time of intensified global interconnectedness, while Mandela had gained the credit for achieving a peaceful transition to democracy.

Democratic challenges and the rise of Jacob Zuma

Given Mbeki's desire to promote moral renewal and his frustrations with the 'get rich quick' attitudes that he saw in the new black elite, it was somewhat ironic that scandal and corruption would shape the political manoeuvres that led to his downfall in 2008. Three years before, Mbeki had dismissed his deputy president, Jacob Zuma, who had been implicated in a corruption scandal connected with a multibillion-dollar arms deal that had been brokered through the Durban businessman Schabir Shaik in 1999. A former Robben Island prisoner and a leading figure in the ANC in exile in the 1970s and 1980s, Zuma had taken prominent roles in Kwazulu-Natal in the 1990s, before being named deputy president in 1999, a post he held until his dismissal in June 2005. As deputy president, he had some success in continental diplomacy, facilitating the start of the peace process in Burundi in 2003.[36]

Throughout the Shaik case, and during a subsequent trial on charges of rape, Zuma received strong support from the youth sections of the ANC and SACP and in December 2007 he was elected President of the ANC. Under Zuma, the ANC National Executive Committee declared that Mbeki was no longer fit to rule South Africa, prompting him to step down as state president in September 2008. After a brief period with Kgalema Motlanthe serving as interim president, Zuma came to power following the elections of 2009.

Investigations into Zuma's dealings with Shaik defined their relationship as one of 'mutually beneficial symbiosis' – a carefully crafted description that raised questions about the nature of the interactions between politics and business in post-apartheid South Africa. The political events of 2008 brought a range of issues, from failure to deliver basic services, unemployment, worsening inequality and the social trauma of HIV/AIDS, to a crisis point. It was Zuma's successful marshalling of a populist coalition of supporters from the political left into a revolt against the distant leadership of Mbeki and his moderate, reformist approach. The wider political challenges to South African were clear, but contemporary observers retained optimism that the independence of the judiciary, media and civil society groups, taken together with the emergence of clear camps within the ANC, meant that 'all [was] not lost for democracy'.[37]

In his contest with Mbeki, Jacob Zuma presented himself effectively at the head of a populist opposition to the faceless and technocratic politics that had developed under Mbeki. He drew on the expressive language of the anti-apartheid struggle, embodied in his performance of the song 'Umshini Wami' ('Bring Me My Machine Gun'), which had connected the township rebels of the 1980s with their comrades in MK camps north of the Limpopo. When Zuma revived the song during the Shaik trial in 2005, he sought to retrieve the symbolic power of the 1980s culture of resistance. But, bringing 'the dancing body and song' back to South African public discourse, Zuma also revealed the instability and unruliness of post-apartheid politics.[38]

Zuma came to power, therefore, as an alternative to the kind of politics represented by Mbeki, backed by left-of-centre elements of the Tripartite Alliance of ANC, SACP and COSATU, combined with ethnic support in KwaZulu-Natal. But he also constructed a web of political and business affiliates around his presidency, and the growth in his personal wealth after 2010 has been presented as evidence of moral dubiousness and corruption. The most prominent illustration of Zuma's alleged misuse of his office for personal gain was the major renovation of his homestead at Nkandla, on which public funds amounting to several millions of Rand were spent, ostensibly on security. At the same time Zuma, and many in his own family, became associated with an array of deals relating to public works and contracts with state institutions. Business connections, such as those with the Gupta family, seemed increasingly central to Zuma's power.[39]

Debates around corruption, however, did not begin or end with Zuma. The idea that South African public officials were tainted and morally dubious was widespread and long-standing; a survey just two years after the election of Mandela found that nearly half of those who responded believed that 'most officials were engaged in corruption'.[40] There was some evidence that, unlike post-colonial governments elsewhere in Africa, the state inherited by the ANC, with a relatively efficient administration and some pre-existing social welfare operations, arguably created a climate that weighed against the development of corruption. Historically, the South African state had remained relatively free from corruption through to the 1970s, but the development of Homelands under Vorster and Botha had resulted in high levels of corruption, characterized by extensive patronage networks, a hollowed-out set of state institutions and the undermining of economic growth.[41] The dysfunction of the late-apartheid state arguably created the conditions for the development of a post-apartheid political culture that allowed the 'instrumentalisation of disorder'.[42] The compromises of transition, allied with a dominant party whose own culture was forged in a political and military struggle not conducive to the development of a culture of transparent accountability, meant that corruption and the politics of patronage would be one of the most pressing challenges to post-apartheid democracy.

'It's Time': South Africa in the post-millennial world

In 2010, the eyes of the world focused on South Africa as the country hosted the sporting mega-event, the FIFA World Cup. Launched under the Sesotho slogan 'Ke Nako' ('It's Time'), the event was lauded by many as a moment of celebration for Africa as a whole. Writing in 2003 in support of the country's bid to host the World Cup, Mbeki declared that hosting the event would serve 'to show that Africa's time has come'; as the first global sporting event to be held on the continent, it was to be a statement of African confidence in accord with his wider vision of African Renaissance. And, as Deputy President Zuma argued, it would also be a major economic boost. Critics noted, however, that spending on infrastructure was directed towards the needs of the FIFA tournament, not necessarily in alignment with the wider social and economic needs of the country.[43] For some the event did at least temporarily foster a 'banal nationalism', in which symbols of South African soccer, from Vuvuzela horns to Bafana Bafana T-shirts, became everyday expressions of national unity that spoke of multiple levels: as a global expression of pan-Africanism, as a claim to South African leadership on the continent, and as a statement to white South Africans.[44]

Although the social and symbolic value of the 2010 World Cup was of greater significance than its economic impact, the country had seen considerable material growth in the first decade of the twenty-first century. From 1994 until 2008, GDP growth had averaged over 3 per cent per year, and over 5 per cent in the years before the global financial crisis of 2008. In the aftermath of the crisis, GDP growth in South Africa fell to around 3 per cent, with further decline to around 1.5 per cent in 2014. Despite significant poverty and inequality, allied with major social challenges that included unemployment and the impact of HIV/AIDS, South Africa under Mbeki had begun to position itself as a significant international power, in both regional associations such as the Southern African Development Community, the continental African Union, and global fora including the Group of Twenty (G20). From 2003, the country joined India and Brazil in a trilateral forum for 'South-South' dialogue. In 2010, South Africa became a formal member of the association of emerging economies known as 'BRICS' (denoting its membership: Brazil, Russia, India, China, South Africa).

From the middle of the first decade of the twenty-first century, South Africa was beginning to position itself in what appeared to be a more uncertain pattern of global governance, in which older forms of liberal internationalist order began to coexist with increased geopolitical competition between powers. A more optimistic vision suggested that a more fluid and indeterminate global order might provide opportunities for South Africa as an influential actor in multiple organizations, from the OECD to the G20 and the BRICS.[45] Observers suggested that how this international status would develop might depend more on its leaders' ambitions and approach rather than its status within global economic and political structures. From 1994, the emphasis in South African foreign policy had supported multilateral efforts to address global challenges within the framework of international law and human rights. This arguably created a widening gap between the country's ambition on the international stage and its domestic goals of economic development and improvement of basic services. Following a tilt to Africa under Mbeki, foreign policy under the Zuma administration was oriented towards Russia and China, with the president visiting the former more than any other power in the first five years of his presidency.[46] South African policy in the second decade of the century began to turn more firmly towards economic interests and an ideological anti-Westernism. Perhaps the most blatant example of the calculus of foreign relations under Zuma came in 2014, when the Tibetan spiritual and political figurehead the Dalai Lama was refused permission to travel to South Africa for a planned conference of Nobel Peace Prize winners, shortly before Zuma undertook an official visit to China.

Insurgent citizens – popular politics, protest and the state under Zuma

In his first term as president, Zuma also faced an increasing volume of popular protest, focused in the main on issues of 'service delivery', poverty and what seemed like an abandonment of the platform that he used in his struggle for the ANC leadership after 2005. Allied with the increasing levels of protest were rising levels of xenophobic violence and attacks on foreigners in informal communities on the margins of major cities. Migrant workers had been targeted in assaults throughout the period since 1994, and research by groups such as the South African Migration Project suggested that immigration was perceived as a significant issue by many South Africans, with nearly 80 per cent of respondents in favour of strict restrictions on foreign workers in the late 1990s.[47] Predictions that this 'underside of democratic nationalism' might become a major social challenge were borne out with a major outbreak of violence in 2008, which originated in Alexandra in northern Johannesburg, but then spread across the country, resulting in over sixty deaths and the displacement of tens of thousands of urban residents.[48] Sporadic episodes of violence against foreigners continued into the following decade, often taking the form of attacks on small-scale retailers and shops in townships, and often targeting specific groups of foreign nationals, including those from Zimbabwe and Somalia.

Analysis of the rise of xenophobia has focused close attention on the definition of citizenship and nation in post-apartheid South Africa, where an inward multicultural inclusivity of the vision of a 'Rainbow Nation' had developed alongside exclusionary practices focused outward on 'illegal' immigrants.[49] A variety of explanatory factors might be deployed in an attempt to understand the attacks, from imagined connections between migrant labour and the apartheid past, through to the culture of self-interest and individualist enrichment fostered by the actions of public officials. Official attempts to address immigration, including the establishment of detention centres such as that at Lindela in Johannesburg, along with suggestions that established groups instigated some occurrences of xenophobic violence, have been seen as evidence of the degree to which the South African state has enabled violence against foreigners to become normalized. Xenophobic attacks might therefore be considered a state discourse centred on the politics of fear that popular movements were unable or unwilling to reject.[50]

There have been notable exceptions, however. In the mid-2000s, a new movement, Abahlali baseMjondolo, emerged in the informal settlements of Durban, subsequently extending into a nationwide campaign in support of shack dwellers, calling for greater provisions of land and improved housing, and protesting against removals and evictions. In some respects, Abahali has drawn on practices of self-improvement and community-based projects that have historical echoes in squatter movements of the mid-twentieth century and Black Consciousness programmes of the 1970s. The movement condemned the xenophobic violence of 2008 unequivocally, releasing a powerful statement declaring that a 'person cannot be illegal. A person is a person wherever they may find themselves'.[51] Alongside Abahlali, protests against the 2008 violence were strongly articulated by groups such as the Anti-Privatisation Forum and the Treatment Action Campaign. The outbreak – and continuation – of xenophobic violence revealed that illiberal and exclusionary political expressions could arise within any sphere, including formal, 'participatory' institutions.

Abahlali baseMjondolo provides an early example of an increasingly intense culture of political protest that emerged in South Africa around the end of the first decade of the twenty-first century. By 2012, South Africa was experiencing an average of around thirty incidents of protest every day, most of which were categorized as 'service delivery protest', that is, small-scale, community-based and rooted in a multiplicity of causes and motivations. In the face of protest, state authorities aggressively sought to restore order, most notoriously in August 2012 when police shot thirty-four striking mineworkers at Marikana, west of Pretoria. The initial shock of the shootings, images of which evoked the apartheid era, was compounded by the revelation that a number of the workers had been killed while attempting to hide from police on a nearby hill. This was no simple matter of a threatening and hostile mob, but brutal suppression of what appeared to have been an orderly protest.[52] The official narrative centred on claims that the strike at heart was a struggle between rival unions, but it appeared that the Marikana strikers had acted, in the first instance, independently of the newly formed Association of Mineworkers and Construction Union (AMCU). The killings, moreover, prompted increased support for the strike, and inspired tens of thousands of workers to join strikes across the mining sector.[53] By the end of the year, strikes had been experienced in manufacturing, building and municipal workers, while farm workers launched a strike across the Western Cape, building on the development of new forms of 'social movement trade union' in the first decade of the century.[54]

Twenty years after the country's first election under a universal franchise, South African political culture faced a number of contradictory dilemmas. On the one hand, support for the ANC remained solid, allowing the party to maintain a commanding, if diminished, majority in the 2014 election. Despite cracks within the Tripartite Alliance, attempts to form political parties that could rival the ANC had limited success. The launch of the Congress of the People party (COPE) in 2008 reflected the divisions in the ANC that had emerged with the battle between Mbeki and Zuma. Under the leadership of the former minister of defence, Mosiuoa Lekota, COPE won over 7 per cent of the popular vote in the 2009 election, but its support declined to less than 1 per cent in 2014. The official parliamentary opposition, the Democratic Alliance (DA), which had its roots in the apartheid-era Progressive Party, was formed in 2000 by a merger between the Democratic Party, New National Party and the Federal Alliance, and increased its support to 22 per cent of the vote in the 2014 election. With the bulk of its supporters in the Western Cape, the DA has struggled to counter the impression that it represented wealthy and largely white interests.

Although some grassroots movements had sought to forge allegiances with mainstream parties (Abahlali received a mixed response when it declared support for the DA in KwaZulu-Natal during the 2014 elections), there was a clear disconnect between popular protest movements and party politics, compounded by an apparent willingness to use formal legal frameworks to supress, rather than regulate, political protest. Some groups nonetheless claimed to represent popular movements in efforts to coordinate new forms of parliamentary opposition, notably the Economic Freedom Fighters, formed in 2013 by former head of the ANC Youth League, Julius Malema. In the elections the following year, it claimed over 6 per cent of the popular vote, becoming the third-largest parliamentary party. With its representatives dressed in red overalls – the uniform of South African domestic workers – the EFF has relied on political spectacle in its confrontations with the ANC in parliament, but its leftist ideology and focus on political education have led some to suggest that its methods have remained within the framework of established politics.[55]

The country's first democratically elected president, Nelson Mandela, had pledged his life to the struggle for equal political rights, and was rightly celebrated for his role in the achievement of this aim following his death in 2013. But at the same time, the future for his legacy was unclear. The derisive reception given to Zuma at the memorial to Mandela at the FNB stadium in Johannesburg, the rise of the EFF, and perhaps more significantly, the emergence of an insurgent politics of protest suggested that the future direction of South African politics was indeterminate. In 2014, the ANC retained an overwhelming majority in parliament, with over 60 per cent of the vote, but its authority to rule had become contingent upon its actions and effectiveness in ways that were markedly different from twenty years previously.

It is possible to argue that it was only in the early years of the twenty-first century that South Africa came into being as a nation distinct from – although still marked by – its apartheid and colonial past. Beginning in the nineteenth century, South Africa had been stitched together as a modern unitary state in a process shaped by the interactions between indigenous and settler populations. With technological and economic advantage and unity, colonial groups were able to build political and social institutions that served the interests of a transnational minority. Through to the middle of the twentieth century, despite the emergence of an undeniably South African settler identities (with Afrikaner nationalism as its most obvious, but by no means only, form), white supremacy was at all times shaped with reference to wider global and imperial political, intellectual and cultural frameworks. But the South African political and social landscape was also shaped by indigenous resistance and cooperation, and by internationalist currents that privileged humanitarianism, Africanism and democracy. Even at the height of the power of the apartheid state in the second half of the twentieth century, when South African policies appeared starkly at odds with the global retreat from formal colonialism, South Africa was never truly isolated. Nevertheless, in the years after 1994, the post-apartheid 'New South Africa' was subject to global influences of a greater intensity than ever before.

The twentieth century saw two 'new' South Africas. The first, in the aftermath of the South African War, centred on attempts to create a national economy centred on the mining industry, to reconcile the two main groups in the settler population and to manage the incorporation of the major fraction of the population into a modern state. The second 'new' South Africa, in the 1990s, sought to overcome the basic inequalities entrenched by the earlier version. The basic political foundation of post-apartheid South Africa – universal democracy – was more easily established. The wider projects of reconstruction, redistribution and reconciliation that made up the contours of the new South Africa were far harder to achieve. In both 1902 and 1994, the moment of reconstruction was powerfully influenced by transnational forces – imperialism at the turn of the twentieth century and the (not unrelated) discourses of globalization and the Washington Consensus at the end of the century. But, whereas in the first decade of the twentieth century, the first 'new' South Africa was established as an outpost of settler colonialism within the British Empire, the opening years of the twenty-first century saw a democratic South Africa seek to make its way as a post-colonial African state in an increasingly interconnected world.

Since 1994, South African politics has struggled with the social legacies of apartheid, as stark inequalities continued to constrain the lives of a large proportion of its population. While post-apartheid politics has remained largely stable, social instabilities and inequalities have remained, and to an extent intensified. South Africa has experienced high levels of crime, poverty and unemployment, while the HIV-AIDS health crisis affected the country on a scale unmatched in the world. South Africans sought to redefine themselves, both against their own past and in a changing continental and global context.

Further reading

Adebajo, Adekeye, Adebayo Adedeji and Chris Landsberg, eds. *South Africa in Africa: The Post-Apartheid Era*. Scottsville, South Africa: University of KwaZulu-Natal Press, 2007.

Asmal, Kader, Louise Asmal and Ronald Suresh Roberts. *Reconciliation through Truth: A Reckoning of Apartheid's Criminal Governance*. New York: St. Martin's Press, 1997.

Bond, Patrick. *Elite Transition: From Apartheid to Neoliberalism in South Africa*. Scottsville, South Africa: University of KwaZulu-Natal Press, 2005.

Coombes, Annie E. *History after Apartheid: Visual Culture and Public Memory in a Democratic South Africa*. Durham, NC: Duke University Press, 2003.

Davenport, Rodney. *The Birth of the New South Africa*. London: University of Toronto Press, 1998.
Gevisser, Mark. *Thabo Mbeki: The Dream Deferred*. Johannesburg: Jonathan Ball, 2007.
Gumede, William. *Thabo Mbeki and the Battle for the Soul of the ANC*. New York: Zed Books, 2007.
Karim, S. S. Abdool and Q. Abdool Karim. *HIV/AIDS in South Africa*. Cambridge: Cambridge University Press, 2010.
Krog, Antjie. *Country of My Skull*. London: Jonathan Cape, 1999.
Lodge, Tom. *Politics in South Africa: From Mandela to Mbeki*. Oxford: James Currey, 2003.
Marais, Hein. *South Africa: Limits to Change: The Political Economy of Transition*. Cape Town: University of Cape Town Press, 1998.
Murray, Martin J. *Revolution Deferred: The Painful Birth of Post-Apartheid South Africa*. New York: Verso, 1994.
Nuttall, Sarah, and Carli Coetzee, eds. *Negotiating the Past: The Making of Memory in South Africa*. Cape Town: Oxford University Press, 1998.
Wilson, Richard. *The Politics of Truth and Reconciliation in South Africa: Legitimizing the Post-Apartheid State*. Cambridge: Cambridge University Press, 2001.

CHRONOLOGY

1795	British occupy Cape Colony
1799	Khoisan rebellion
1803	Foundation of Bethelsdorp mission station
1806	Formal establishment of British rule in Cape Colony
1811–12	British force leads expedition against Xhosa in Zuurveld
c. 1816	Zulu kingdom established
1818–19	'War of Nxele'; British forces extend boundary of Cape to Keiskamma River
1820	British settlers arrive in Zuurveld
1822	Foundation of Kuruman mission
1823	Formation of Anti-Slavery Society in London
1824	Sotho kingdom established under Moshoeshoe; foundation of Port Natal
c. 1826	Mzilikazi establishes Ndebele power in Highveld
1828	Publication of John Philip's *Researches in South Africa*; Ordinance 50; death of Shaka
1829	Establishment of the Kat River Settlement
1834	Emancipation of slaves in British Empire
1834–35	British–Xhosa war; Queen Adelaide Province
1835	Murder of Hintsa
1834–40	Beginnings of movement of Voortrekkers away from Cape
1836	Voortrekker forces defeat Mzilikazi
1836–37	Select Committee on Aborigines meets in London
1838	Battle of Ncome River; formation of Republic of Natalia
1841	Foundation of Lovedale College
1843	British annexation of Natal
1846–47	'War of the Axe' between British and Xhosa; establishment of British Kaffraria
1852	Establishment of Zuid-Afrikaansche Republiek (ZAR)
1850–53	War between British and Xhosa in the Eastern Cape; Kat River Rebellion
1853	Cape Colony granted Representative Government, elected under non-racial franchise
1854	Establishment of Orange Free State
1856–57	Xhosa Cattle Killing
1856	Natal granted representative government
1860	First indentured workers arrive in Natal from India
1866	British Kaffraria (Ciskei) incorporated into Cape Colony
1867	Discovery of diamonds in Griqualand West

1875	Black Flag revolt in Kimberley
1877	Annexation of South African Republic; Paul Kruger elected President of South African Republic
1877–78	Anglo-Xhosa War
1879	Anglo-Zulu War; Pedi War
1881	South African War; defeat of British at Majuba Hill
1884	*Imvo Zabantsundu* launched
1886	Discovery of gold on Witwatersrand
1888	Formation of de Beers mining company
1889	British South Africa Company granted Royal Charter
1890	Cecil Rhodes elected prime minister of Cape Colony
1894	Formation of Natal Indian Congress; Cecil Rhodes introduces 'Glen Grey' Act
1895	Opening of Delagoa Bay Railway
1895–96	Jameson Raid
1896	Gandhi publishes his 'Green Pamphlet' on Indians in South Africa
1897	'Nkosi Sikelel' i Africa' composed by Eric Sontonga
1899–1902	South African War
1903–5	South African Native Affairs Commission. Report presented in 1905.
1904	Importation of Chinese indentured labourers to Witwatersrand
1906	Bambatha rebellion; 'Chinese slavery' becomes key issue in British general election
1907	Het Volk Party wins elections in Transvaal
1908	National Convention discusses Union
1910	Union of South Africa
1911	Gandhi launches satyagraha campaign in Natal
1912	Formation of South African Natives' National Congress
1913	Natives Land Act establishes 'reserves'; mass civil disobedience in Natal led by Gandhi
1914	Afrikaner rebellion
1915	International Socialist League formed in Johannesburg
1917	Sinking of SS *Mendi*
1918	Formation of Afrikaner Broederbond
1919	Formation of Industrial and Commercial Workers' Union; black workers strike in Johannesburg
1921	Formation of Communist Party of South Africa
1922	Rand Revolt
1923	Natives (Urban Areas) Act comes into effect
1924	J.B.M. Hertzog becomes prime minister
1927	Kadalie travels to Europe; Native Administration Act came into effect
1928	Communist Party adopts 'Native Republic' policy
1929	Formation of Institute for Race Relations
1933	Formation of 'Purified' National Party under D. F. Malan

1936	Hertzog Bills passed
1938	*Eufees* celebration of centenary of Great Trek
1943	Formation of ANC Youth League; publication of 'African Claims in South Africa'
1945	Formation of United Nations
1946	Government of India brings complaint against treatment of South African Indians to the UN General Assembly; African mineworkers' strike
1948	National Party under Malan elected to power; Universal Declaration of Human Rights adopted by the UN General Assembly
1950	Group Areas Act and Population Registration Act enacted
1952	Defiance campaign of civil disobedience against apartheid; Albert Lutuli elected president of ANC
1953	Formation of American Committee on Africa in New York; Bantu Education Act enacted
1955	Freedom Charter adopted by the Congress of the People; first removals from Sophiatown
1956	Start of Treason Trial; launch of Defence and Aid Fund in London
1958	Alexandra Bus Boycott; All-African Peoples' Assembly in Accra
1959	Formation of Pan-Africanist Congress; launch of Boycott Movement in UK; promotion of Bantu Self-Government Act
1960	Sharpeville Massacre; banning of ANC and PAC; formation of British Anti-Apartheid Movement
1961	South Africa withdraws from Commonwealth after becoming a republic; formation of Umkhonto wi Sizwe and launch of armed struggle by ANC/SACP
1962	Mandela addresses Pan-African conference in Addis Ababa
1963	First meeting of the UN Special Committee against apartheid; UN Security Council imposes voluntary arms embargo
1964	Rivonia trial of leading members of Umkhonto wi Sizwe including Mandela and Sisulu; sanctions conference in London
1966	Death of Verwoerd
1967	MK fighters engage in military skirmishes in Rhodesia
1968	South Africa banned from Mexico Olympics
1969	Formation of South African Students Organisation; launch of Stop the Seventy Tour sports boycott campaign
1970	South Africa expelled from International Olympic Committee
1973	Strikes in Durban
1974	Fall of Estado Novo regime in Portugal
1975	Angola and Mozambique achieve independence
1976	Soweto Uprising
1977	Gleneagles Accord; UN mandatory arms embargo; death of Biko
1978	P. W. Botha succeeds Vorster as Prime Minister
1978–79	International Anti-Apartheid Year

1983 Tricameral Constitution; launch of United Democratic Front
1984 Vaal Uprising; first state of emergency; P. W. Botha visits UK and other European states
1985 Formation of Congress of South African Trades Unions; Botha's 'Rubicon' speech
1986 US and Commonwealth sanctions imposed; abolition of Pass Laws
1988 Nelson Mandela birthday concert, London
1989 P. W. Botha resigns
1990 F. W. de Klerk announces lifting of bans on ANC, PAC and SACP; release of Nelson Mandela
1991 Launch of Convention for a Democratic South Africa
1992 Boipateng massacre
1994 Fully-democratic elections; Nelson Mandela inaugurated as president
1996 First hearings under the Truth and Reconciliation Commission; launch of Growth, Employment and Redistribution strategy by ANC government
1998 Formation of Black Economic Empowerment Commission; launch of Treatment Action Campaign
1999 Thabo Mbeki elected president
2000 World AIDS conference, Durban; formation of Democratic Alliance
2001 Launch of New Partnership for Africa's Development
2002 Launch of African Union
2007 Jacob Zuma elected president of ANC; Mbeki resigns as state president
2008 Wave of xenophobic violence
2009 Jacob Zuma elected president
2010 FIFA World Cup held in South Africa; South Africa joins 'BRICS' association of emerging economies
2012 Marikana shootings
2013 Formation of Economic Freedom Fighters; death of Mandela
2014 Zuma elected for second term as president

NOTES

Chapter 1: Introduction

1. Thabo Mbeki, 'Speech at the Funeral of Sarah Bartmann', 9 August 2002, http://www.dfa.gov.za/docs/speeches/2002/mbek0809.htm
2. Stephen Jay Gould. *The Flamingo's Smile*. London: Penguin Books, 1991, pp. 291–301. See also Stephen Jay Gould. *The Mismeasure of Man*. Rev. and expanded edn. London: Penguin, 1996, pp. 117–18.
3. Andrew Bank. 'Of "Native Skulls" and "Noble Caucasians": Phrenology in Colonial South Africa'. *Journal of Southern African Studies*, 22 (3) (1 September 1996): 387–403; Saul Dubow. *Scientific Racism in Modern South Africa*. New York: Cambridge University Press, 1995.
4. Sander L. Gilman. 'Black Bodies, White Bodies: Toward an Iconography of Female Sexuality in Late Nineteenth-Century Art, Medicine, and Literature'. *Critical Inquiry*, 12 (1) (1985): 204–42.
5. Ciraj Rassool. 'Human Remains, the Disciplines of the Dead, and the South African Memorial Complex'. In *The Politics of Heritage in Africa: Economies, Histories, and Infrastructures*, ed. Derek R. Peterson, Kodzo Gavua and Ciraj Rassool, 133–56. New York: Cambridge University Press, 2015.
6. Clifton C. Crais and Pamela Scully. *Sara Baartman and the Hottentot Venus: A Ghost Story and a Biography*. Princeton, NJ: Oxford: Princeton University Press.
7. Lydie Moudileno. 'Returning Remains: Saartjie Baartman, or the "Hottentot Venus" as Transnational Postcolonial Icon'. *Forum for Modern Language Studies*, 45 (2) (1 April 2009): 200–12.
8. Pierre-Yves Saunier. *Transnational History*. Houndmills, Basingstoke: Palgrave Macmillan, 2013, p. 3.
9. Saul Dubow. 'South Africa and South Africans: Nationality, Belonging, Citizenship'. In *The Cambridge History of South Africa*, Vol. 2: *1885–1994*, ed. Robert Ross, Anne Kelk Mager and Bill Nasson. Cambridge: Cambridge University Press, 2011, p. 65.
10. Annie E. Coombes, ed. *Rethinking Settler Colonialism: History and Memory in Australia, Canada, Aotearoa New Zealand and South Africa*. Manchester: Manchester University Press, 2006, p. 3.
11. Jean Comaroff and John L. Comaroff. *Of Revelation and Revolution*. Vol. 1: *Christianity, Colonialism, and Consciousness in South Africa*. Chicago and London: University of Chicago Press, 1991, p. 313; Jean-François Bayart and Stephen Ellis. 'Africa in the World: A History of Extraversion'. *African Affairs*, 99 (395) (1 April 2000): 217–67.
12. Shula Marks and Richard Rathbone. 'Introduction'. In *Industrialisation and Social Change in South Africa: African Class Formation, Culture, and Consciousness, 1870–1930*, edited by Shula Marks and Richard Rathbone. Harlow: Longman, 1982, p. 13.
13. Saul Dubow. 'How British Was the British World? The Case of South Africa'. *Journal of Imperial and Commonwealth History*, 37 (1) (2009): 1–27.
14. Bill Schwarz. *Memories of Empire*. Vol. 1: *The White Man's World*. Oxford: Oxford University Press, 2011, pp. 277–340.

15. Kerry Ward. *Networks of Empire: Forced Migration in the Dutch East India Company*. Cambridge: Cambridge University Press, 2009. Ward's work builds on studies of the nineteenth century, notably Alan Lester. *Imperial Networks: Creating Identities in Nineteenth-Century South Africa and Britain*. London and New York: Routledge, 2001.
16. Isabel Hofmeyr and Michelle Williams. 'South Africa–India: Connections and Comparisons'. *Journal of Asian and African Studies*, 44 (1) (1 February 2009): 5–17.
17. Isabel Hofmeyr. 'The Idea of "Africa" in Indian Nationalism: Reporting the Diaspora in *The Modern Review* 1907–1929'. *South African Historical Journal*, 57 (1) (2007): 60–81.

Chapter 2: South Africa in the Colonial World

1. Himanshu Prabha Ray and Edward A. Alpers, eds. *Cross Currents and Community Networks: The History of the Indian Ocean World*. New Delhi; New York: Oxford University Press, 2007.
2. Simon Hall. 'Farming Communities of the Second Millennium: Internal Frontiers, Identity, Continuity and Change'. In *The Cambridge History of South Africa*. Vol. 1: *From Early Times to 1885*, ed. Carolyn Hamilton, Bernard Mbenga and Robert Ross, 112–67. New York: Cambridge University Press, 2010.
3. Robert Ross. 'Khoesan and Immigrants: The Emergence of Colonial Society in the Cape, 1500–1800'. In *The Cambridge History of South Africa*. Vol. 1: *From Early Times to 1885*, ed. Carolyn Hamilton, Bernard Mbenga and Robert Ross, 168–210. New York: Cambridge University Press, 2010; Richard Elphick and Hermann Giliomee, eds. *The Shaping of South African Society, 1652–1820*. Cape Town: Longman, 1979.
4. David Coplan. *In Township Tonight! South Africa's Black City Music and Theatre*. London: Longman, 1985, p. 9.
5. Norman Etherington. *The Great Treks: The Transformation of Southern Africa, 1815–1854*. Harlow: Longman, 2001.
6. James McCann. *Maize and Grace: Africa's Encounter with a New World Crop, 1500–2000*. First Harvard University Press paperback edn. Cambridge, MA: Harvard University Press, 2005.
7. Julian Cobbing. 'The Mfecane as Alibi: Thoughts on Dithakong and Mbolompo'. *The Journal of African History*, 29 (3) (1 January 1988): 487–519; Carolyn Hamilton. *The Mfecane Aftermath: Reconstructive Debates in Southern African History*. Johannesburg; Pietmaritzburg: Witwatersrand University Press; University of Natal Press, 1995.
8. Etherington, *Great Treks*, p. 346.
9. John Wright. 'Turbulent Times: Political Transformations in the North and East, 1760s-1830s'. In *The Cambridge History of South Africa*. Vol. 1: *From Early Times to 1885*, ed. Carolyn Hamilton, Bernard Mbenga and Robert Ross, 211–52. New York: Cambridge University Press, 2010.
10. Carolyn Hamilton. *Terrific Majesty: The Power of Shaka Zulu and the Limits of Historical Invention*. Cambridge, MA: Harvard University Press, 1998, pp. 36–71.
11. C. A. Bayly. *Imperial Meridian: The British Empire and the World 1780–1830*. Cambridge: Cambridge University Press, 1989.
12. C. A. Bayly. *The Birth of the Modern World, 1780–1914: Global Connections and Comparisons*. Oxford: Blackwell, 2004, p. 115.
13. Charles A. Jones. *International Business in the Nineteenth Century: The Rise and Fall of a Cosmopolitan Bourgeoisie*. Brighton: Wheatsheaf, 1987.
14. Morewood, *Philosophical and Statistical History of the Inventions and Customs of Ancient and Modern Nations in the Manufacture and Use of Inebriating Liquors*, Dublin, 1838.

15. Timothy J. Keegan. *Colonial South Africa and the Origins of the Racial Order*. Cape Town: David Philip Publishers, 1996, pp. 59–60; 158–61.
16. William Beinart. *The Rise of Conservation in South Africa: Settlers, Livestock, and the Environment 1770–1950*. Oxford: Oxford University Press, 2003.
17. Martin Legassick and Robert Ross. 'From Slave Economy to Settler Capitalism: The Cape Colony and Its Extensions, 1800–1854'. In *The Cambridge History of South Africa*. Vol. 1: *From Early Times to 1885*, ed. Carolyn Hamilton, Bernard Mbenga and Robert Ross. New York: Cambridge University Press, 2010, p. 256.
18. Etherington, *Great Treks*, p. 320.
19. Bayly, Imperial *Meridian*, pp. 202–3; Bayly, *Birth of the Modern World*, p. 144.
20. Hermann Giliomee. 'The Eastern Frontier, 1770–1812'. In *The Shaping of South African Society, 1652–1820*, ed. Richard Elphick and Hermann Giliomee. Cape Town: Maskew Miller Longman, 1979, p. 448.
21. Bayly, *Imperial Meridian*, p. 10.
22. Legassick and Ross, 'From Slave Economy to Settler Capitalism', p. 257; Keegan, Colonial *South Africa*, p. 144.
23. Alan Lester. *Imperial Networks: Creating Identities in Nineteenth-Century South Africa and Britain*. New York: Routledge, 2001, p. 16.
24. Christopher Saunders and Iain R. Smith. 'Southern Africa, 1795–1901'. In *The Oxford History of the British Empire*. Vol. III: *The Nineteenth Century*, ed. Andrew Porter. Oxford: Oxford University Press, 1999, p. 598.
25. Keegan, *Colonial South Africa*, p. 67.
26. Clifton C. Crais. *White Supremacy and Black Resistance in Pre-Industrial South Africa: The Making of the Colonial Order in the Eastern Cape, 1770–1865*. Cambridge: Cambridge University Press, 1992, pp. 92–5.
27. Ibid., p. 259. See also Elizabeth Elbourne. *Blood Ground: Colonialism, Missions, and the Contest for Christianity in the Cape Colony and Britain, 1799–1853*. Montreal: McGill-Queen's University Press, 2002.
28. Jean Comaroff and John L. Comaroff. *Of Revelation and Revolution*. Vol. 1: *Christianity, Colonialism, and Consciousness in South Africa*. London: University of Chicago Press, 1991.
29. Elizabeth Elbourne. 'Concerning Missionaries: The Case of Van Der Kemp'. *Journal of Southern African Studies*, 17 (1) (1 March 1991): 153–64.
30. Legassick and Ross, 'From Slave Economy to Settler Capitalism', pp. 260–1.
31. Julia C. Wells. 'The Scandal of Rev James Read and the Taming of the London Missionary Society by 1820'. *South African Historical Journal*, 42 (1) (1 May 2000): 136–60.
32. Jared McDonald. 'James Read: Towards a New Reassessment'. *South African Historical Journal*, 62 (3) (2010): 514–33.
33. Legassick and Ross, 'From Slave Economy to Settler Capitalism', p. 267.
34. Elbourne, *Blood Ground*, p. 241.
35. John Philip. *Researches in South Africa: Illustrating the Civil, Moral, and Religious Condition of the Native Tribes: Including Journals of the Author's Travels in the Interior*. London: J. Duncan, 1828, p. 381.
36. Lester, *Imperial Networks*, p. 33.
37. Ibid., p. 27.
38. Zoë Laidlaw. 'Investigating Empire: Humanitarians, Reform and the Commission of Eastern Inquiry'. *The Journal of Imperial and Commonwealth History*, 40 (5) (19 November 2012): 749–68. See also Zoë Laidlaw. *Colonial Connections, 1815–45: Patronage, the Information Revolution and Colonial Government*. Manchester: Manchester University Press, 2005.
39. J. B. Peires. 'The British and the Cape, 1814–1834'. In *The Shaping of South African Society, 1652–1820*, ed. Richard Elphick and Hermann Giliomee. Cape Town: Maskew Miller Longman, 1979, p. 495.

40. Julie Evans, Patricia Grimshaw, David Phillips and Shurlee Swain. *Equal Subjects, Unequal Rights: Indigenous Peoples in British Settler Colonies, 1830–1910*. Manchester: Manchester University Press, 2003, pp. 94–5.
41. Lisa Ford and Andrew Roberts. 'Expansion, 1820–50'. In *The Cambridge History of Australia*, ed. Alison Bashford and Stuart Macintyre, 142–8. Cambridge: Cambridge University Press, 2013.
42. Crais, *White Supremacy*, pp. 62–3.
43. Keegan, *Colonial South Africa*, p. 140.
44. Lester, *Imperial Networks*, pp. 124–5.
45. Legassick and Ross, 'From Slave Economy to Settler Capitalism', pp. 282–3; Crais, *White Supremacy*, p. 117.
46. E. Elbourne, 'The Sin of the Settler: The 1835-36 Select Committee on Aborigines and Debates over Virtue and Conquest in the Early Nineteenth-Century British White Settler Empire'. *Journal of Colonialism and Colonial History*, 4 (3) (2003). *Project MUSE*, doi:10.1353/cch.2004.0003; see also Elbourne, *Blood Ground*, pp. 288–92.
47. Lester, *Imperial Networks*, p. 105.
48. Ibid., p. 114; Andrew Porter. '"Commerce and Christianity": The Rise and Fall of a Nineteenth-Century Missionary Slogan'. *The Historical Journal*, 28 (3) (1 September 1985): 597–621.
49. Roger S. Levine. 'Cultural Innovation and Translation in the Eastern Cape: Jan Tzatzoe, Xhosa Intellectual and the Making of an African Gospel, 1817–1833'. *African Historical Review*, 42 (2) (1 November 2010): 84–101. See also Roger S. Levine. *A Living Man from Africa: Jan Tzatzoe, Xhosa Chief and Missionary, and the Making of Nineteenth-Century South Africa*. New Haven, CT: Yale University Press, 2011.
50. Lester, *Imperial Networks*, p. 122.
51. Elbourne, 'Sin of the Settler'.
52. Crais. *White Supremacy*, pp. 127–38.
53. Lester, *Imperial Networks*, p. 76.
54. Martin Legassick. *The Politics of a South African Frontier: The Griqua, the Sotho-Tswana and the Missionaries, 1780–1840*. Basel: Basler Afrika Bibliographien, 2010.
55. Comaroff and Comaroff, *Of Revelation and Revolution*, vol.1, p. 266.
56. Guy Hartley. 'The Battle of Dithakongand the "Mfecane" Theory'. In *The Mfecane Aftermath: Reconstructive Debates in Southern African History*, ed. Carolyn Hamilton, 395–416. Johannesburg; Pietmaritzburg: Witwatersrand University Press; University of Natal Press, 1995; Hartley and others have sought to downplay the role of the Griqua as the primary catalyst for violence on the Highveld suggested by Julian Cobbing. See Cobbing, 'Mfecane as Alibi', 487–519.
57. Keegan, *Colonial South Africa*, pp. 180–2.
58. Etherington, *Great Treks*, pp. 192–3.
59. Keegan, *Colonial South Africa*, p. 184; Legassick and Ross, 'From Slave Economy to Settler Capitalism', p. 288.
60. Hermann Giliomee. *The Afrikaners: Biography of a People*. London: Hurst, 2011, pp. 144–53; Keegan, *Colonial South Africa*, pp. 184–91.
61. Legassick and Ross, 'From Slave Economy to Settler Capitalism', pp. 288–9.
62. Keegan, *Colonial South Africa*, pp. 191–3; Norman A. Etherington. 'An American Errand into the South African Wilderness'. *Church History*, 39 (1) (1970): 62–71.
63. Etherington, *Great Treks*, pp. 279–85.
64. Keegan, *Colonial South Africa*, p. 205; Giliomee, *Afrikaners*, p. 168.
65. Lester, *Imperial Networks*, pp. 138–75.
66. Keegan, *Colonial South Africa*, p. 205.
67. Crais, *White Supremacy*, p. 134.
68. Ibid., pp. 138–41; see also Keegan, *Colonial South Africa*, pp. 126–7.

69. Keegan, *Colonial South Africa*, pp. 211–13.
70. Legassick and Ross, 'From Slave Economy to Settler Capitalism', pp. 296–8; Keegan, *Colonial South Africa*, pp. 217–19.
71. Etherington, *Great Treks*, p. 313.
72. Keegan, *Colonial South Africa*, p. 220.
73. Lester, *Imperial Networks*, p. 151.
74. Legassick and Ross, 'From Slave Economy to Settler Capitalism', pp. 302–3.
75. Keegan, *Colonial South Africa*, pp. 248–52.
76. Etherington. *Great Treks*, p. 323.
77. Keegan, *Colonial South Africa*, pp. 225–30; Legassick and Ross, 'From Slave Economy to Settler Capitalism', pp. 306–7.
78. J. B. Peires. *The Dead Will Arise: Nongqawuse and the Great Xhosa Cattle-Killing Movement of 1856–7*. Johannesburg: Jonathan Ball, 2003, pp. 9–15.
79. Legassick and Ross, 'From Slave Economy to Settler Capitalism', pp. 309–10.
80. Andrew Bank. 'Losing Faith in the Civilizing Mission: The Premature Decline of Humanitarian Liberalism at the Cape, 1840–60'. In *Empire and Others: British Encounters with Indigenous Peoples, 1600–1850*, ed. Martin Daunton and Rick Halpern. London: UCL Press, 1999, p. 380.
81. Paul Young. *Globalization and the Great Exhibition: The Victorian New World Order*. Basingstoke: Palgrave Macmillan, 2009.
82. 'Some Moral Aspects of the Exhibition', *Economist*, 17 May 1851; Young, *Globalization and the Great Exhibition*, p. 352.
83. *Times*, 21 June 1851; see also J. S. Galbraith. *Reluctant Empire: British Policy on the South African Frontier, 1834–1854*. Berkeley, CA: California University Press, 1963, pp. 248–9; Etherington, *Great Treks*, p. 312.
84. Quoted in Peires, *Dead Will Arise*, p. 12; Legassick and Ross, 'From Slave Economy to Settler Capitalism', p. 311.
85. Norman Etherington, Patrick Harries and Bernard Mbenga. 'From Colonial Hegemonies to Imperial Conquest, 1840–1880'. In *The Cambridge History of South Africa*. Vol. 1: *From Early Times to 1885*, ed. Carolyn Hamilton, Bernard Mbenga and Robert Ross, 325–6. New York: Cambridge University Press, 2010.
86. Peires, *Dead Will Arise*, pp. 286–96.
87. John Laband. 'From Mercenaries to Military Settlers: The British German Legion, 1854–1861'. In *Soldiers and Settlers in Africa, 1850–1918*, ed. Stephen M. Miller, 85–122. Leiden: Brill, 2009.
88. Peires, *Dead Will Arise*, pp. 316–19.
89. David Lambert and Alan Lester, eds. *Colonial Lives across the British Empire: Imperial Careering in the Long Nineteenth Century*. New York: Cambridge University Press, 2006; Catherine Hall. *Civilising Subjects: Metropole and Colony in the English Imagination, 1830–1867*. Oxford: Polity, 2002.
90. Saul Dubow. 'South Africa and South Africans: Nationality, Belonging, Citizenship'. In *The Cambridge History of South Africa*, Vol. 2: *1885–1994*, ed. Robert Ross, Anne Kelk Mager and Bill Nasson. Cambridge: Cambridge University Press, 2011, p. 23.
91. Giliomee, *Afrikaners*, pp. 175–81.
92. Stanley Trapido. '"The Friends of the Natives": Merchants, Peasants and the Political and Ideological Structure of Liberalism in the Cape, 1854–1910'. In *Economy and Society in Pre-Industrial South Africa*, ed. Shula Marks and Anthony Atmore. London: Longman, 1980, p. 251.
93. Saul Dubow. *A Commonwealth of Knowledge: Science, Sensibility, and White South Africa, 1820–2000*. Oxford: Oxford University Press, 2006, pp. 35–44.
94. Elbourne, *Blood Ground*, pp. 343–4; Bank, 'Losing Faith in the Civilizing Mission', pp. 364–83.

95. Evans, Grimshaw, Phillips and Swain, *Equal Subjects, Unequal Rights*, p. 90.
96. On the development of African consciousness and 'resistance', see Comaroff and Comaroff, *Of Revelation and Revolution*, vol. 1; Jean Comaroff and John L. Comaroff. *Of Revelation and Revolution*. Vol. 2: *The Dialectics of Modernity on a South African Frontier*. London: University of Chicago Press, 1997.
97. Saunders and Smith, 'Southern Africa, 1795–1901', p. 597.
98. Bayly, *Birth of the Modern World*, p. 132.
99. Kenneth Pomeranz. *The Great Divergence: Europe, China, and the Making of the Modern World Economy*. Princeton, NJ: Princeton University Press, 2000.

Chapter 3: Minerals and Modernity

1. Christopher Saunders and Iain R. Smith. 'Southern Africa, 1795–1901'. In *The Oxford History of the British Empire*. Vol. III: *The Nineteenth Century*, ed. Andrew Porter. Oxford: Oxford University Press, 1999, p. 598.
2. James Belich. *Replenishing the Earth: The Settler Revolution and the Rise of the Anglo-World, 1783–1939*. Oxford: Oxford University Press, 2009, p. 373.
3. Shula Marks and Richard Rathbone, eds. *Industrialisation and Social Change in South Africa: African Class Formation, Culture, and Consciousness, 1870–1930*. Harlow: Longman, 1982, p. 14.
4. C. H. Feinstein. *An Economic History of South Africa : Conquest, Discrimination and Development*. Cambridge: Cambridge University Press, 2005, p. 55.
5. David Welsh. *The Roots of Segregation : Native Policy in Colonial Natal, 1845–1910*. Oxford: Oxford University Press, 1971, p. 23.
6. Welsh, *Roots of Segregation*; see also Mahmood Mamdani. *Citizen and Subject : Contemporary Africa and the Legacy of Late Colonialism*. Princeton, NJ: Princeton University Press, 1996; for alternative precedents for segregation see Saul Dubow. *Racial Segregation and the Origins of Apartheid in South Africa, 1919–36*. Basingstoke: Macmillan, 1989.
7. Thomas McClendon. 'The Man Who Would Be Inkosi: Civilising Missions in Shepstone's Early Career1'. *Journal of Southern African Studies*, 30 (2) (1 June 2004): 339–58.
8. Jeremy Martens. '"Civilised Domesticity", Race and European Attempts to Regulate African Marriage Practices in Colonial Natal, 1868–1875'. *The History of the Family*, 14 (4) (26 October 2009): 340–55.
9. Goolam Vahed. 'Race or Class? Community and Conflict amongst Indian Municipal Employees in Durban, 1914–1949'. *Journal of Southern African Studies*, 27 (1) (1 March 2001): 105–25.
10. Jo Beall. 'Women under Indenture in Colonial Natal, 1860–1911'. In *South Asians Overseas : Migration and Ethnicity*, ed. Colin G. Clarke, Ceri Peach and Steven Vertovec, 57–74. Cambridge: Cambridge University Press, 1990.
11. John Darwin. *The Empire Project: The Rise and Fall of the British World-System, 1830–1970*. Cambridge: Cambridge University Press, 2009, pp. 221–3.
12. Robert Turrell. *Capital and Labour on the Kimberley Diamond Fields 1871–1890*. Cambridge: Cambridge University Press, 1987.
13. See Ged Martin. *Britain and the Origins of Canadian Confederation, 1837–67*. Basingstoke: Macmillan, 1995.
14. R. L. Cope. 'Local Imperatives and Imperial Policy: The Sources of Lord Carnarvon's South African Confederation Policy'. *The International Journal of African Historical Studies*, 20 (4) (1 January 1987): 601–26; Norman A. Etherington. 'Labour Supply and the Genesis of South African Confederation in the 1870s'. *The Journal of African History*, 20 (2) (1 January

1979): 235–53; Clement Francis Goodfellow. *Great Britain and South African Confederation, 1870–1881*. Cape Town ; London: Oxford University Press, 1966.

15. Darwin, *Empire Project*, p. 229.
16. Alan Lester. *Imperial Networks: Creating Identities in Nineteenth-Century South Africa and Britain*. New York: Routledge, 2001, pp. 173–5.
17. Bill Schwarz. *The White Man's World*. Oxford: Oxford University Press, 2011, pp. 71–84.
18. Froude to Carnarvon 11 October 1874, BL, quoted in R. L. Cope. 'C. W. de Kiewiet, the Imperial Factor, and South African "Native Policy"'. *Journal of Southern African Studies*, 15 (3) (1 April 1989): 498.
19. Norman Etherington, Patrick Harries and Bernard Mbenga. 'From Colonial Hegemonies to Imperial Conquest, 1840–1880'. In *The Cambridge History of South Africa 1: From Early Times to 1885*, ed. Carolyn Hamilton, Bernard Mbenga and Robert Ross, 379–80. New York : Cambridge University Press, 2010. Hermann Giliomee. *The Afrikaners: Biography of a People*. London: Hurst, 2011, p. 188.
20. Saul Dubow. 'South Africa and South Africans: Nationality, Belonging, Citizenship'. In *The Cambridge History of South Africa*. Vol. 2: *1885–1994*, ed. Robert Ross, Anne Kelk Mager and Bill Nasson, 20–2. Cambridge: Cambridge University Press, 2011.
21. Saul Dubow. *A Commonwealth of Knowledge: Science, Sensibility, and White South Africa, 1820–2000*. Oxford: Oxford University Press, 2006.
22. Belich, *Replenishing the Earth*, pp. 383–5.
23. Etherington, Harries and Mbenga, 'From Colonial Hegemonies to Imperial Conquest', pp. 334–5.
24. Ibid., p. 383.
25. Peter Delius. *The Land Belongs to Us: The Pedi Polity, the Boers and the British in the Nineteenth-Century Transvaal*. London: Heinemann, 1984.
26. Jeff Guy. *The Destruction of the Zulu Kingdom: The Civil War in Zululand, 1879–1884*. London: Longman, 1979.
27. Giliomee. *The Afrikaners*, pp. 229–31.
28. Marks and Rathbone. *Industrialisation and Social Change in South Africa*, p. 11.
29. Feinstein. *Economic History of South Africa*, p. 93.
30. Turrell. *Capital and Labour*, pp. 146–73.
31. David Coplan. *In Township Tonight! South Africa's Black City Music and Theatre*. London: Longman, 1985, pp. 14–22.
32. Ibid., p. 46.
33. Rob Turrell. 'Kimberley: Labour and Compounds, 1871–1888'. In *Industrialisation and Social Change in South Africa: African Class Formation, Culture, and Consciousness, 1870–1930*, ed. Shula Marks and Richard Rathbone. Harlow: Longman, 1982, p. 51.
34. Lionel Forman. *Chapters in the History of the March to Freedom*. Cape Town: Real Printing & Publishing Co., 1959, p. 6.
35. Etherington. 'Labour Supply', pp. 235–53.
36. Patrick Harries. *Work, Culture, and Identity: Migrant Laborers in Mozambique and South Africa, c.1860–1910*. London: James Currey, 1994.
37. Stanley Trapido. 'Imperialism, Settler Identities and Colonial Capitalism: The Hundred-Year Origins of the 1899 South African War'. In *The Cambridge History of South Africa. Vol. 2: 1885–1994*, ed. Robert Ross, Anne Kelk Mager and Bill Nasson, 66–101. Cambridge: Cambridge University Press, 2011.
38. Marks and Rathbone, *Industrialisation and Social Change in South Africa*, p. 10.
39. Wheatcroft provides a general assessment of the emergence of mining capital on the Rand: Geoffrey Wheatcroft. *The Randlords: The Men Who Made South Africa*. London: Weidenfeld and Nicolson, 1985. See also Donald Denoon. 'Capital and Capitalists in the Transvaal in the 1890s and 1900s'. *The Historical Journal*, 23 (1) (1980): 111–32; Jean Jacques Van-Helten.

'Empire and High Finance: South Africa and the International Gold Standard 1890–1914'. *The Journal of African History*, 23 (4) (1982): 529–48.

40. Pratt Ambrose, quoted in Charles van Onselen. *Studies in the Social and Economic History of the Witwatersrand, 1886–1914*. Vol. 1: *New Babylon*. New York: Longman, 1982, p. 2; see also Frederick A. Johnstone. *Class, Race and Gold : A Study of Class Relations and Racial Discrimination in South Africa*. London: Routledge and Kegan Paul, 1976.
41. Susan Lee Johnson. *Roaring Camp: The Social World of the California Gold Rush*. 1st edn. New York: W.W. Norton, 2001. Peter Richardson and Jean-Jacques van Helten. 'The Development of the South African Gold-Mining Industry, 1895–1918'. *The Economic History Review*, 37 (3) (1984): 319–40.
42. P. J. Cain and A. G. Hopkins. *British Imperialism, 1688–2000*. London: Longman, 2001, p. 322.
43. Trapido, 'Imperialism, Settler Identities and Colonial Capitalism', pp. 83–4.
44. Cain and Hopkins, *British Imperialism*, p. 308.
45. Andrew Porter. 'Britain, the Cape Colony, and Natal, 1870–1914: Capital, Shipping, and the Imperial Connexion'. *The Economic History Review*, New Series, 34 (4) (1 November 1981): 554–77.
46. Thomas J. Noer. *Briton, Boer and Yankee : The United States and South Africa, 1870–1914*. Kent, OH: Kent State University Press, 1978.
47. Turrell, *Capital and Labour*, pp. 138–42.
48. Pule Phoofolo. 'Epidemics and Revolutions: The Rinderpest Epidemic in Late Nineteenth-Century Southern Africa'. *Past & Present*, (138) (1 February 1993): 112–43.
49. C. van Onselen. 'Reactions to Rinderpest in Southern Africa 1896–97'. *The Journal of African History*, 13 (3) (1 January 1972): 473–88.
50. Randall M. Packard. *White Plague, Black Labor: Tuberculosis and the Political Economy of Health and Disease in South Africa*. Pietermaritzburg: University of Natal Press, 1990.
51. Karen Jochelson. *The Colour of Disease: Syphilis and Racism in South Africa, 1880–1950*. Basingstoke: Palgrave in association with St. Antony's College, Oxford, 2001; Maynard W. Swanson. 'The Sanitation Syndrome: Bubonic Plague and Urban Native Policy in the Cape Colony, 1900–1909'. *The Journal of African History*, 18 (3) (1 January 1977): 387–410.
52. Coplan, *In Township Tonight*, pp. 4–42.
53. Charles van Onselen. *Studies in the Social and Economic History of the Witwatersrand, 1886–1914*. Vol. 1: *New Babylon*. New York: Longman, 1982, pp. 108–11.
54. Jonathan S. Crush and Charles H. Ambler, eds. *Liquor and Labor in Southern Africa*. Athens, OH: Ohio University Press, 1992. Charles van Onselen. 'Randlords and Rotgut 1886–1903: An Essay on the Role of Alcohol in the Development of European Imperialism and Southern African Capitalism, with Special Reference to Black Mineworkers in the Transvaal Republic'. *History Workshop*, 2 (1976): 33–89.
55. Van Onselen, *Studies in the Social and Economic History*, pp. 52–5.
56. Martin Kröger. 'Imperial Germany and the Boer War'. In *The International Impact of the Boer War*, ed. Keith M. Wilson. Chesham: Acumen, 2001, pp. 25–6.
57. Patrick Furlong. *Between Crown and Swastika : The Impact of the Radical Right on the Afrikaner Nationalist Movement in the Fascist Era*. Hanover, NH: University Press of New England, 1991, pp. 71–2.
58. Bill Nasson. *The South African War, 1899–1902*. London: Arnold, 1999, pp. 49, 60.
59. Robert I. Rotberg. *The Founder: Cecil Rhodes and the Pursuit of Power*. New York; Oxford: Oxford University Press, 1988; M. Tamarkin. *Cecil Rhodes and the Cape Afrikaners: The Imperial Colossus and the Colonial Parish Pump*. London: Cass, 1996; Paul Maylam. *The Cult of Rhodes : Remembering an Imperialist in Africa*. Claremont, South Africa: David Philip, 2005.
60. Rotberg, *Founder*, p. 289.
61. Rotberg, *Founder*, p. 469.

62. Ronald Edward Robinson and John Gallagher. *Africa and the Victorians: The Official Mind of Imperialism*. London: Macmillan, 1961, p. 418.
63. Cain and Hopkins, *British Imperialism*, p. 321.
64. Robinson and Gallagher, *Africa and the Victorians*, p. 427.
65. Noer, *Briton, Boer and Yankee*, pp. 31, 34.
66. *New York Times*, 1 May 1896, quoted in Noer, *Briton, Boer and Yankee*, p. 53.
67. See for example, Poultney Bigelow. *White Man's Africa*. 2nd edn. London: Harper, 1900.
68. 'London Audiences and the Transvaal'. *Times* [London, England] 13 January 1896: 9; see also Keir Waddington. '"We Don't Want Any German Sausages Here!" Food, Fear, and the German Nation in Victorian and Edwardian Britain'. *Journal of British Studies,* 52 (4) (2013): 1028–9.
69. Nasson, *South African War*, p. 78.
70. Robinson and Gallagher, *Africa and the Victorians* , pp. 439–40.
71. Van Onselen, *Studies in the Social and Economic History*, p. 23.
72. M. Tamarkin. 'The Cape Afrikaners and the British Empire from the Jameson Raid to the South African War'. In *The South African War Reappraised*, ed. Donal Lowry, 121–39. Manchester: Manchester University Press, 2000.
73. Denis Judd and Keith Terrance Surridge. *The Boer War*. London: John Murray, 2002, p. 1; Robinson and Gallagher, *Africa and the Victorians*, p. 461. Darwin, *Empire Project*, pp. 242–5; Trapido, 'Imperialism, Settler Identities and Colonial Capitalism', pp. 66–101.
74. Keith M. Wilson, ed. *The International Impact of the Boer War*. Chesham: Acumen, 2001.
75. Wolfgang Mommsen. 'Introduction'. In *The International Impact of the Boer War*, ed. Keith M. Wilson, 1–7. Chesham: Acumen, 2001.
76. See Simon Potter. *News and the British World: The Emergence of an Imperial Press System, 1876–1922*. Oxford: Clarendon Press, 2003.
77. Robert Bickers. *The Scramble for China: Foreign Devils in the Qing Empire, 1832–1914*. London: Penguin, 2012.
78. Wilson, *International Impact of the Boer War*, p. 5.
79. Mommsen, 'Introduction', pp. 6–7.
80. See, for example, F. Hale. 'The Scandinavian Corps in the Second Anglo-Boer War'. *Historia,* 45 (1) (2000): 220–36.
81. Donal Lowry. '"The Boers Were the Beginning of the End"?: The Wider Impact of the South African War'. In *The South African War Reappraised*, ed. Donal Lowry, pp. 212–13. Manchester: Manchester University Press, 2000.
82. Nasson, *South African War*, pp. 191, 195.
83. Lowry, '"The Boers Were the Beginning of the End"?', p. 236.
84. Donal Lowry. '"The World's No Bigger than a Kraal": The War and International Opinion in the First Age of "Globalization"'. In *The Impact of the South African War*, ed. David E. Omissi and Andrew Thompson, 268–87. Basingstoke: Palgrave, 2002.
85. David E. Omissi and Andrew Thompson, eds. *The Impact of the South African War*. New York: Palgrave, 2002, p. 13.
86. Phillip A. Buckner, 'Canada'. In *The Impact of the South African War*, ed. David E. Omissi and Andrew Thompson, 233–50. Basingstoke: Palgrave, 2002.
87. Nasson, *South African War*, pp. 306–7.
88. Lowry, '"The Boers Were the Beginning of the End"?', pp. 207, 215.
89. Vincent Kuitenbrouwer. *War of Words: Dutch Pro-Boer Propaganda and the South African War (1899–1902)*. Amsterdam: Amsterdam University Press, 2012. See also Martin Bossenbroek. 'The Netherlands and the Boer War'. In *The International Impact of the Boer War*, ed. Keith M. Wilson, 123–39. Chesham: Acumen, 2001.
90. Lowry, '"The Boers Were the Beginning of the End"?', pp. 215–16.
91. Nasson, *South African War*, pp. 180–3.

92. Luc Sante. *The Other Paris: An Illustrated Journey through a City's Poor and Bohemian Past.* London: Faber & Faber, 2015, p. 201.
93. Bradford Perkins. *The Great Rapprochement: England and the United States, 1895–1914.* New York: Atheneum, 1968; Lowry, '"The Boers Were the Beginning of the End"?', p. 209; William N. Tilchin. 'The United States and the Boer War'. In *The International Impact of the Boer War*, ed. Keith M. Wilson, 107–22. Chesham: Acumen, 2001.
94. Noer, *Briton, Boer and Yankee*, p. 90.
95. Nasson, *South African War*, p. 273; David E. Omissi. 'India: Some Perceptions of Race and Empire'. In *The Impact of the South African War*, ed. David E. Omissi and Andrew Thompson. New York: Palgrave, 2002, p. 216.
96. Bill Nasson. *Abraham Esau's War: A Black South African War in the Cape, 1899–1902.* Cambridge: Cambridge University Press, 1991, p. 13.
97. Peter Warwick. *Black People and the South African War, 1899–1902.* Cambridge: Cambridge University Press, 1983, pp. 18–19.
98. Warwick, *Black People*, pp. 19–26.
99. Nasson, *Abraham Esau's War*, pp. 189–92.
100. Sol T. Plaatje. *The Boer War Diary of Sol T. Plaatje : An African at Mafeking*, ed. John L. Comaroff. London: Cardinal, 1976.
101. Quoted in Warwick, *Black People*, p. 112.
102. Christopher Saunders. 'African Attitudes to Britain and the Empire before and after the South African War'. In *The South African War Reappraised*, ed. Donal Lowry. Manchester: Manchester University Press, 2000, p. 143.
103. Balasubramanyam Chandramohan. '"Hamlet with the Prince of Denmark Left out"?: The South African War, Empire and India'. In *The South African War Reappraised*, ed. Donal Lowry. Manchester: Manchester University Press, 2000, pp. 157, 159.
104. Pradip Kumar Datta. 'The Interlocking Worlds of the Anglo-Boer War in South Africa/India'. *South African Historical Journal*, 57 (1) (1 January 2007): 35–59.
105. Gareth Stedman Jones. 'Working-Class Culture and Working-Class Politics in London, 1870–1900; Notes on the Remaking of a Working Class'. *Journal of Social History*, 7 (4) (1974): 460–508.
106. Greg Cuthbertson. 'Pricking the "Nonconformist Conscience": Religion against the South African War'. In *The South African War Reappraised*, ed. Donal Lowry, 169–87. Manchester: Manchester University Press, 2000.
107. Paul Readman. 'The Conservative Party, Patriotism, and British Politics: The Case of the General Election of 1900'. *Journal of British Studies*, 40 (1) (2001): 107–45. See also Richard Price. *An Imperial War and the British Working Class: Working- Class Attitudes and Reactions to the Boer War, 1899–1902.* London: Routledge and Kegan Paul, 1972.
108. See Hope Hay Hewison. *Hedge of Wild Almonds : South Africa, the pro-Boers & the Quaker Conscience, 1890–1910.* London: J. Currey, 1989; also Bernard Porter. *Critics of Empire: British Radicals and the Imperial Challenge.* New edn. London: I. B. Tauris, 2008.
109. John Fisher. *That Miss Hobhouse: The Life of a Great Feminist.* London: Secker and Warburg, 1971.
110. S. B. Spies. 'Women and the War'. In *The South African War : The Anglo-Boer War 1899–1902*, ed. Peter Warwick, 161–85. Harlow: Longman, 1980; London: Secker and Warburg, 1971.
111. Quoted in Rhiannon Vickers. *The Labour Party and the World.* Manchester: Manchester University Press, 2003, p. 43.
112. J. A. (John Atkinson) Hobson. *The War in South Africa : Its Causes and Effects.* London: J. Nisbet, 1900, p. 240.
113. Iain R. Smith. 'A Century of Controversy over Origins'. In *The South African War Reappraised*, ed. Donal Lowry, 23–49. Manchester: Manchester University Press, 2000.

114. For an overview, see Norman Etherington. *Theories of Imperialism: War, Conquest & Capital*. London, 1984. On Hobson, see P. J. Cain. *Hobson and Imperialism : Radicalism, New Liberalism, and Finance 1887–1938*. Oxford: Oxford University Press, 2002.
115. William Beinart. *Twentieth-Century South Africa*. Oxford: Oxford University Press, 1994, p. 51.

Chapter 4: Race and Segregation

1. Charles van Onselen. *Studies in the Social and Economic History of the Witwatersrand, 1886–1914*. Vol. 1: *New Babylon*. New York: Longman, 1982, pp. 24–6.
2. Gary Kynoch. '"Your Petitioners Are in Mortal Terror": The Violent World of Chinese Mineworkers in South Africa, 1904–1910'. *Journal of Southern African Studies*, 31 (3) (1 September 2005): 531–46.
3. Peter Richardson. 'Coolies, Peasants and Proletarians: The Origins of Chinese Indentured Labour in South Africa, 1904–1907'. In *International Labour Migration: Historical Perspectives*, ed. Shula Marks and Peter Richardson, 167–85. London: Institute of Commonwealth Studies, 1984.
4. Rachel Bright. *Chinese Labour in South Africa, 1902–10: Race, Violence, and Global Spectacle*. Basingstoke: Palgrave Macmillan, 2013, pp. 42–4.
5. Kevin Grant. *A Civilised Savagery: Britain and the New Slaveries in Africa, 1884–1926*. New York: Routledge, 2005, pp. 90–2.
6. Andrew Thompson. *The Empire Strikes Back?: The Impact of Imperialism on Britain from the Mid-Nineteenth Century*. First edn. Harlow, England: Pearson Longman, 2005, pp. 70–3.
7. Grant, *Civilised Savagery*, p. 98; James Thompson. '"Pictorial Lies"? Posters and Politics in Britain C. 1880–1914'. *Past & Present*, (197) (2007): 177–210.
8. Ronald Hyam and Peter Henshaw. *The Lion and the Springbok: Britain and South Africa since the Boer War*. Cambridge: Cambridge University Press, 2003, pp. 52–75.
9. Saul Dubow. 'South Africa and South Africans: Nationality, Belonging, Citizenship'. In *The Cambridge History of South Africa*. Vol. 2: *1885–1994*, ed. Robert Ross, Anne Kelk Mager and Bill Nasson, 17–65. Cambridge: Cambridge University Press, 2011.
10. Julie Evans, Patricia Grimshaw, David Phillips and Shurlee Swain. *Equal Subjects, Unequal Rights: Indigenous Peoples in British Settler Colonies, 1830–1910*. Manchester: Manchester University Press, 2003, p. 190.
11. Thompson, *Empire Strikes Back*, 158–92. See especially Fig. 8, p. 159.
12. Peter Richardson. 'Coolies, Peasants and Proletarians: The Origins of Chinese Indentured Labour in South Africa, 1904–1907'. In *International Labour Migration: Historical Perspectives*, ed. Shula Marks and Peter Richardson, 167–85. London: Institute of Commonwealth Studies, 1984.
13. Jonathan Hyslop. 'Scottish Labour, Race, and Southern African Empire c.1880–1922: A Reply to Kenefick'. *International Review of Social History*, 55 (1) (2010): 63–81; William Kenefick. 'Confronting White Labourism: Socialism, Syndicalism, and the Role of the Scottish Radical Left in South Africa before 1914'. *International Review of Social History*, 55 (1) (2010): 29–62; Harold Jack Simons and Ray Esther Simons. *Class and Colour in South Africa, 1850–1950*. Harmondsworth: Penguin, 1969, p. 99.
14. Wulf D. Hund, Jeremy Krikler and David R. Roediger. *Wages of Whiteness & Racist Symbolic Capital*. Berlin: LIT, 2010.
15. Rachel Bright. *Chinese Labour in South Africa, 1902–10: Race, Violence, and Global Spectacle*. Basingstoke: Palgrave Macmillan, 2013.

16. Jonathan Hyslop. 'A Scottish Socialist Reads Carlyle in Johannesburg Prison, June 1900: Reflections on the Literary Culture of the Imperial Working Class'. *Journal of Southern African Studies,* 29 (3) (1 September 2003): 639–55.
17. Jonathan Hyslop. 'The World Voyage of James Keir Hardie: Indian Nationalism, Zulu Insurgency and the British Labour Diaspora 1907–1908'. *Journal of Global History,* 1 (3) (2006): 343–62.
18. On the 1913 general strike, see Elaine N. Katz. *A Trade Union Aristocracy: A History of White Workers in the Transvaal and the General Strike of 1913.* Johannesburg: African Studies Institute, University of the Witwatersrand, 1976; Jeremy Krikler. *White Rising: The 1922 Insurrection and Racial Killing in South Africa.* Manchester: Manchester University Press, 2005, pp. 37–8.
19. Jonathan Hyslop. 'The Strange Death of Liberal England and the Strange Birth of Illiberal South Africa: British Trade Unionists, Indian Labourers and Afrikaner Rebels, 1910–1914'. *Labour History Review,* 79 (1) (1 January 2014): 97–120.
20. Jonathan Hyslop. 'The Imperial Working Class Makes Itself "White": White Labourism in Britain, Australia, and South Africa Before the First World War'. *Journal of Historical Sociology,* 12 (4) (1999): 398–421.
21. Peter Cole and Lucien van der Walt. 'Crossing the Color Lines, Crossing the Continents: Comparing the Racial Politics of the IWW in South Africa and the United States, 1905–1925'. *Safundi,* 12 (1) (2011): 69–96.
22. See Peter L. Wickins. 'The One Big Union Movement among Black Workers in South Africa'. *The International Journal of African Historical Studies,* 7 (3) (1 January 1974): 391–416.
23. Anthony Lemon. 'The Political Position of Indians in South Africa'. In *South Asians Overseas: Migration and Ethnicity,* ed. Colin G. Clarke, Ceri Peach and Steven Vertovec. Cambridge: Cambridge University Press, 1990, p. 131.
24. Evans, Grimshaw, Phillips and Swain. *Equal Subjects, Unequal Rights,* p. 168.
25. Balasubramanyam Chandramohan. '"Hamlet with the Prince of Denmark Left out"?: The South African War, Empire and India'. In *The South African War Reappraised,* ed. Donal Lowry, 150–68. Manchester: Manchester University Press, 2000.
26. 'The Grievances of the British Indians in South Africa – The Green Pamphlet' in Mahatma Gandhi. *The Collected Works of Mahatma Gandhi 2: (1896–1897).* Delhi: Ministry of Information and Broadcasting Government of India, 1958, p. 43.
27. M. K. Gandhi, 'Speech at a Meeting in Madras', 26 October 1896, in Mahatma Gandhi. *The Collected Works of Mahatma Gandhi.* 3rd edn. New Delhi: The Publications Division, Ministry of Information and Broadcasting, Government of India, 1979, pp. 426–48.
28. Mahatma Gandhi. *The South African Gandhi: An Abstract of the Speeches and Writings of M.K. Gandhi, 1893–1914,* ed. Meer Fatima and Hassim Seedat. 2nd edn. Durban: Madiba Publishers, Institute for Black Research, University of Natal, 1996, p. 744.
29. David E. Omissi. 'India: Some Perceptions of Race and Empire'. In *The Impact of the South African War,* ed. David E. Omissi and Andrew Thompson. New York: Palgrave, 2002, p. 220; Bill Nasson. *The South African War, 1899–1902.* London: Arnold, 1999, p. 160.
30. Omissi, 'India', p. 226.
31. S. R. Bakshi. *Gandhi and Indians in South Africa.* New Delhi: Antique Publishers, 1988, p. 253.
32. M. K. Gandhi, 'Speech at Calcutta Meeting', 19 January 1902, in Mahatma Gandhi. *The Collected Works of Mahatma Gandhi.* 3rd rev. edn. New Delhi: Ministry of Information and Broadcasting, Government of India, 2000, p. 434.
33. Maureen Swan. *Gandhi, the South African Experience.* Johannesburg: Ravan Press, 1985.
34. Parvathi Raman. 'Yusuf Dadoo: Transnational Politics, South African Belonging'. *South African Historical Journal,* 50 (1) (2004): 27–48.
35. Swan, *Gandhi,* pp. 226–56.
36. Pixley Seme, 'Native Union' in *Imvo Zabantsundu,* 24 October, 1911.

37. P. Walshe. *The Rise of African Nationalism in South Africa: The African National Congress, 1912–1952*. London: C. Hurst, 1970, p. 3.
38. Evans, Grimshaw, Phillips and Swain, *Equal Subjects, Unequal Rights*, pp. 161–2.
39. André Odendaal. *The Founders: The Origins of the ANC and the Struggle for Democracy in South Africa*. Auckland Park, South Africa: Jacana Media, 2012, pp. 67–9.
40. Dubow, 'South Africa and South Africans', p. 29.
41. Odendaal, *Founders*; Walshe, *Rise of African Nationalism*, pp. 4–7.
42. See Neil Parsons and African chief Kwama. *King Khama, Emperor Joe, and the Great White Queen: Victorian Britain through African Eyes*. Chicago, IL: University of Chicago Press, 1998.
43. Walshe, *Rise of African Nationalism*, pp. 10–12.
44. H. Pretorius and L Jafta. '"A Branch Springs Out": African Initiated Churches'. In *Christianity in South Africa – A Political, Social and Cultural History*, ed. Richard Elphick and Rodney Davenport, 211–26. Cape Town: David Phillip, 1997.
45. Pretorius and Jafta, '"A Branch Springs Out"', pp. 211–26; N. A. Etherington. 'The Historical Sociology of Independent Churches in South East Africa'. *Journal of Religion in Africa*, 10 (2) (1979): 108–26.
46. J. T. Campbell. *Songs of Zion : The African Methodist Episcopal Church in the United States and South Africa*. Chapel Hill, NC: University of North Carolina Press, 1998.
47. Shula Marks. *Reluctant Rebellion: The 1906–8 Disturbances in Natal*. Oxford: Clarendon Press, 1970.
48. Robert Trent Vinson and Robert Edgar. 'Zulus Abroad: Cultural Representations and Educational Experiences of Zulus in America, 1880–1945'. *Journal of Southern African Studies*, 33 (1) (1 March 2007): 43–62.
49. Thomas J. Noer. *Briton, Boer and Yankee: The United States and South Africa, 1870–1914*. Kent, OH: Kent State University Press, 1978, p. 42.
50. Robert Trent Vinson. '"Sea Kaffirs": "American Negroes" and the Gospel of Garveyism in Early Twentieth-Century Cape Town'. *The Journal of African History*, 47 (2) (1 January 2006): 281–303.
51. Noer, *Briton, Boer and Yankee*, pp. 122–7.
52. Christopher Saunders. 'African Attitudes to Britain and the Empire before and after the South African War'. In *The South African War Reappraised*, ed. Donal Lowry. Manchester: Manchester University Press, 2000, p. 144.
53. Dubow, 'South Africa and South Africans', p. 31.
54. Resolutions of the South African Native Convention, 1909, in Sheridan Johns, Thomas Karis and Gwendolen Margaret Carter, eds. *From Protest to Challenge: A Documentary History of African Politics in South Africa, 1882–1964*. Vol. 1: *Protest and Hope, 1882–1934*. Stanford, CA: Hoover Institution Press, 1972, p. 53.
55. Odendaal, *Founders*, p. 422.
56. Ronald Hyam and Peter Henshaw. *The Lion and the Springbok : Britain and South Africa since the Boer War*. Cambridge: Cambridge University Press, 2003, pp. 82–3.
57. William Cross, quoted in Solomon Tshekisho Plaatje. *Native Life in South Africa, before and since the European War and the Boer Rebellion*. London: P. S. King, 1916, p. 228.
58. Odendaal, *Founders*, p. 477.
59. Brian Willan. *Sol Plaatje : South African Nationalist 1876–1932*. London: Heinemann, 1984.
60. Plaatje, *Native Life in South Africa*, p. 15.
61. Walshe, *Rise of African Nationalism*, pp. 52–3.
62. Bill Nasson. 'A Great Divide: Popular Responses to the Great War in South Africa'. *War and Society*, 12 (1) (1 May 1994): 47–64; 248–76.
63. T. R. H. Davenport. 'The South African Rebellion, 1914'. *The English Historical Review*, 78 (306) (1 January 1963): 73–94.

64. Hermann Giliomee. *The Afrikaners: Biography of a People*. London: Hurst, 2011, p. 380; Sandra Swart. '"A Boer and His Gun and His Wife Are Three Things Always Together": Republican Masculinity and the 1914 Rebellion'. *Journal of Southern African Studies,* 24 (4) (1 December 1998): 737–51.
65. Bill Nasson. 'War Opinion in South Africa, 1914'. *The Journal of Imperial and Commonwealth History,* 23 (2) (1 May 1995): 248–76.
66. Ibid.; see also Simons and Simons, *Class and Colour in South Africa,* 182–4.
67. Albert Grundlingh. *Fighting Their Own War: South African Blacks and the First World War*. Johannesburg: Ravan Press, 1987, p. 96.
68. B. P. Willan. 'The South African Native Labour Contingent, 1916–1918'. *The Journal of African History,* 19 (1) (1978): 61–86.
69. Howard Phillips. *'Black October': The Impact of the Spanish Influenza Epidemic of 1918 on South Africa*. Pretoria: Government Printer, 1990; Howard Phillips. 'Why Did It Happen?: Religious Explanations of the "Spanish" Flu Epidemic in South Africa'. *Historically Speaking,* 9 (7) (2008): 34–6.
70. Jonathan Hyslop. '"Segregation Has Fallen on Evil Days": Smuts' South Africa, Global War, and Transnational Politics, 1939–46'. *Journal of Global History,* 7 (3) (2012): 438–60.
71. Krikler, *White Rising*, pp. 39–42.
72. Frederick A. Johnstone. *Class, Race and Gold: A Study of Class Relations and Racial Discrimination in South Africa*. London: Routledge and Kegan Paul, 1976.
73. Peter Alexander. 'Race, Class Loyalty and the Structure of Capitalism: Coal Miners in Alabama and The Transvaal, 1918–1922'. *Journal of Southern African Studies,* 30 (1) (2004): 115–32; Krikler, *White Rising*, pp. 115–29.
74. Alexander, 'Race, Class Loyalty', pp. 115–32.
75. Adam Ashforth. *The Politics of Official Discourse in Twentieth-Century South Africa*. Oxford: Clarendon, 1990.
76. 'Report of the South African Native Affairs Commission'. Cape Town, 1905, p. 96.
77. Saul Dubow. *Racial Segregation and the Origins of Apartheid in South Africa, 1919–36*. Basingstoke: Macmillan, 1989, pp. 23–5.
78. David Welsh. *The Roots of Segregation : Native Policy in Colonial Natal, 1845–1910*. Oxford: Oxford University Press, 1971.
79. Martin Legassick. 'British Hegemony and the Origins of Segregation in South Africa, 1901–14'. In *Segregation and Apartheid in Twentieth-Century South Africa*, ed. William Beinart and Saul Dubow. London: Routledge, 1995.
80. P. B. Rich. 'Ministering to the White Man's Needs: The Development of Urban Segregation in South Africa 1913–1923'. *African Studies,* 37 (2) (1978): 177–92.
81. Dubow, *Racial Segregation.*
82. John W. Cell. *The Highest Stage of White Supremacy: The Origins of Segregation in South Africa and the American South*. Cambridge: Cambridge University Press, 1982; Mahmood Mamdani. *Citizen and Subject : Contemporary Africa and the Legacy of Late Colonialism*. Princeton, NJ: Princeton University Press, 1996.
83. US Chief Justice John Marshall, 1831, quoted in Ian R. Tyrrell. *Transnational Nation: United States History in Global Perspective since 1789*. Basingstoke: Palgrave Macmillan, 2007.
84. Kevin Grant. *A Civilised Savagery : Britain and the New Slaveries in Africa, 1884–1926*. New York: Routledge, 2005.
85. Susan Pedersen. 'Settler Colonialism at the Bar of the League of Nations'. In *Settler Colonialism in the Twentieth Century: Projects, Practices, Legacies*, ed. Caroline Elkins and Susan Pedersen, 113–34. New York: Routledge, 2005; Mark Mazower. 'An International Civilization? Empire, Internationalism and the Crisis of the Mid-Twentieth Century'. *International Affairs (Royal Institute of International Affairs 1944-),* 82 (3) (1 May 2006): 553–66.
86. Jan Christiaan Smuts. *Africa and Some World Problems*. Oxford: Clarendon Press, 1930.

87. Cell, *Highest Stage*, pp. 247–9.
88. Saul Dubow. *A Commonwealth of Knowledge: Science, Sensibility, and White South Africa, 1820–2000*. Oxford: Oxford University Press, 2006.
89. Saul Dubow. *Scientific Racism in Modern South Africa*. New York: Cambridge University Press, 1995, pp. 39–47.
90. Gareth Cornwell. 'George Webb Hardy's The Black Peril and the Social Meaning of "Black Peril" in Early Twentieth-Century South Africa'. *Journal of Southern African Studies*, 22 (3) (1 September 1996): 441–53.
91. Dubow, *Scientific Racism*, pp. 210–14.
92. Cell, *Highest Stage*, p. 221.
93. Quoted in Philip Bonner. 'The Transvaal Native Congress 1917–1920: The Radicalisation of the Black Petty Bourgeoisie on the Rand'. In *Industrialisation and Social Change in South Africa: African Class Formation, Culture, and Consciousness, 1870–1930*, ed. Shula Marks and Richard Rathbone, 270–313. London: Longman, 1982.
94. Lloyd George to Smuts, 1920 – quoted in Willan, *Sol Plaatje*, p. 245.
95. Erez Manela. *The Wilsonian Moment: Self-Determination and the International Origins of Anticolonial Nationalism*. Oxford: Oxford University Press, 2007.
96. Petition to King George IV, 16 December 1918, in Sheridan Johns, Thomas Karis and Gwendolen Margaret Carter, eds. *From Protest to Challenge: A Documentary History of African Politics in South Africa, 1882–1964*. Vol. 1: *Protest and Hope, 1882–1934*. Stanford, CA: Hoover Institution Press, 1972, p. 142.
97. Willan, *Sol Plaatje*, pp. 259–81.
98. Ibid., p. 293.
99. See Bonner, 'The Transvaal Native Congress', pp. 297–8.
100. Robert Edgar. 'The Prophet Motive: Enoch Mgijima, the Israelites, and the Background to the Bullhoek Massacre'. *The International Journal of African Historical Studies*, 15 (3) (1 January 1982): 401–22.
101. Les Switzer. 'The Ambiguities of Protest in South Africa: Rural Politics and the Press during the 1920s'. *The International Journal of African Historical Studies*, 23 (1) (1 January 1990): 87–109; and Hill and Pirio, '"Africa for the Africans"'.
102. William Beinart and Colin Bundy. *Hidden Struggles in Rural South Africa: Politics & Popular Movements in the Transkei & Eastern Cape 1890–1930*. London: Currey, 1987.
103. Oswin Bull, quoted in Hill and Pirio, '"Africa for the Africans"', p. 225; F. Bridgman, quoted in a letter from C. H. Patton to E. C. Jenkins, 7 May 1921, YMCA, Yergan Papers, South Africa/Max Yergan, 1915–38.
104. W. E. B. Du Bois. 'Thomas Jesse Jones'. *The Crisis*, 22 (6) (1921).
105. Walshe, *Rise of African Nationalism*, p. 166.
106. Hill and Pirio, '"Africa for the Africans"', p. 228.
107. Vinson, '"Sea Kaffirs"', 281–303.
108. Quoted in Hill and Pirio, '"Africa for the Africans"', p. 214.
109. C. Kadalie. 'African Labour Congress'. *The Workers' Herald*, 21 December 1923.
110. See Johns, Karis and Margaret Carter, *From Protest to Challenge*, pp. 154–6; Walshe, *Rise of African Nationalism*, pp. 93–4.
111. W. Holtby to F. Brockway, 26 April 1929, UCT Ballinger papers, BC 347/D2.1.1.6; E. Lewis to J. B. M. Hertzog, UCT, Ballinger Papers, BC 347/D2.I.1.1.
112. Clements Kadalie. *My Life and the ICU: The Autobiography of a Black Trade Unionist in South Africa*. London: Cass, 1970, pp. 102–23.
113. 'Open letter to Blackpool', *The New Leader*, 30 September 1927, in Johns, Karis and Margaret Carter, *From Protest to Challenge*, pp. 328–31.
114. Helen Bradford. *A Taste of Freedom: The ICU in Rural South Africa, 1924–1930*. New Haven, CT: Yale University Press, 1987.

115. Ibid.
116. Tom Lodge. *Black Politics in South Africa since 1945*. London: Longman, 1983, p. 7.
117. Catherine Coquery-Vidrovitch. *Africa : Endurance and Change South of the Sahara*, tr. David Maisel. Berkeley, CA; London: University of California Press, 1988, p. 241.
118. Vladimir Shubin and Marina Traikova. 'There Is No Threat from the Eastern Bloc'. In *The Road to Democracy in South Africa*. Vol. 3: *International Solidarity*, Part 2, ed. South African Democracy Education Trust, 985–1066. Pretoria: University of South Africa, 2008, p. 987.
119. Walshe, *Rise of African Nationalism*, pp. 169–80.
120. Edward Johanningsmeier. 'Communists and Black Freedom Movements in South Africa and the US: 1919–1950'. *Journal of Southern African Studies*, 30 (1) (1 March 2004): 155–80.
121. Philip Bonner. 'South African Society and Culture, 1910–1948'. *The Cambridge History of South Africa. Vol. 2: 1885–1994. Cambridge*, ed. Robert Ross, Anne Kelk Mager and Bill Nasson: Cambridge University Press, 2011, p. 286.
122. Bill Freund. *The African City – A History*. Cambridge: Cambridge University Press, 2007, pp. 65–106.
123. See for example, J. Merle Davis. *Modern Industry and the African*. London: Macmillan and Co. Ltd, 1933; William Malcolm Hailey. *An African Survey: A Study of Problems Arising in Africa South of the Sahara*. London: Oxford University Press, 1938.
124. Ellen Hellmann. *Rooiyard. A Sociological Survey of an Urban Native Slum Yard*. Cape Town: Oxford University Press, 1948, p. 117.
125. Freund, *African City*, pp. 83–9.
126. T. Dunbar Moodie and Vivienne Ndatshe. *Going for Gold: Men, Mines, and Migration*. Berkeley, CA: University of California Press, 1994; T. Dunbar Moodie, Vivienne Ndatshe and British Sibuyi. 'Migrancy and Male Sexuality on the South African Gold Mines'. *Journal of Southern African Studies*, 14 (2) (1 January 1988): 228–56.
127. William Beinart. 'Worker Consciousness, Ethnic Particularism and Nationalism: The Experiences of a South African Migrant'. In *The Politics of Race, Class and Nationalism in Twentieth-Century South Africa*, ed. Shula Marks and Stanley Trapido. Harlow: Longman, 1987, pp. 306–7.
128. Anthony Sampson. *Drum: A Venture into the New Africa*. London: Collins, 1956, p. 109.
129. Philip Bonner. 'The Russians on the Reef, 1947–57'. In *Apartheid's Genesis, 1935–1962*, ed. Philip Bonner, Peter Delius and Deborah Posel. Johannesburg: Witwatersrand University Press, 1993, p. 186.
130. Phillip Bonner. 'African Urbanisation on the Rand between the 1930s and 1960s: Its Social Character and Political Consequences'. *Journal of Southern African Studies*, 21 (1) (1 March 1995): 126.
131. Sampson, *Drum*, pp. 106–7.
132. Christopher John Ballantine. *Marabi Nights : Jazz, 'Race' and Society in Early Apartheid South African*. Scottsville, South Africa: University of KwaZulu-Natal Press, 2012.
133. David B. Coplan. *In Township Tonight! South Africa's Black City Music and Theatre*. 2nd edn. Chicago, IL: University of Chicago Press, 2007.
134. Ibid.
135. Rian Malan. *The Lion Sleeps Tonight*. London: Grove Press UK, 2014.
136. Paul B. Rich. *State Power and Black Politics in South Africa, 1912–51*. Basingstoke: Macmillan, 1996. See also Cell, *Highest Stage*.

Chapter 5: Empire, Nation and War

1. C. H. Feinstein. *An Economic History of South Africa: Conquest, Discrimination and Development*. Cambridge: Cambridge University Press, 2005, pp. 94, 140.

2. William Beinart. *Twentieth-Century South Africa*. Oxford: Oxford University Press, 1994, p. 175.
3. Bill Freund. 'South Africa: The Union Years, 1910–1948'. *The Cambridge History of South Africa. Vol. 2: 1885–1994*, ed. Robert Ross, Anne Kelk Mager and Bill Nasson. Cambridge: Cambridge University Press, 2011, pp. 247–9.
4. Feinstein, *Economic History of South Africa*, pp. 132–5.
5. Freund, 'South Africa', 211–53.
6. Alex Thomson. 'Balancing Interests beyond the Water's Edge: Identifying the Key Interests That Determined US Foreign Policy towards Apartheid South Africa'. *Politikon*, 32 (1) (2005): 131; see also Kevin Danaher. *The Political Economy of U.S. Policy toward South Africa*. Boulder: Westview Press, 1985.
7. John Darwin. *After Tamerlane: How Empires Rise and Fall*. London: Penguin, 2008, pp. 402–8; 422–3.
8. Much of the following section follows the framework set out by Barbara Bush in her account of interwar liberal groups. See Barbara Bush. *Imperialism, Racism and Resistance*. London: Routledge, 1999.
9. Paul Rich. 'Race, Science, and the Legitimization of White Supremacy in South Africa, 1902–1940'. *The International Journal of African Historical Studies*, 23 (4) (1990): 683–5.
10. Ray Edmund Phillips. *The Bantu Are Coming: Phases of South Africa's Race Problem*. London: Student Christian Movement Press, 1930, p. 59.
11. Richard Elphick. 'The Benevolent Empire and the Social Gospel: Missionaries and South African Christians in the Age of Segregation'. In *Christianity in South Africa: A Political, Social and Cultural History*, ed. Richard Elphick and Rodney Davenport. Cape Town: David Phillip, 1997, p. 359.
12. Alan Wilkinson. *The Community of the Resurrection: A Centenary History*. London: SCM, 1992.
13. David Goodhew. 'Working-Class Respectability: The Example of the Western Areas of Johannesburg, 1930–55'. *The Journal of African History*, 41 (2) (1 January 2000): 241–66.
14. David B. Coplan. *In Township Tonight! South Africa's Black City Music and Theatre*. 2nd edn. Chicago, IL: University of Chicago Press, 2007, p. 172.
15. Joseph Houldsworth Oldham. *White and Black in Africa: A Critical Examination of the Rhodes Lectures of General Smuts*. London: Longmans, Green, 1930.
16. Morag Bell. 'American Philanthropy, the Carnegie Corporation and Poverty in South Africa'. *Journal of Southern African Studies*, 26 (3) (1 September 2000): 481–504.
17. Bush, *Imperialism, Racism and Resistance*, p. 182.
18. John Darwin. *The Empire Project: The Rise and Fall of the British World-System, 1830–1970*. Cambridge: Cambridge University Press, 2009, pp. 439–49.
19. Donal Lowry. '"The Boers Were the Beginning of the End"?: The Wider Impact of the South African War'. In *The South African War Reappraised*, ed. Donal Lowry, 203–46. Manchester: Manchester University Press, 2000.
20. Ronald Hyam and Peter Henshaw. *The Lion and the Springbok: Britain and South Africa since the Boer War*. Cambridge: Cambridge University Press, 2003, p. 126.
21. Darwin, *Empire Project*, p. 460.
22. See for example, J. Merle Davis. *Modern Industry and the African*. London: Macmillan and Co. Ltd, 1933; William Malcolm Hailey. *An African Survey: A Study of Problems Arising in Africa South of the Sahara*. London: Oxford University Press, 1938.
23. Hermann Giliomee. *The Afrikaners: Biography of a People*. London: Hurst, 2011, pp. 345–7.
24. E. G. Malherbe quoted in Marita Golden. *Carnegie Corporation in South Africa: A Difficult Past Leads to a Commitment to Change*. Carnegie Corporation of New York, 2004.
25. Giliomee, *Afrikaners*, pp. 350–64.

26. Isabel Hofmeyr. 'Building a Nation from Words: Afrikaans Language, Literature and Ethnic Identity, 1902–1924'. In *The Politics of Race, Class and Nationalism in Twentieth-Century South Africa*, ed. Shula Marks and Stanley Trapido. Harlow: Longman, 1987, p. 105.
27. Jonathan Hyslop. 'White Working-Class Women and the Invention of Apartheid: "Purified" Afrikaner Nationalist Agitation for Legislation against "Mixed" Marriages, 1934–9'. *The Journal of African History*, 36 (1) (1 January 1995): 57–81.
28. Leslie Witz. 'Solly Sachs, the Great Trek and Jan van Riebeeck: Settler Pasts and Racial Identities in the Garment Workers' Union, 1938–52'. In *Rethinking Settler Colonialism: History and Memory in Australia, Canada, Aotearoa New Zealand and South Africa*, ed. Annie E. Coombes. Manchester University Press, 2006, p. 49.
29. Alan Paton. *Hofmeyr*. London; Cape Town: Oxford University Press, 1964, p. 301.
30. *Times*, 16 December 1938, p. 17.
31. *Times*, 17 December 1938, p. 13.
32. Darwin, *Empire Project*, p. 461.
33. Joanne L. Duffy. *The Politics of Ethnic Nationalism: Afrikaner Unity, the National Party, and the Radical Right in Stellenbosch, 1934–1948*. London: Routledge, 2006.
34. T. Dunbar Moodie. *The Rise of Afrikanerdom: Power, Apartheid, and the Afrikaner Civil Religion*. Berkeley, CA: University of California Press, 1975, p. 166.
35. Patrick Furlong. *Between Crown and Swastika: The Impact of the Radical Right on the Afrikaner Nationalist Movement in the Fascist Era*. Hanover, NH: University Press of New England, 1991, pp. 53–4; Moodie, *Rise of Afrikanerdom*, p. 168.
36. Milton Shain. *The Roots of Antisemitism in South Africa*. Charlottesville, VA; London: University Press of Virginia, 1994; see also Duffy, *Politics of Ethnic Nationalism*, p. 83.
37. Charles Bloomberg. *Christian-Nationalism and the Rise of the Afrikaner Broederbond, in South Africa, 1918–48*, ed. Saul Dubow. London: Macmillan Press, 1990, p. 150; Furlong, *Between Crown and Swastika*, pp. 87–96.
38. Duffy, *Politics of Ethnic Nationalism*, p. 97.
39. Elphick, 'Benevolent Empire', pp. 360–1.
40. Saul Dubow. *Scientific Racism in Modern South Africa*. New York: Cambridge University Press, 1995, pp. 259–60; see also Gerrit J. Schutte. 'The Netherlands, Cradle of Apartheid?'. *Ethnic and Racial Studies*, 10 (4) (1 October 1987): 392–414.
41. Moodie, *Rise of Afrikanerdom*, pp. 52–72.
42. Schutte, 'Netherlands, Cradle of Apartheid?', pp. 392–414; see also Dubow, *Scientific Racism*, p. 262.
43. Moodie, *Rise of Afrikanerdom*, pp. 150–61.
44. Furlong, *Between Crown and Swastika*, p. 239.
45. Dubow, *Scientific Racism*, p. 250.
46. W. K. Hancock. *Smuts – Fields of Force, 1919–1950*. Cambridge: Cambridge University Press, 1968, pp. 320–4.
47. Jeanne Morefield. *Empires Without Imperialism: Anglo-American Decline and the Politics of Deflection*. New York: Oxford University Press, 2014.
48. Hancock, *Smuts*, p. 357; see also Bill Schwarz. *The White Man's World*. Oxford: Oxford University Press, 2011, pp. 277–340.
49. L. Grundlingh. 'The Recruitment of South African Blacks for Participation in the Second World War'. In *Africa and the Second World War*, ed. D. Killingray and R. Rathbone. London: Palgrave MacMillan, 1986.
50. Jonathan Hyslop. '"Segregation Has Fallen on Evil Days": Smuts' South Africa, Global War, and Transnational Politics, 1939–46'. *Journal of Global History*, 7 (3) (2012): 438–60.
51. *Road to a New South Africa*. Cape Town: Propaganda Committee of the National Party, 1940. On Nationalist plans for social welfare, see Deborah Posel. 'The Case for a Welfare State: Poverty & the Politics of the Urban African Family in the 1930s & 1940s'. In *South Africa's*

1940s: Worlds of Possibilities, ed. Saul Dubow and Alan Jeeves, 64–86. Cape Town: Double Storey, 2005.

52. Saul Dubow. 'Introduction: South Africa's 1940s'. In *South Africa's 1940s: Worlds of Possibilities*, ed. Saul Dubow and Alan Jeeves, 1–19. Cape Town: Double Storey, 2005, p. 8.
53. William Temple. *Christianity and Social Order*. Harmondsworth: Penguin Books, 1942. See also Adrian Hastings. *A History of English Christianity 1920–1985*. London: Collins, 1986, pp. 397–8.
54. Saul Dubow. 'Scientism, Social Research and the Limits of "South Africanism": The Case of Ernst Gideon Malherbe'. *South African Historical Journal*, 44 (1) (1 May 2001): 130–4.
55. Hancock, *Smuts*, p. 384.
56. Hyslop, '"Segregation Has Fallen"', pp. 438–60.
57. Jeremy Seekings. 'Visions, Hopes & Views about the Future: The Radical Moment of South African Welfare Reform'. In *South Africa's 1940s: Worlds of Possibilities*, ed. Saul Dubow and Alan Jeeves, 44–63. Cape Town: Double Storey, 2005.
58. David Killingray and Richard Rathbone. 'Introduction'. In *Africa and the Second World War*, ed. D. Killingray and R. Rathbone, 1–19. London: Macmillan, 1986.
59. Nicoli Nattrass. 'Economic Growth and Transformation in the 1940s'. In *South Africa's 1940s: Worlds of Possibilities*, ed. Saul Dubow and Alan Jeeves, 20–43. Cape Town: Double Storey, 2005.
60. Ibid., pp. 24–25; Grundlingh, 'Recruitment of South African Blacks', p. 196.
61. A. W. Stadler. 'Birds in the Cornfield: Squatter Movements in Johannesburg, 1944–1947'. *Journal of Southern African Studies*, 6 (1) (1 October 1979): 93–123.
62. Tom Lodge. *Black Politics in South Africa since 1945*. London: Longman, 1983, pp. 11–16.
63. Killingray and Rathbone, 'Introduction', p. 5.
64. Rob Skinner. 'Christian Reconstruction, Secular Politics: Michael Scott and the Campaign for Right and Justice, 1943–1945'. In *South Africa's 1940s: Worlds of Possibilities*, ed. Saul Dubow and Alan Jeeves, 246–66. Cape Town: Double Storey, 2005.
65. Peter Alexander. *Workers, War & the Origins of Apartheid: Labour & Politics in South Africa, 1939–48*. Cape Town: D. Philip, 2000.
66. T. Dunbar Moodie. 'The Moral Economy of the Black Miners' Strike of 1946'. *Journal of Southern African Studies*, 13 (1) (1 October 1986): 1–35.
67. D. Killingray and R. Rathbone, eds. *Africa and the Second World War*. London: Macmillan, 1986.
68. Lodge, *Black Politics*, p. 22.
69. 'African Claims in South Africa', in *From Protest to Challenge: A Documentary History of African Politics in South Africa 1882–1964*. Vol. 2: *Hope and Challenge, 1935–52*, ed. Thomas Karis and Gwendolen Margaret Carter. Stanford, CA: Hoover Institution Press, 1973, pp. 209–22.
70. Saul Dubow. 'South Africa and South Africans: Nationality, Belonging, Citizenship'. In *The Cambridge History of South Africa*. Vol. 2: *1885–1994*, ed. Robert Ross, Anne Kelk Mager and Bill Nasson. Cambridge: Cambridge University Press, 2011, p. 50.
71. David Henry Anthony. *Max Yergan: Race Man, Internationalist, Cold Warrior*. New York: New York University Press, 2006.
72. Anthony Lemon. 'The Political Position of Indians in South Africa'. In *South Asians Overseas: Migration and Ethnicity*, ed. Colin G. Clarke, Ceri Peach and Steven Vertovec. Cambridge: Cambridge University Press, 1990, p. 132.
73. Goolam Vahed. 'Race, Empire, and Citizenship: Sarojini Naidu's 1924 Visit to South Africa'. *South African Historical Journal*, 64 (2) (2012): 319–42.
74. Parvathi Raman. 'Being Indian the South African Way: The Development of Indian Identity in 1940s Durban'. In *Rethinking Settler Colonialism: History and Memory in Australia, Canada, Aotearoa New Zealand and South Africa*, ed. Annie E. Coombes. Manchester University Press, 2006, p. 196.

75. Ibid., p. 202.
76. Parvathi Raman. 'Yusuf Dadoo: Transnational Politics, South African Belonging'. *South African Historical Journal,* 50 (1) (2004): 27–48.
77. Brij Maharaj. 'The Local State and Residential Segregation'. *South African Geographical Journal,* 77 (1) (1995): 33–41.
78. Karthigasen Gopalan. 'The Role of Visiting Indian Hindu Missionaries in Their Attempts to "Reform" Hinduism in South Africa, 1933–1935'. *South African Historical Journal,* 64 (2) (2012): 273–94.
79. Raman, 'Being Indian', p. 206.
80. Hilary Sapire. 'African Loyalism and Its Discontents: The Royal Tour of South Africa, 1947'. *The Historical Journal,* 54 (1) (2011): 215–40.
81. Uma Dhupelia-Mesthrie. 'Cultural Crossings from Africa to India: Select Travel Narratives of Indian South Africans from Durban and Cape Town, 1940s to 1990s'. *South African Historical Journal,* 64 (2) (2012): 295–312.
82. Saul Dubow. 'Smuts, the United Nations and the Rhetoric of Race and Rights'. *Journal of Contemporary History,* 43 (1) (1 January 2008): 45–74.
83. Mark Mazower. *No Enchanted Palace: The End of Empire and the Ideological Origins of the United Nations.* Woodstock, UK: Princeton University Press, 2009.
84. Carol Anderson. *Eyes off the Prize: The United Nations and the African American Struggle for Human Rights, 1944–1955.* Cambridge; New York: Cambridge University Press, 2003.
85. Hyslop, '"Segregation Has Fallen"', 438–60.
86. UN General Assembly Resolution 44(I), 8 December 1946.
87. Lorna Lloyd. '"A Family Quarrel". The Development of the Dispute over Indians in South Africa'. *The Historical Journal,* 34 (3) (1991): 703–25.
88. Raman, 'Yusuf Dadoo', 45.
89. Corrie Gerald Haines. 'The United Nations Challenge to Racial Discrimination in South Africa 1946–1950'. *African Studies,* 60 (2) (2001): 185–204.
90. Hyslop, '"Segregation Has Fallen"', pp. 455–7.
91. Michael Crowder. 'Tshekedi Khama, Smuts, and South West Africa'. *The Journal of Modern African Studies,* 25 (1) (1 March 1987): 25–42.
92. Christopher Saunders. 'Michael Scott and Namibia'. *African Historical Review,* 39 (2) (2007): 25–40.
93. Freda Troup. *In Face of Fear. Michael Scott's Challenge to South Africa. [With Plates, Including a Portrait.].* London: Faber & Faber, 1950.

Chapter 6: Apartheid and Cold War

1. Deborah Posel. *The Making of Apartheid, 1948–1961: Conflict and Compromise.* Oxford: Clarendon Press, 1991.
2. Tim Rooth. 'Britain, South African Gold, and the Sterling Area, 1945–50'. *The Journal of Imperial and Commonwealth History,* 32 (1) (2004): 93–114.
3. Posel, *Making of Apartheid.*
4. See ibid. and also Ivan Thomas Evans. *Bureaucracy and Race: Native Administration in South Africa.* Berkeley, CA: University of California Press, 1997.
5. Frederick Cooper. 'A Parting of the Ways: Colonial Africa and South Africa, 1946–48'. *African Studies,* 65 (1) (2006): 27–44.
6. Ann Laura Stoler. 'Sexual Affronts and Racial Frontiers'. In *Tensions of Empire: Colonial Cultures in a Bourgeois World,* ed. Frederick Cooper and Ann Laura Stoler. Berkeley, CA: University of California Press, 1997, p. 199.

7. Deborah Posel. 'What's in a Name? Racial Categorisations under Apartheid and Their Afterlife'. *Transformation,* 47 (50-74) (2001): 59–82.
8. Jonathan Hyslop. '"A Destruction Coming In": Bantu Education as a Response to Social Crisis'. In *Apartheid's Genesis, 1935–1962*, ed. Philip Bonner, Peter Delius and Deborah Posel. Johannesburg: Witwatersrand University Press, 1993.
9. *Times*, 26 May 1948, p. 5.
10. Michael Scott. *A Time to Speak*. Garden City, NY: Doubleday, 1958, p. 246.
11. E. S. Sachs. 'Will South Africa Go Fascist?' *New Statesman*, 24 August 1946.
12. Brian Bunting. *The Rise of the South African Reich*. Harmondsworth: Penguin Books, 1964.
13. Saul Dubow. 'Ethnic Euphemisms and Racial Echoes'. *Journal of Southern African Studies,* 20 (3) (1 September 1994): 355–70.
14. David B. Coplan. *In Township Tonight! South Africa's Black City Music and Theatre*. 2nd edn. Chicago, IL: University of Chicago Press, 2007, pp. 176–7.
15. Ibid., p. 212.
16. Carol Polsgrove. *Ending British Rule in Africa: Writers in a Common Cause*. Manchester, UK: Manchester University Press, 2009, p. 83.
17. Paul B. Rich. *Hope and Despair: English-Speaking Intellectuals and South African Politics, 1896–1976*. London: British Academic Press, 1993, pp. 125–8.
18. Paul Gready. 'The Sophiatown Writers of the Fifties: The Unreal Reality of Their World'. *Journal of Southern African Studies,* 16 (1) (1990): 139–64.
19. Tom Lodge. 'The Destruction of Sophiatown'. *The Journal of Modern African Studies,* 19 (1) (1 March 1981): 107–32.
20. Bill Freund. *The African City – A History*. Cambridge: Cambridge University Press, 2007.
21. David Goodhew. *Respectability and Resistance: A History of Sophiatown*. Westport, CT: Praeger, 2004.
22. Tom Lodge. *Black Politics in South Africa since 1945*. London: Longman, 1983, pp. 26–7.
23. Elizabeth Williams. *The Politics of Race in Britain and South Africa: Black British Solidarity and the Anti-Apartheid Struggle*. London: I.B. Tauris, 2012, pp. 20–2.
24. Ciraj Rassool and Leslie Witz. 'The 1952 Jan Van Riebeeck Tercentenary Festival: Constructing and Contesting Public National History in South Africa'. *The Journal of African History,* 34 (3) (1 January 1993): 447–68.
25. Lutuli, A. 'The Road to Freedom is Via the Cross'. In *From Protest to Challenge: A Documentary History of African Politics in South Africa 1882–1964*. Vol. 2: *Hope and Challenge, 1935–52*, ed. Thomas Karis and Gwendolen Margaret Carter. Stanford, CA: Hoover Institution Press, 1973, pp. 486–9.
26. Lodge, *Black Politics,* p. 68.
27. Peter Delius. 'Sebatakgomo and the Zoutpansberg Balemi Association: The ANC, the Communist Party and Rural Organization, 1939–55'. *The Journal of African History,* 34 (2) (1 January 1993): 293–313.
28. Z. K. Matthews, 'Presidential Address to Cape ANC', reproduced in Thomas Karis, Gwendolen Margaret Carter, and Gail M. Gerhart. *From Protest to Challenge: A Documentary History of African Politics in South Africa 1882–1964. Vol. 3: Challenge and Violence, 1953–1964.* Stanford, CA: Hoover Institution Press, 1977, p. 105.
29. Lodge, *Black Politics*, pp. 68–73.
30. Julia C. Wells. *We Now Demand! The History of Women's Resistance to Pass Laws in South Africa*. Johannesburg: Witwatersrand University Press, 1993.
31. Neil Gavin Ross Overy. '"These Difficult Days" : Mission Church Reactions to Bantu Education in South Africa, 1949–56'. PhD, School of Oriental and African Studies (University of London), 2002.
32. Lodge, 'Destruction of Sophiatown', pp. 107–32.

33. Ibid., pp. 153–87; Derek Catsam. 'Marching in the "Dark City": Bus Boycotts in South Africa in the 1940s and the Limits and Promise of Comparative History'. *Safundi,* 8 (3) (2007): 315–25.
34. David Hostetter. '"An International Alliance of People of All Nations Against Racism": Nonviolence and Solidarity in the Antiapartheid Activism of the American Committee on Africa, 1952–19651'. *Peace & Change,* 32 (2) (1 April 2007): 134–52.
35. Francis Njubi Nesbitt. *Race for Sanctions: African Americans against Apartheid, 1946–1994.* Bloomington, IN: Indiana University Press, 2004.
36. Rob Skinner. *The Foundations of Anti-Apartheid: Liberal Humanitarianism and Transnational Activism in Britain and the United States, C. 1919–64.* Basingstoke: Palgrave Macmillan, 2010, pp. 125–32.
37. Trevor Huddleston. *Naught for Your Comfort.* London: Collins, 1956.
38. *Suppression of Communism Act* (No. 44 of 1950). Cape Town: Government of South Africa.
39. Ronald Hyam and Peter Henshaw. *The Lion and the Springbok: Britain and South Africa since the Boer War.* Cambridge: Cambridge University Press, 2003, p. 116.
40. James Sanders. *Apartheid's Friends: The Rise and Fall of South Africa's Secret Service.* London: John Murray, 2006.
41. See Geoff R. Berridge. *South Africa, the Colonial Powers and "African Defence": The Rise and Fall of the White Entente, 1948–60.* London: Macmillan, 1992.
42. Ibid.
43. Joshua N. Lazerson. *Against the Tide: Whites in the Struggle against Apartheid / Joshua N. Lazerson.* Boulder, CO; Oxford: Westview Press, 1994; Neil Roos. *Ordinary Springboks: White Servicemen and Social Justice in South Africa, 1939–1961.* Aldershot: Ashgate, 2005; Rob Skinner. 'Christian Reconstruction, Secular Politics: Michael Scott and the Campaign for Right and Justice, 1943–1945'. In *South Africa's 1940s: Worlds of Possibilities,* ed. Saul Dubow and Alan Jeeves, 246–66. Cape Town: Double Storey, 2005.
44. Parvathi Raman. 'Yusuf Dadoo: Transnational Politics, South African Belonging'. *South African Historical Journal,* 50 (1) (2004): 27–48.
45. Edward Johanningsmeier. 'Communists and Black Freedom Movements in South Africa and the US: 1919–1950'. *Journal of Southern African Studies,* 30 (1) (1 March 2004): 155–80.
46. Randolph Vigne. *Liberals against Apartheid: A History of the Liberal Party of South Africa, 1953–68.* Basingstoke: Macmillan, 1997.
47. Thomas Karis, Gwendolen Margaret Carter and Gail M. Gerhart. *From Protest to Challenge: A Documentary History of African Politics in South Africa 1882–1964.* Vol. 3: *Challenge and Violence, 1953–1964.* Stanford, CA: Hoover Institution Press, 1977, pp. 310–15.
48. 'Manifesto of the Africanist Movement', reproduced in Karis, Margaret Carter and Gerhart, *From Protest to Challenge,* p. 523; Tom Lodge. *Sharpeville: An Apartheid Massacre and Its Consequences.* Oxford: Oxford University Press, 2011, p. 67.
49. Vladimir Shubin and Marina Traikova. 'There Is No Threat from the Eastern Bloc'. In *The Road to Democracy in South Africa,* Vol. 3: *International Solidarity,* ed. South African Democracy Education Trust. Pretoria: University of South Africa, 2008.
50. Ryan M. Irwin. *Gordian Knot: Apartheid and the Unmaking of the Liberal World Order.* Oxford: Oxford University Press, 2012, p. 7.
51. Thomas Borstelmann. *The Cold War and the Color Line: American Race Relations in the Global Arena.* Cambridge, MA: Harvard University Press, 2001, p. 115.
52. Christopher J. Lee, ed. *Making a World after Empire: The Bandung Moment and Its Political Afterlives.* Athens, OH: Ohio University Press, 2010.
53. Frederick Cooper. *Citizenship between Empire and Nation: Remaking France and French Africa, 1945–1960.* Princeton, NJ: Princeton University Press, 2014.
54. James Leslie and Elisabeth Leake, eds. *Decolonization and the Cold War: Negotiating Independence.* New Approaches to International History. London: Bloomsbury, 2015.

55. John D. Hargreaves. *Decolonization in Africa*. London: Longman, 1988, pp. 200–3.
56. Saul Dubow. 'Macmillan, Verwoerd, and the 1960 "Wind Of Change" Speech'. *The Historical Journal,* 54 (4) (2011): 1087–114.
57. Wellesley College, Symposium on Africa, 16–17 February 1960, quoted in Ladun Anise. 'The African Redefined: The Problems of Collective Black Identity'. *Issue: A Journal of Opinion,* 4 (4) (1 December 1974): 26–32.
58. 'The Pan Africanist Congress Has a Message for the Down Trodden Black Masses of Afrika', reproduced in Karis, Margaret Carter and Gerhart, *From Protest to Challenge*, pp. 560–1.
59. Simon Stevens. 'Strategies of Struggle: Boycotts, Sanctions, and the War Against Apartheid'. PhD, Columbia University, 2015.
60. See Lodge, *Sharpeville*, pp. 104–7.
61. C. J. Driver. *Patrick Duncan: South African and Pan-African*. Oxford: James Currey, 2000, pp. 176–81; see also Lodge, *Sharpeville*, pp. 110–62.
62. Christabel Gurney. '"A Great Cause": The Origins of the Anti-Apartheid Movement, June 1959-March 1960'. *Journal of Southern African Studies,* 26 (1) (1 March 2000): 123–44.
63. Peter Limb. 'The Anti-Apartheid Movements in Australia and Aotearoa/New Zealand'. In *The Road to Democracy in South Africa*. Vol. 3: *International Solidarity*, Part 1, ed. South African Democracy Education Trust, 907–82. Pretoria: Unisa Press, 2008.
64. Lodge, *Sharpeville*, p. 172; see James Barber, John Barratt and South African Institute of International Affairs. *South Africa's Foreign Policy: The Search for Status and Security 1945-1988.* Cambridge: Cambridge University Press, 1990.
65. Lodge, *Sharpeville,* p. 172.
66. Saul Dubow. 'Were There Political Alternatives in the Wake of the Sharpeville-Langa Violence in South Africa, 1960?'. *The Journal of African History,* 56 (1) (2015): 119–42.
67. C. Saunders. 'Hammarskjöld's Visit to South Africa'. *African Journal on Conflict Resolution,* 11 (1) (2011): 15–34.
68. *Voice of Africa*, 22 September 1960, p. 3; on Reeves see John Stuart Peart-Binns. *Ambrose Reeves*. London: Gollancz, 1973; R. Ambrose Reeves. *Shooting at Sharpeville: The Agony of South Africa*. London: V. Gollancz, 1960.
69. Ronald Hyam. 'The Parting of the Ways: Britain and South Africa's Departure from the Commonwealth, 1951–61'. *The Journal of Imperial and Commonwealth History,* 26 (2) (1 May 1998): 157–75.
70. Sanders, *Apartheid's Friends*; Neil Parsons. 'The Pipeline: Botswana's Reception of Refugees, 1956–68'. *Social Dynamics,* 34 (1) (1 March 2008): 17–32.
71. Lodge, *Black Politics*, pp. 196–7.
72. Charles Hooper. *Brief Authority*. First edn. London: Collins, 1960; Peter Delius. 'Sebatakgomo; Migrant Organization, the ANC and the Sekhukhuneland Revolt'. *Journal of Southern African Studies,* 15 (4) (1 October 1989): 581–615; Thembela Kepe and Lungisile Ntsebeza, eds. *Rural Resistance in South Africa: The Mpondo Revolts after Fifty Years*. Cape Town: UCT Press, 2012. See also Govan Mbeki. *South Africa: The Peasant's Revolt*. Harmondsworth: Penguin, 1964.
73. Vigne, *Liberals against Apartheid*, pp. 203–4.
74. Lodge, *Black Politics*, p. 241.
75. Gready, 'Sophiatown Writers', pp. 139–64.
76. Roger Pfister. 'Gateway to International Victory: The Diplomacy of the African National Congress in Africa, 1960–1994'. *The Journal of Modern African Studies,* 41 (1) (1 March 2003): 51–73.
77. Thami ka Plaatjie. 'The PAC in Exile'. In *The Road to Democracy in South Africa*. Vol. 2: *1970–80*, ed. South African Democracy Education Trust. Pretoria: Unisa Press, 2006.
78. Karis, Carter and Gerhart, *From Protest to Challenge*, p. 351; see also Skinner, *Foundations*, p. 181.

79. See Nelson Mandela. *No Easy Walk to Freedom. Articles, Speeches, and Trial Addresses of Nelson Mandela*, ed. Ruth First. London: Heinemann, 1965.
80. Mark Gevisser. *Thabo Mbeki: The Dream Deferred*. Johannesburg: Jonathan Ball, 2007, pp. 251–86.
81. Shubin and Traikova, 'There Is No Threat', 985–1066.
82. Denis Herbstein. *White Lies: Canon John Collins and the Secret War against Apartheid*. Oxford: James Currey, 2004.
83. Lodge, *Black Politics*, pp. 296–8.
84. Shubin and Traikova, 'There Is No Threat', 991–2.
85. Lodge, *Black Politics*, p. 298.
86. Ibid., pp. 299–300.
87. *Times*, 22 July 1967.
88. Stephen Ellis and Tsepo Sechaba. *Comrades against Apartheid: The ANC and the South African Communist Party in Exile*. London: James Currey, 1992, p. 64.
89. Ken Keable. *London Recruits: The Secret War against Apartheid*. Pontypool, UK: Merlin Press, 2012.
90. Lodge, *Black Politics*, p. 313.
91. Pfister, 'Gateway to International Victory', pp. 51–73.
92. UN General Assembly Resolution 1761, 6 November 1962; Newell Maynard Stultz. 'Evolution of the United Nations Anti-Apartheid Regime'. *Human Rights Quarterly*, 13 (1) (1 February 1991): 1–23.
93. UN Security Council Resolution 181, 7 August 1963.
94. Irwin, *Gordian Knot*, pp. 87–9.
95. Skinner, *Foundations*, pp. 192–4.
96. Alex Thomson. 'Balancing Interests beyond the Water's Edge: Identifying the Key Interests That Determined US Foreign Policy towards Apartheid South Africa'. *Politikon*, 32 (1) (2005): 123–37.
97. Irwin, *Gordian Knot*, p. 7.
98. Thomas Borstelmann. *Apartheid's Reluctant Uncle: The United States and Southern Africa in the Early Cold War*. Oxford: Oxford University Press, 1993.
99. Christian M. De Vos. 'Balancing Acts: John Kennedy, the Cold War and the African National Congress'. *Politikon*, 32 (1) (2005): 103–22.
100. 'Address by Martin Luther King', 7 December 1964, Amistad Center, Tulane University, New Orleans, ACOA papers, 007/0545-6. See also Nesbitt, *Race for Sanctions*, p. 61.
101. Malcolm X. *The Autobiography of Malcolm X: With the Assistance of Alex Haley*. London: Hutchinson, 1966, p. 470.
102. Irwin, *Gordian Knot*, pp. 11–13.
103. Thomson, 'Balancing Interests', 123–37; Saki Dockrill. *Britain's Retreat from East of Suez: The Choice between Europe and the World?* Basingstoke: Palgrave Macmillan, 2002; Jeffrey Pickering. *Britain's Withdrawal from East of Suez: The Politics of Retrenchment*. Basingstoke: Macmillan, 1998.
104. Robert Archer and Antoine Bouillon. *The South African Game: Sport and Racism*. London: Zed Press, 1982; Douglas Booth. *The Race Game: Sport and Politics in South Africa*. London; Portland, OR: F. Cass, 1998.
105. Richard Edward Lapchick. *The Politics of Race and International Sport: The Case of South Africa*. Westport, CT: Greenwood Press, 1975.
106. Dennis Brutus and Bernth Lindfors. *The Dennis Brutus Tapes: Essays at Autobiography*. Oxford: James Currey, 2011.
107. Bruce K. Murray. 'Politics and Cricket: The D'Oliveira Affair of 1968'. *Journal of Southern African Studies*, 27 (4) (2001): 667–84.

108. Peter Hain. *Don't Play with Apartheid: The Background to the Stop the Seventy Tour Campaign*. London: Allen & Unwin, 1971.
109. Lapchick, *Politics of Race*, p. 158.
110. Ibid., 174–9.
111. David Black and John Nauright. *Rugby and the South African Nation: Sport, Cultures, Politics, and Power in the Old and New South Africas*. Manchester: Manchester University Press, 1998, pp. 84–5.
112. William Beinart. *Twentieth-Century South Africa*. Oxford: Oxford University Press, 1994, p. 182.
113. The 'revisionist' interpretation of segregation and apartheid, as compatible with the capitalism economy, developed in the early 1970s – see Stanley Trapido. 'South Africa in a Comparative Study of Industrialization'. *The Journal of Development Studies*, 7 (3) (1 April 1971): 309–20; Harold Wolpe. 'Capitalism and Cheap Labour-Power in South Africa: From Segregation to Apartheid 1'. *Economy and Society*, 1 (4) (1 November 1972): 425–56.
114. C. H. Feinstein. *An Economic History of South Africa: Conquest, Discrimination and Development*. Cambridge: Cambridge University Press, 2005, pp. 165–84.
115. Beinart, *Twentieth-Century South Africa*, p. 176.
116. Feinstein, *Economic History of South Africa*, pp. 182–3.
117. Beinart, *Twentieth-Century South Africa*, pp. 176–7.
118. Henk van Woerden. *A Mouthful of Glass*, tr. Dan Jacobson. London: Granta, 2000.
119. Saul Dubow. *Apartheid, 1948–1994*. First edn. Oxford Histories. Oxford: Oxford University Press, 2014, pp. 105–9.
120. Ibid., p. 112; Laurine Platzky and Cherryl Walker. *The Surplus People: Forced Removals in South Africa*. Johannesburg: Ravan Press, 1985.
121. Deborah Posel. 'The Apartheid Project, 1948–1970'. *The Cambridge History of South Africa*. Vol. 2: *1885–1994*, ed. Robert Ross, Anne Kelk Mager and Bill Nasson, 319–68. Cambridge: Cambridge University Press, 2011.
122. Beinart, *Twentieth-Century South Africa*, p. 354.
123. Lodge, *Black Politics*, p. 321.
124. Colin Murray. 'Displaced Urbanization: South Africa's Rural Slums'. *African Affairs*, 86 (344) (1 July 1987): 311–29; Cosmas Desmond. *The Discarded People: An Account of African Resettlement*. Braamfontein: Christian Institute of South Africa, 1969.
125. Ruth First, Jonathan Steele and Christabel Gurney. *The South African Connection: Western Investment in Apartheid*. London: Temple Smith, 1972, p. 281.

Chapter 7: Liberation Struggles

1. Steve Biko. *I Write What I like*. London: Penguin Books, 1988, p. 117.
2. C. R. D. Halisi. 'Biko and Black Consciousness Philosophy: An Interpretation'. In *Bounds of Possibility: Legacy of Steve Biko and Black Consciousness*, ed. Barney Pityana, pp. 108–9. London: Zed Books, 1992.
3. Lindy Wilson. 'Bantu Steven Biko: A Life'. In *Bounds of Possibility: Legacy of Steve Biko and Black Consciousness*, ed. Barney Pityana. London: Zed Books, 1992, pp. 28–9.
4. Anthony Lemon. 'The Political Position of Indians in South Africa'. In *South Asians Overseas: Migration and Ethnicity*, ed. Colin G. Clarke, Ceri Peach and Steven Vertovec. Cambridge: Cambridge University Press, 1990, pp. 134–8.
5. David B. Coplan. *In Township Tonight! South Africa's Black City Music and Theatre*. 2nd edn. Chicago, IL: University of Chicago Press, 2007, pp. 250–8.

6. Nozipho J. Diseko. 'The Origins and Development of the South African Student's Movement (SASM): 1968–1976'. *Journal of Southern African Studies*, 18 (1) (1 March 1992): 40–62.
7. Saul Dubow. *Apartheid, 1948–1994*. First edn. Oxford Histories. Oxford: Oxford University Press, 2014, pp. 167–71.
8. William Beinart. *Twentieth-Century South Africa*. Oxford: Oxford University Press, 1994, pp. 239–42.
9. C. H. Feinstein. *An Economic History of South Africa: Conquest, Discrimination and Development*. Cambridge: Cambridge University Press, 2005, pp. 200–20.
10. Nicoli Nattrass and Elisabeth Ardington, eds. *The Political Economy of South Africa*. Oxford: Oxford University Press, 1990.
11. Gary Baines. 'The Master Narrative of South Africa's Liberation Struggle: Remembering and Forgetting June 16, 1976'. *The International Journal of African Historical Studies*, 40 (2) (2007): 283–302.
12. Tom Lodge. *Black Politics in South Africa since 1945*. London: Longman, 1983, pp. 328–30.
13. John Kane-Berman. *Soweto: Black Revolt, White Reaction*. Johannesburg: Ravan Press, 1978.
14. Dubow, *Apartheid*, pp. 182–3.
15. Roger Pfister. 'Gateway to International Victory: The Diplomacy of the African National Congress in Africa, 1960–1994'. *The Journal of Modern African Studies*, 41 (1) (1 March 2003): p. 63.
16. Roger Pfister. *Apartheid South Africa and African States: From Pariah to Middle Power, 1961–1994*. London; New York: Tauris Academic Studies, 2005; see also Deon Geldenhuys. *The Diplomacy of Isolation: South African Foreign Policy Making*. Johannesburg: Macmillan South Africa for the South African Institute of International Affairs, 1984.
17. David Birmingham. *Portugal and Africa*. Basingstoke: Macmillan, 1999.
18. Joseph Hanlon. *Mozambique: The Revolution under Fire*. London: Zed, 1984.
19. James Sanders. *Apartheid's Friends: The Rise and Fall of South Africa's Secret Service*. London: John Murray, 2006.
20. Pfister, 'Gateway to International Victory', 57–8.
21. UN Security Council Resolution 418, 4 November 1977.
22. James A. Sanders. *South Africa and the International Media, 1972–1979: A Struggle for Representation*. London: F. Cass, 2000.
23. Robert M. Price. *The Apartheid State in Crisis: Political Transformation in South Africa, 1975–1990*. New York: Oxford University Press, 1991.
24. Phyllis Johnson and David Martin, eds. *Destructive Engagement: Southern Africa at War*. Harare, Zimbabwe: Zimbabwe Publishing House for the Southern African Research and Documentation Centre, 1986.
25. Philip H. Frankel. *Pretoria's Praetorians: Civil-Military Relations in South Africa*. Cambridge: Cambridge University Press, 1984.
26. Price, *Apartheid State in Crisis*, p. 82.
27. Stanley B. Greenberg. *Legitimating the Illegitimate: State, Markets, and Resistance in South Africa*. London: University of California Press, 1987.
28. Deborah Posel. 'The Language of Domination, 1978–83'. In *The Politics of Race, Class and Nationalism in Twentieth-Century South Africa*, ed. Shula Marks and Stanley Trapido. Harlow: Longman, 1987.
29. Shula Marks and Stanley Trapido. 'South Africa Since 1976: An Historical Perspective'. In *South Africa: No Turning Back*, ed. Shaun Johnson. Basingstoke: Macmillan, 1988, p. 28.
30. William Cobbett. 'Apartheid's Army and the Arms Embargo'. In *War and Society: The Militarisation of South Africa*, ed. Jacklyn Cock and Laurie Nathan. Cape Town: David Philip, 1989, pp. 239–40; Sanders, *Apartheid's Friends*.

31. Mark Swilling and Mark Phillips. 'State Power in the 1980s: From "Total Strategy" to "Counter-Revolutionary Warfare"'. In *War and Society: The Militarisation of South Africa*, ed. Jacklyn Cock and Laurie Nathan, 134–48. Cape Town: David Philip, 1989.
32. Lemon, 'Political Position of Indians'.
33. Tom Lodge and Bill Nasson. *All, Here, and Now: Black Politics in South Africa in the 1980s*. London: Hurst, 1992, pp. 35–42.
34. John W. De Gruchy. *The Church Struggle in South Africa*. Minneapolis, MN: Fortress Press, 2005.
35. Peter Walshe. *Church versus State in South Africa: The Case of the Christian Institute*. Maryknoll, NY: Orbis Books, 1983; Basil Moore. *Black Theology: The South African Voice*. London: C. Hurst, 1973; Dwight Hopkins. 'Steve Biko, Black Consciousness and Black Theology'. In *Bounds of Possibility: Legacy of Steve Biko and Black Consciousness*, ed. Barney Pityana, 194–200. London: Zed Books, 1992.
36. Lemon, 'Political Position of Indians'.
37. Lodge and Nasson, *All, Here, and Now*, pp. 65–77.
38. Jeremy Seekings. '"Trailing behind the Masses": The United Democratic Front and Township Politics in the Pretoria-Witwatersrand-Vaal Region, 1983–84'. *Journal of Southern African Studies*, 18 (1) (1 March 1992): 93–114. See also Jeremy Seekings. 'From Quiescence to "People's Power": Township Politics in Kagiso, 1985–1986'. *Social Dynamics*, 18 (1) (1 June 1992): 20–41; Jeremy Seekings. *The UDF: A History of the United Democratic Front in South Africa, 1983–1991*. Oxford: James Currey, 2000.
39. Johnson and Martin, *Destructive Engagement*.
40. Pfister, 'Gateway to International Victory', pp. 51–73.
41. Stephen R. Davis. 'The African National Congress, Its Radio, Its Allies and Exile*'. *Journal of Southern African Studies*, 35 (2) (1 June 2009): 349–73.
42. Paul Trewhela. *Inside Quatro: Uncovering the Exile History of the ANC and SWAPO*. Auckland Park, South Africa: Jacana Media, 2009. See also Stephen Ellis. *External Mission: The ANC in Exile, 1960–1990*. London: Hurst, 2012.
43. Lodge and Nasson, *All, Here, and Now*, pp. 127–40.
44. De Gruchy, *Church Struggle*.
45. John W. De Gruchy. 'Grappling with a Colonial Heritage: The English-Speaking Churches under Imperialism and Apartheid'. In *Christianity in South Africa: A Political, Social, and Cultural History*, ed. Richard Elphick and T. R. H. (Thomas Rodney Hope) Davenport, 155–72. Berkeley, CA: University of California Press, 1997.
46. Allen A. Anderson and G. J. Pillay. 'The Segregated Spirit: The Pentecostals'. In *Christianity in South Africa: A Political, Social, and Cultural History*, ed. Richard Elphick and T. R. H. (Thomas Rodney Hope) Davenport, 227–41. Berkeley, CA: University of California Press, 1997.
47. Diane Sandler. 'The Psychological Experiences of White Conscripts in the Black Townships'. In *War and Society: The Militarisation of South Africa*, ed. Jacklyn Cock and Laurie Nathan, 79–89. Cape Town: David Philip, 1989.
48. Swilling and Phillips, 'State Power in the 1980s', p. 147.
49. From the early 1960s, South African security forces were taking note of the tactics employed by French forces in Algeria; see Brian Bunting. *The Rise of the South African Reich*. Harmondsworth: Penguin Books, 1964. More recently, James Sanders has detailed the extensive connections between the South African intelligence services and their Western counterparts, Sanders, *Apartheid's Friends*.
50. Rob Nixon. 'Apartheid on the Run: The South African Sports Boycott'. *Transition*, 58 (1992): 68–88; Douglas Booth. *The Race Game: Sport and Politics in South Africa*. London; Portland, OR: F. Cass, 1998.

51. Margaret E. Keck and Kathryn Sikkink. *Activists beyond Border: Advocacy Networks in International Politics*. Ithaca, NY: Cornell University Press, 1998.
52. Håkan Thörn. *Anti-Apartheid and the Emergence of a Global Civil Society*. Basingstoke: Palgrave Macmillan, 2006.
53. Audie Klotz. *Norms in International Relations: The Struggle against Apartheid*. Ithaca, NY: Cornell University Press, 1995. See also Neta Crawford and Audie Klotz, eds. *How Sanctions Work: South Africa in Comparative Perspective*. Basingstoke: Macmillan, 1998.
54. Thörn, *Anti-Apartheid*, pp. 77–9.
55. Tore Linné Eriksen, ed. *Norway and National Liberation in Southern Africa*. Uppsala, Sweden: Nordic Institute of African Studies, 1999.
56. Kevin O'Sullivan. *Ireland, Africa and the End of Empire: Small State Identity in the Cold War, 1955–75*. Manchester: Manchester University Press, 2012.
57. Sietse Bosgra. 'From Jan van Riebeeck to Solidarity with the Struggle: The Netherlands, South Africa and Apartheid'. In *The Road to Democracy in South Africa*. Vol. 3: *International Solidarity*, ed. South African Democracy Education Trust. Pretoria: University of South Africa, 2008. On the CZA, see Alex Lichtenstein. 'The Dutch Antiapartheid Movement: An Interview with Sietse Bosgra'. *Radical History Review*, 2014 (119) (20 March 2014): 24–51.
58. South African Democracy Education Trust, ed. *The Road to Democracy in South Africa*. Vol. 3: *International Solidarity*. Pretoria: University of South Africa, 2008.
59. Genevieve Lynette Klein. 'The Anti-Apartheid Movement in Britain and Support for the African National Congress, 1976–1990'. DPhil dissertation. St. Antony's College (University of Oxford), 2007.
60. Shula Marks. '"Half-Ally, Half-Untouchable at the Same Time": Britain and South Africa since 1959'. London: Anti-Apartheid Archives Committee, 1999.
61. Chester A. Crocker. 'In Defense of American Policy'. In *The Anti-Apartheid Reader: The Struggle against White Racist Rule in South Africa*, ed. David Mermelstein. New York: Grove Press, 1987. See also J. E. Davies. *Constructive Engagement?: Chester Crocker & American Policy in South Africa, Namibia & Angola, 1981–8*. Oxford: James Currey, 2007.
62. Elizabeth Schmidt. 'The Sullivan Principles: A Critique'. In *The Anti-Apartheid Reader: The Struggle against White Racist Rule in South Africa*, ed. David Mermelstein, 387–99. New York: Grove Press, 1987.
63. Charles Hamm. *Putting Popular Music in Its Place*. Cambridge: Cambridge University Press, 1995; Louise Meintjes. 'Paul Simon's Graceland, South Africa, and the Mediation of Musical Meaning'. *Ethnomusicology*, 34 (1) (1990): 37–73.
64. Gavin Brown and Helen Yaffe. 'Practices of Solidarity: Opposing Apartheid in the Centre of London'. *Antipode*, 46 (1) (2014): 34–52; see also Gavin Brown and Helen Yaffe. *Youth Activism and Solidarity: The Non-Stop Picket Against Apartheid*. London: Routledge, (forthcoming).
65. Elizabeth Williams. *The Politics of Race in Britain and South Africa: Black British Solidarity and the Anti-Apartheid Struggle*. London: I.B. Tauris, 2012.
66. 'The Thatcher-Botha Papers'. *History Workshop Online*. N.p., 5 January 2014.
67. Robin Renwick. *The End of Apartheid: Diary of a Revolution*. London: Biteback Publishing, 2015.
68. Rob Skinner. 'Anti-Apartheid'. In *NGOs in Contemporary Britain: Non-State Actors in Society and Politics since 1945*, ed. N. J. Crowson, Matthew Hilton and James McKay, 129–46. Basingstoke: Palgrave Macmillan, 2009.
69. Roger Fieldhouse. *Anti-Apartheid: A History of the Movement in Britain*. London: Merlin Press, 2005, pp. 360–1.
70. Nerys John. 'The Campaign Against British Bank Involvement In Apartheid South Africa'. *African Affairs*, 99 (396) (1 July 2000): 415–33.

71. Christine Jennett. 'Signals to South Africa: The Australian Anti-Apartheid Movement'. In *Politics of the Future: The Role of Social Movements*, ed. Christine Jennett and Randal G. Stewart, 98–155. South Melbourne: MacMillan, 1989.
72. Commonwealth Group of Eminent Persons. *Mission to South Africa: The Commonwealth Report*. Harmondsworth: Penguin for the Commonwealth Secretariat, 1986.
73. Thomas J. Redden. 'The US Comprehensive Anti-Apartheid Act of 1986: Anti-Apartheid or Anti-African National Congress?" *African Affairs*, 87 (349) (1 October 1988): 595–605.
74. Donald R. Culverson. *Contesting Apartheid: U.S. Activism, 1960–1987*. Boulder, CO: Westview, 1999, p. 160.
75. 'Address by State President P. W. Botha, 15 August 1985 – The O'Malley Archives'. https://www.nelsonmandela.org/omalley/index.php/site/q/03lv01538/04lv01600/05lv01638/06lv01639.htm (accessed 21 October 2015).
76. 'Response to PW Botha's "Rubicon" Speech – The O'Malley Archives'. https://www.nelsonmandela.org/omalley/index.php/site/q/03lv03445/04lv04015/05lv04016/06lv04025/07lv04026.htm (accessed 21 October 2015).
77. Feinstein, *Economic History of South Africa*, pp. 227–30.
78. Ibid.
79. Vella Pillay. 'Rising Cost of Apartheid: The Economic Crisis'. In *Destructive Engagement: Southern Africa at War*, ed. Phyllis Johnson and David Martin, 221–44. Harare, Zimbabwe: Zimbabwe Publishing House for the Southern African Research and Documentation Centre, 1986.
80. Robert Davies. 'After Cuito Cuanavale – The New Regional Conjuncture and the Sanctions Question'. In *Sanctions against Apartheid*, ed. Mark Orkin, 198–206. Cape Town: D. Philip, 1989.
81. N. Haysom. 'Vigilantes and Militarisation of South Africa'. In *War and Society: The Militarisation of South Africa*, ed. Jacklyn Cock and Laurie Nathan. Cape Town: David Philip, 1989.
82. *New York Times*, 18 November 1986.
83. Nkosinathi Gwala. 'Political Violence and the Struggle for Control in Pietermaritzburg'. *Journal of Southern African Studies*, 15 (3) (1 April 1989): 506–24.
84. Feinstein, *Economic History of South Africa*, p. 244.
85. Pádraig Carmody. 'Between Globalisation and (Post) Apartheid: The Political Economy of Restructuring in South Africa'. *Journal of Southern African Studies*, 28 (2) (1 June 2002): 262.
86. Joseph Hanlon. *Beggar Your Neighbours: Apartheid Power in Southern Africa*. London: Catholic Institute for International Relations in collaboration with Currey, 1986, pp. 53–4.
87. Pfister, 'Gateway to International Victory', pp. 51–73.
88. Aletta J. Norval. *Deconstructing Apartheid Discourse*. New York: Verso, 1996, p. 257.
89. Mark Gevisser. *Thabo Mbeki: The Dream Deferred*. Johannesburg: Jonathan Ball, 2007.
90. Anthony Sampson. *Mandela: The Authorised Biography*. London: Harper Collins, 1999.
91. Vladimir Shubin and Marina Traikova. 'There Is No Threat from the Eastern Bloc'. *The Road to Democracy in South Africa. Vol. 3: International Solidarity, Part 2*, pp. 1052–3. South African Democracy Education Trust. Pretoria: University of South Africa, 2008.
92. Pfister, 'Gateway to International Victory', p. 67.
93. Sampson, *Mandela*, p. 407.
94. William Gumede. *Thabo Mbeki and the Battle for the Soul of the ANC*. New York: Zed Books, 2007, pp. 69–70.
95. Patti Waldmeir. *Anatomy of a Miracle: The End of Apartheid and the Birth of the New South Africa*. London: W.W. Norton & Co, 1997, pp. 214–15.
96. South Africa. Truth and Reconciliation Commission. *Report*. Vol. 2. Cape Town: Juta, 1999, p. 625.
97. Ellis, *External Mission*, pp. 268–9.

98. 'Where a Massacre Is a Way of Life | News | M&G', 3 July 1992, http://mg.co.za/article/1992-07-03-00-where-a-massacre-is-a-way-of-life (accessed 16 June 2016).
99. Pfister, 'Gateway to International Victory', pp. 51–73.
100. M. J. Evans. *Broadcasting the End of Apartheid: Live Television and the Birth of the New South Africa*. London: I.B. Tauris, 2014.
101. Linda Melvern. 'Missing the Story: The Media and the Rwandan Genocide'. In *The Media and the Rwanda Genocide*, ed. Allan Thompson, 198–210. London: Ann Arbor, MI: Pluto Press, 2007.

Chapter 8: Globalization and the New South Africa

1. Heinz Klug. *Constituting Democracy: Law, Globalism, and South Africa's Political Reconstruction*. Cambridge: Cambridge University Press, 2000, p. 28.
2. Roland Burke. 'From Individual Rights to National Development: The First UN International Conference on Human Rights, Tehran, 1968'. *Journal of World History*, 19 (3) (2008): 275–96.
3. Amadou-Mahatar M'Bow. 'Apartheid, the Vilest Form of Modern Slavery'. *The UNESCO Courier*, November 1977.
4. Barney Pityana. 'Medical Ethics and South Africa's Security Laws: A Sequel to Death of Steve Biko'. In *Bounds of Possibility: Legacy of Steve Biko and Black Consciousness*, ed. Barney Pityana, 78–98. London: Zed Books, 1992. See also Mandisa Mbali. '"A Matter of Conscience": The Moral Authority of the World Medical Association and the Readmission of the South Africans, 1976–1994'. *Medical History*, 58 (2) (2014): 257–77.
5. Alex Thomson. 'Balancing Interests beyond the Water's Edge: Identifying the Key Interests That Determined US Foreign Policy towards Apartheid South Africa'. *Politikon*, 32 (1) (2005): 123–37.
6. Samuel Moyn. *The Last Utopia: Human Rights in History*. London: Belknap Press of Harvard University Press, 2010.
7. Simon Stevens. 'Why South Africa? The Politics of Anti-Apartheid Activism in Britain in the Long 1970s'. In *The Breakthrough: Human Rights in the 1970s*, ed. Jan Eckel and Samuel Moyn, first edn. Philadelphia, PA: University of Pennsylvania Press, 2014, p. 204.
8. Tom Lodge. *Sharpeville: An Apartheid Massacre and Its Consequences*. Oxford: Oxford University Press, 2011, p. 43.
9. Saul Dubow. *South Africa's Struggle for Human Rights*. Athens, OH: Ohio University Press, 2012, p. 84.
10. Desmond Tutu. *No Future without Forgiveness*. London: Rider, 1999.
11. Mahmood Mamdani. 'Amnesty or Impunity? A Preliminary Critique of the Report of the Truth and Reconciliation Commission of South Africa (TRC)'. *Diacritics*, 32 (3–4) (2002): 33–59.
12. Richard Wilson. *The Politics of Truth and Reconciliation in South Africa: Legitimizing the Post-Apartheid State*. Cambridge: Cambridge University Press, 2001.
13. Ibid.
14. Pádraig Carmody. 'Between Globalisation and (Post) Apartheid: The Political Economy of Restructuring in South Africa'. *Journal of Southern African Studies*, 28 (2) (1 June 2002): 255–75.
15. Patrick Bond. *Elite Transition: From Apartheid to Neoliberalism in South Africa*. Scottsville, South Africa: University of KwaZulu-Natal Press, 2005.
16. William Gumede. *Thabo Mbeki and the Battle for the Soul of the ANC*. New York: Zed Books, 2007.
17. African National Congress. *The Reconstruction and Development Programme: A Policy Framework*. Johannesburg: Umanyano Publications, for African National Congress, 1994, p. 90.

18. Gumede, *Thabo Mbeki*, pp. 86–91.
19. Carmody, 'Between Globalisation and (Post) Apartheid', p. 263.
20. Evangelos A. Calamitsis. 'How Has the Asian Crisis Affected Other Regions?' *Finance and Development*, September 1998.
21. Isabel Hofmeyr and Michelle Williams. 'South Africa – India: Connections and Comparisons'. *Journal of Asian and African Studies*, 44 (1) (1 February 2009): 5–17.
22. Jonathan Hyslop. 'The African Renaissance Meets the Asian Renaissance? The Malaysian Impact on Contemporary South Africa'. Paper presented at the University of Sussex, Centre for Southern African Studies, February 1998.
23. Mark Gevisser. *Thabo Mbeki: The Dream Deferred*. Johannesburg: Jonathan Ball, 2007, pp. 588–9.
24. 'Black Economic Empowerment – The O'Malley Archives'. https://www.nelsonmandela.org/omalley/index.php/site/q/03lv03445/04lv04206/05lv04220/06lv04221/07lv04222.htm (accessed 27 October 2015).
25. Thabo Mbeki. 'Statement on Behalf of the ANC on the Occasion of the Adoption by the Constitutional Assembly of "The Republic of South Africa Constitution Bill 1996", Cape Town, 1996/05/08', Thabo Mbeki Foundation. http://www.mbeki.org/2016/06/06/statement-on-behalf-of-the-anc-on-the-occasion-of-the-adoption-by-the-constitutional-assembly-of-the-republic-of-south-africa-constitution-bill-1996-cape-town-19960508/ (accessed 1 May 2016).
26. Thabo Mbeki. 'Speech at the Launch of the African Renaissance Institute, Pretoria – 1999/10/11', Thabo Mbeki Foundation. http://www.mbeki.org/2016/06/09/speech-at-the-launch-of-the-african-renaissance-institute-pretoria-19991011/ (accessed 4 May 2016.)
27. Gumede, *Thabo Mbeki*.
28. Gevisser, *Thabo Mbeki*.
29. Ibid., p. 730.
30. Alexander Rödlach. *Witches, Westerners, and HIV: AIDS and Cultures of Blame in Africa*. Walnut Creek, CA: Left Coast, 2006. On South Africa in particular, see Deborah Posel. 'Sex, Death and the Fate of the Nation: Reflections on the Politicization of Sexuality in Post-Apartheid South Africa'. *Africa: Journal of the International African Institute*, 75 (2) (1 January 2005): 125–53.
31. *South African National HIV Prevalence, Incidence and Behaviour Survey, 2012*. Cape Town: HSRC Press, 2014, p. 41.
32. Dubow, *South Africa's Struggle*, p. 124.
33. *South African National HIV Prevalence, Incidence and Behaviour Survey, 2012*. Cape Town: HSRC Press, 2014, p. 41.
34. Deborah Posel. 'AIDS'. In *New South African Keywords*, ed. Nick Shepherd and Steven Robinson. Johannesburg: Jacana, 2008.
35. Gevisser, *Thabo Mbeki*, pp. 740–1.
36. René Lemarchand. 'Consociationalism and Power Sharing in Africa: Rwanda, Burundi, and the Democratic Republic of the Congo'. *African Affairs*, 106 (422) (2007): 1–20; Kristina A. Bentley and Roger Southall. *An African Peace Process: Mandela, South Africa, and Burundi*. Cape Town: HSRC Press, 2005.
37. William M. Gumede. 'South Africa: Jacob Zuma and the Difficulties of Consolidating South Africa's Democracy'. *African Affairs*, 107 (427) (2008): 261–71.
38. Liz Gunner. 'Jacob Zuma, the Social Body and the Unruly Power of Song'. *African Affairs*, 108 (430) (1 January 2009): 27–48.
39. Roger Southall. 'Family and Favour at the Court of Jacob Zuma'. *Review of African Political Economy*, 38 (130) (1 December 2011): 617–26.
40. Tom Lodge. 'Political Corruption in South Africa'. *African Affairs*, 97 (387) (1998): 157–87.
41. Jonathan Hyslop. 'Political Corruption: Before and After Apartheid'. *Journal of Southern African Studies*, 31 (4) (2005): 773–89.

42. Patrick Chabal and Jean-Pascal Daloz. *Africa Works: Disorder as Political Instrument*. Oxford: International African Institute in association with James Currey, 1999. See also Hyslop, 'Political Corruption'.
43. Ashwin Desai and Goolam Vahed. 'World Cup 2010: Africa's Turn or the Turn on Africa?' *Soccer & Society*, 11 (1–2) (2010): 154–67.
44. Sabelo J. Ndlovu-Gatsheni. 'The World Cup, Vuvuzelas, Flag-Waving Patriots and the Burden of Building South Africa'. *Third World Quarterly*, 32 (2) (2011): 279–93; see also Udesh Pillay, Richard Tomlinson and Orli Bass, eds. *Development and Dreams: The Urban Legacy of the 2010 Football World Cup*. Cape Town, South Africa: HSRC Press, 2009.
45. Alan S. Alexandroff. 'South Africa in a Complex Global Order: How and Where to Fit In?' *South African Journal of International Affairs*, 22 (2) (2015): 249–68.
46. Mzukisi Qobo and Memory Dube. 'South Africa's Foreign Economic Strategies in a Changing Global System'. *South African Journal of International Affairs*, 22 (2) (2015): 145–64.
47. Jonathan Crush. 'The Dark Side of Democracy: Migration, Xenophobia and Human Rights in South Africa'. *International Migration*, 38 (6) (2001): 103–33.
48. M. Neocosmos. *From 'Foreign Natives' to 'Native Foreigners': Explaining Xenophobia in Post-Apartheid South Africa: Citizenship and Nationalism, Identity and Politics*. Dakar, Senegal: CODESRIA, 2006.
49. Aidan Mosselson. '"There Is No Difference between Citizens and Non-Citizens Anymore": Violent Xenophobia, Citizenship and the Politics of Belonging in Post-Apartheid South Africa'. *Journal of Southern African Studies*, 36 (3) (2010): 641–55.
50. Michael Neocosmos. 'The Politics of Fear and the Fear of Politics: Reflections on Xenophobic Violence in South Africa'. *Journal of Asian and African Studies*, 43 (6) (2008): 586–94.
51. Abahlali baseMjondolo. 'Statement on the Xenophobic Attacks in Johannesburg', 21 May 2008, http://abahlali.org/node/3582/ (accessed 20 June 2016).
52. Greg Marinovich. 'The Murder Fields of Marikana'. *Daily Maverick*, 8 September 2012.
53. Peter Alexander. 'Marikana, Turning Point in South African History'. *Review of African Political Economy*, 40 (138) (2013): 605–19.
54. Fiona White. 'Deepening Democracy: A Farm Workers' Movement in the Western Cape'. *Journal of Southern African Studies*, 36 (3) (2010): 673–91.
55. Julian Brown. *South Africa's Insurgent Citizens: On Dissent and the Possibility of Politics*. London: Zed Books, 2015.

INDEX